Windows Vista for Starters

THE MISSING MANUAL

Your best friend for answers

David Pogue

POGUE PRESS™
O'REILLY®

Beijing • Cambridge • Farnham • Köln • Paris • Sebastopol • Taipei • Tokyo

Windows Vista for Starters: THE MISSING MANUAL

by David Pogue

Copyright © 2007 David Pogue. All rights reserved.
Printed in the United States of America.

Published by O'Reilly Media, Inc., 1005 Gravenstein Highway North, Sebastopol, CA 95472.

O'Reilly Media books may be purchased for educational, business, or sales promotional use. Online editions are also available for most titles: *safari.oreilly.com*. For more information, contract our corporate/institutional sales department: 800-998-9938 or *corporate@oreilly.com*.

Printing History:

January 2007:	First Edition.
February 2007:	Second Printing.
August 2007:	Third Printing.
October 2007:	Fourth Printing.

RepKover.
This book uses RepKover™, a durable and flexible lay-flat binding.

ISBN-10: 0-596-52826-4
ISBN-13: 978-0-596-52826-3

Windows Vista
for Starters
THE MISSING MANUAL

TABLE OF CONTENTS

PART TWO: THE PIECES OF VISTA

PART THREE: VISTA ONLINE

THE MISSING CREDITS

About the Author

 **David Pogue** is the weekly tech columnist for the *New York Times,* an Emmy-winning correspondent for CBS News Sunday Morning, and the creator of the Missing Manual series. He's the author or co-author of 40 books, including 17 in this series and six in the "For Dummies" line (including *Macs, Magic, Opera, and Classical Music*). In his other life, David is a former Broadway show conductor, a magician, and a pianist. News, photos, links to his columns and weekly videos await at *www.davidpogue.com.* He welcomes feedback about his books by email at *david@pogueman.com.*

About the Creative Team

Teresa Noelle Roberts (copy editor) is a freelance copy editor and proofreader, as well as a published fiction writer and poet. When she can tear herself away from the computer, she may be found gardening, belly dancing, or enjoying the beautiful beaches of New England.

On this edition, she was joined in her editorial duties by Missing Manuals editorial veteran John Cacciatore.

Lesa Snider King (production editor and graphics goddess) assists David Pogue on many projects. As Chief Evangelist for iStockphoto.com and a veteran writer for international graphics publications, Lesa is on a mission to teach the world how to create beautiful graphics. You can see more of her work at *TheGraphicReporter.com,* and catch her live at many conferences. Email: *lesa@graphicreporter.com.*

Shawn King (graphics assistance and beta reader) is the host of a popular Internet broadcast called Your Mac Life, and has been using computers since several years B.D. (Before DOS). Having grabbed a PC mouse and literally followed every single step on every single page of this book to test for accuracy, he can safely say that he now knows more about Windows Vista than he ever hoped to know. Email: *shawn@yourmaclife.com*.

Phil Simpson (design and layout) works out of his office in Southbury, Connecticut, where he has had his graphic design business since 1982. He is experienced in many facets of graphic design, including corporate identity/branding, publication design, and corporate and medical communications. Email: *pmsimpson@earthlink.net*.

Acknowledgments

The Missing Manual series is a joint venture between the dream team introduced on these pages and O'Reilly Media. I'm grateful to all of them, and also to a few people who did massive favors for this book. They include Matt Parretta and Frank Kane, PR guys for Microsoft who devoted themselves to helping me find information; Windows Vista product manager Greg Sullivan, who tolerated being henpecked with my questions; HP and Motion for loaning me testing gear; and proofreaders Sohaila Abdulali, John Cacciatore, Genevieve d'Entremont, Jamie Peppard, and Sada Preisch.

Incidentally, this book is adapted from a much heavier, fatter, more advanced tome called *Windows Vista: The Missing Manual.* That 850-page monster featured contributions from some of the best technical writers in Windows-dom, and some of their prose still inhabits these pages: Joli Ballew, C.A. Callahan, Preston Gralla, and Brian Jepson. I was honored to work with them.

Thanks to David Rogelberg for believing in the idea, and above all, to Jennifer, Kelly, Tia, and Jeffrey, who make these books—and everything else—possible.

—David Pogue

The Missing Manual Series

The Missing Manuals are superbly written guides to computer products that don't come with printed manuals (which is just about all of them). Each book features a hand-crafted index; cross-references to specific page numbers (not just "See Chapter 14"); and RepKover, a detached-spine binding that lets the book lie perfectly flat without the assistance of weights or cinder blocks. Recent and upcoming titles include:

- *Windows Vista: The Missing Manual,* by David Pogue
- *Windows XP Home Edition: The Missing Manual, 2nd Edition* by David Pogue

- *GarageBand 2: The Missing Manual* by David Pogue

- *iLife '05: The Missing Manual* by David Pogue

- *iMovie 6 & iDVD: The Missing Manual* by David Pogue

- *iPhoto 6: The Missing Manual* by David Pogue and Derrick Story

- *iPod & iTunes: The Missing Manual, 4th Edition* by J.D. Biersdorfer

- *iWork '05: The Missing Manual* by Jim Elferdink

- *Office 2004 for Macintosh: The Missing Manual* by Mark H. Walker, Franklin Tessler, and Paul Berkowitz

For Starters

The "For Starters" books contain only the most essential information from their larger counterparts—in larger type, with a more spacious layout, and none of those advanced sidebars. Recent titles include:

- *Windows Vista for Starters: The Missing Manual* by David Pogue

- *Windows XP for Starters: The Missing Manual* by David Pogue

- *Access 2007 for Starters: The Missing Manual* by Matthew MacDonald

- *Excel 2007 for Starters: The Missing Manual* by Matthew MacDonald

- *Quicken 2006 for Starters: The Missing Manual* by Bonnie Biafore

- *Word 2007 for Starters: The Missing Manual* by Chris Grover

- *PowerPoint 2007 for Starters: The Missing Manual* by Emily A. Vander Veer

- *Mac OS X for Starters, Leopard Edition: The Missing Manual* by David Pogue

INTRODUCTION

▶ About This Book

▶ About MissingManuals.com

Let's face it: in the last few years, all the fun went out of using a PC. Viruses, spyware, spam, pop-ups, and other Web nastiness had turned us all into cowering system administrators, spending far too much time trying to shore up our computers rather than using them to get things done.

Why on earth didn't Microsoft do something?

Of course, now we know: Microsoft *was* doing something. It just took five years to finish doing it.

That something was Windows Vista, a new version (well, OK, five versions) that comes with every porthole sealed, every backdoor nailed shut, and every design flaw reworked by a newly security-conscious squad of Microsofties.

Microsoft won't go as far as saying that Vista is invulnerable; nothing with 50 million lines of code could possibly be bulletproof. The bad guys are going to do their best.

But it's safe to say that Vista is by far the most secure Windows yet, and that the sociopaths of the Internet will have a much, much harder time.

That's not all Microsoft accomplished in writing Vista, though. As you'll notice within the first 5 seconds, the company also gave the operating system a total overhaul, both in its capabilities and its look. Vista is the best-looking version of Windows ever.

Version Chaos

You thought Windows XP was bad, with its two different versions (Home and Pro)?

Windows Vista comes in *five* different versions: Home Basic, Home Premium, Business, Enterprise, and Ultimate. And that's not even counting the Starter edition, sold exclusively in poor countries outside North America, or the two "N" versions (like Home Basic N), which are sold in Europe to comply with a different set of antitrust laws.

___ Tip _____
This book series, "for Starters," has nothing to do with Windows Vista, Starter Edition. In fact, we thought of it first. :)
_____

Microsoft says that each version is perfectly attuned to a different kind of customer, as though each edition had been somehow conceived differently. In fact, though, the main thing that distinguishes the editions is the suite of programs that comes with each one. For example:

▶ **Home Premium** comes with Movie Maker (edit your camcorder footage), DVD Maker (turn home movies into simple video DVDs), Media Center (displays your photos and videos on a TV set), and parental controls (lets you limit what your kids do online and what programs they use). None of this is included with the Business or Enterprise versions, on the assumption that busy corporate executives don't have kids, camcorders, or TVs at work.

▶ **Business** and **Enterprise** versions, on the other hand, come with certain goodies that are most useful in corporations. They include Complete PC Backup (makes a snapshot of your entire hard drive), password protection for individual files and folders, Windows Fax and Scan (for faxing and scanning, of course), Remote Desktop (lets you control another PC from across the Internet), and lots of hyper-technical networking features.

▶ And then there's the expensive **Ultimate** version, which, as you'd guess, includes everything from all versions.

Except where noted, every word in this book applies equally well to every Vista version. Meanwhile, if some feature makes you salivate, fear not. Microsoft is only too happy to let you upgrade your copy of Windows Vista to a more expensive edition, essentially "unlocking" features for a fee.

— Tip —
> Vista Enterprise is not sold in any store. It's sold directly to corporations for mass installation by highly paid network geeks.

About This Book

Windows Vista comes with no printed user guide at all. To learn about the thousands of pieces of software that make up this operating system, you're supposed to read the online help screens.

Unfortunately, as you'll quickly discover, these help screens are tersely written, offer very little technical depth, and lack examples. You can't even mark your place, underline, or read them in the bathroom.

The purpose of this book, then, is to serve as the startup manual that should have accompanied Windows Vista. In these pages, you'll find step-by-step instructions for using almost every important Windows feature.

About the Outline

This book is divided into seven parts, each containing several chapters:

▶ Part 1, **The Vista Desktop**, covers everything you see on the screen when you turn on a Windows Vista computer: icons, windows, menus, scroll bars, the Recycle Bin, shortcuts, the Start menu, shortcut menus, and so on. It also covers the juicy new system-wide, instantaneous Search feature.

▶ Part 2, **The Pieces of Vista,** is dedicated to the proposition that an operating system is little more than a launch pad for *programs.* Chapter 6 describes how to work with programs and documents in Windows—launch them, switch among them, swap data between them, use them to create and open files, and so on—and how to use the new micro-programs called *gadgets.*

This part also offers an item-by-item discussion of the individual software nuggets that make up this operating system. These include not just the items in your Control Panel, but also the most important free programs that Microsoft threw in: Windows Media Player, Photo Gallery, Movie Maker, and so on.

▶ Part 3, **Vista Online,** covers all the special Internet-related features of Windows, including setting up your Internet account, Windows Mail (for email), Internet Explorer 7 (for Web browsing), and so on. Chapter 8 also covers Vista's Internet fortification features: the firewall, anti-spyware software, parental controls, and on and on.

▶ Part 4, **Beyond the Basics,** describes the operating system's relationship with equipment you can attach to your PC—scanners, cameras, disks, printers, and so on. It also explores Vista's greatly beefed-up backup and troubleshooting tools.

▶ Part 5, **The Vista Network,** is for the millions of households and offices that contain more than one PC. These chapters show you how to build your own network. File sharing, accounts and passwords are here, too.

At the end of the book, three appendixes provide a guide to installing this operating system, the "Where'd It Go?" Dictionary, which lists every feature Microsoft moved or deleted on the way to Windows Vista, and a master list keyboard shortcuts in Vista.

About→These→Arrows

Throughout this book, and throughout the Missing Manual series, you'll find sentences like this: "Open the Start→Computer→Local Disk (C:)→Windows folder." That's shorthand for a much longer instruction that directs you to open three nested icons in sequence, like this: "Click the Start menu to open it. Click Computer in the Start menu. Inside the Computer window is a disk labeled Local Disk (C:); double-click it to open it. Inside *that* window is yet *another* icon called Windows. Double-click to open it, too."

Similarly, this kind of arrow shorthand helps to simplify the business of choosing commands in menus, as shown in Figure I-1.

Figure I-1: In this book, arrow notations help to simplify folder and menu instructions. For example, "Choose Start→Control Panel→AutoPlay" is a more compact way of saying, "Click the Start button. When the Start menu opens, point to Control Panel; without clicking, now slide to the right onto AutoPlay," as shown here.

About MissingManuals.com

You're invited and encouraged to submit corrections and updates to this book's Web page at *www.missingmanuals.com*. (Click the book's name, and then click the Errata link.) In an effort to keep the book as up-to-date and accurate as possible, each time we print more copies of this book, we'll make any corrections you've suggested.

Even if you have nothing to report, you should check that Errata page now and then. That's where we'll post a list of the corrections and updates we've made, so that you can mark important corrections into your own copy of the book, if you like.

In the meantime, we'd love to hear your suggestions for new books in the Missing Manual line. There's a place for that on the Web site, too, as well as a place to sign up for free email notification of new titles in the series.

PART ONE:
THE VISTA DESKTOP

THE VERY BASICS

▶ About Windows

▶ Mouse and Keyboard Essentials

As any good teacher can tell you, it's best not to put the cart before the horse—or to start flinging computer jargon around without first explaining the lay of the land. And with Windows Vista, there's a heck of a lot of land to survey. The following pages don't actually show you how to do very much—but the do prepare you, psychologically and philosophically, for what your Windows PC holds in store.

About Windows

Windows is an *operating system,* the software that controls your computer. It's designed to serve you in several ways:

▶ **It's a launching bay.** At its heart, Windows is a home base, a remote-control clicker that lets you call up the various software programs (applications) you use to do work or kill time. When you get right down to it, applications are the real reason you bought a PC.

Windows Vista is a well-stocked software pantry unto itself; for example, it comes with a Web browser, email program, simple word processor, and calculator. Vista comes with a suite of games, too.

If you were stranded on a desert island, the built-in Windows programs could suffice for everyday operations. But if you're like most people, sooner or later, you'll buy and install more software. That's one of the luxuries of using Windows: you can choose from a staggering number of add-on programs. Whether you're a left-handed bee-keeper or a German-speaking nun, some company somewhere is selling Windows software designed just for you, its target audience.

▶ **It's a file cabinet.** Every application on your machine, as well as every document you create, is represented on the screen by an *icon,* a little picture that symbolizes the underlying file or container. You can organize these icons into onscreen file folders. You can make backups (safety copies) by dragging file icons onto a floppy disk or blank CD, or send files to people by email. You can also trash icons you longer need by dragging them onto the Recycle Bin icon.

▶ **It's your equipment headquarters.** What you can actually see of Windows is only the tip of the iceberg. An enormous chunk of Windows is behind-the-scenes plumbing that controls the various functions of your computer—its modem, screen, keyboard, printer, and so on.

Mouse and Keyboard Essentials

To use almost any kind of computer, you need to know a few basics. You won't get far without mastering a few terms and concepts:

▶ **Clicking.** This book gives you three kinds of instructions that require you to use the Mac's mouse. To *click* means to point the arrow cursor at something on the screen and then—without moving the cursor—press and release the clicker button on the mouse (or your laptop trackpad). To *double-click,* of course, means to click twice in rapid succession, again without moving the cursor at all. And to *drag* means to move the cursor while holding down the button.

When you're told to *Ctrl-click* something, you click while pressing the Ctrl key (which is next to the Space bar). *Shift-clicking* and *Alt-clicking* work the same way— just click while pressing the corresponding key.

▶ **Icons.** The colorful inch-tall pictures that appear in your various desktop folders are the graphic symbols that represent each program, disk, and document on your computer. See Figure 1-1.

Contacts Desktop Documents Jensen Project

Pictures Saved Games Searches (I've Been) Searchin' ...

Figure 1-1: These are just a few of the icons you'll encounter in Window. If you click an icon one time, it darkens, indicating that you've just *highlighted* or *selected* it. Now you're ready to manipulate it by using, for example, a menu command. If you double-click an icon, on the other hand, you open it (usually into a window or a program).

▶ **Menus.** The *menus* are the words that appear in a row at the top of many windows: File, Edit, and so on. Click one to make a list of commands appear.

Some people click and release to open a menu and then, after reading the choices, click again on the one they want. Other people like to press the mouse button continuously after the initial click on the menu title, drag down the list to the desired command, and only then release the mouse button. Either method works fine.

▶ **Keyboard shortcuts.** If you're typing along in a burst of creative energy, it's disruptive to have to grab the mouse to use a menu. That's why many experienced PC fans prefer to trigger menu commands by pressing certain combinations on the keyboard.

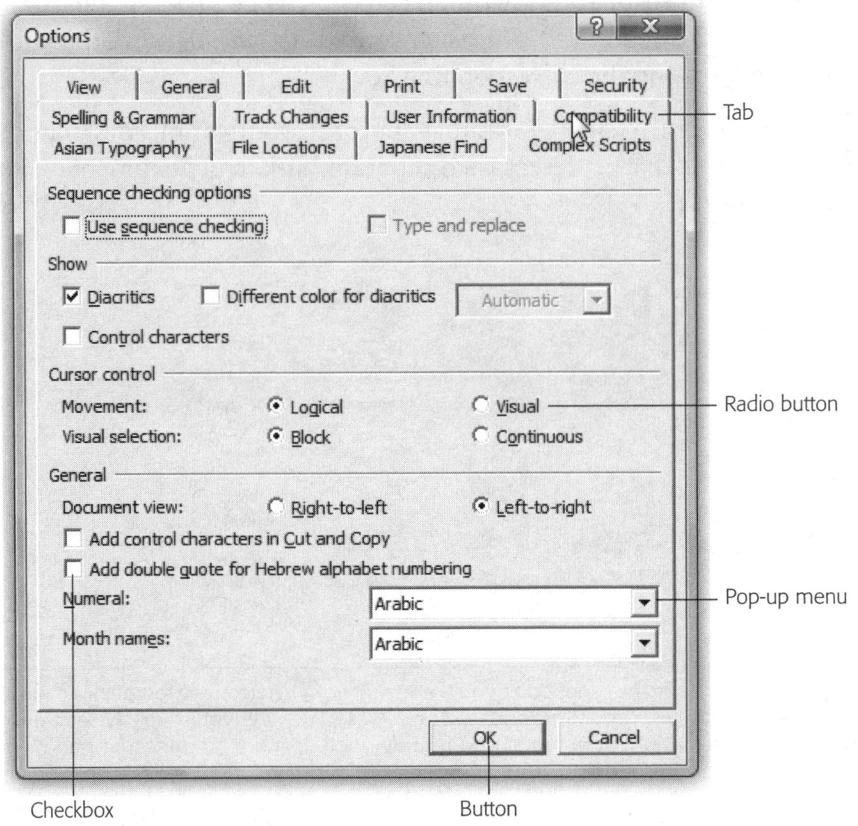

Figure 1-2: You'll find certain components recurring throughout Windows. Checkboxes, for example, let you turn on as many features as you want. Radio buttons are different; like the radio preset buttons on a car, only one can be selected at a time.

For example, in word processors, you can press Ctrl+B to produce a boldface word. When you read an instruction like "press Ctrl+B," start by pressing the Ctrl key; then, while it's down, type the letter B; and finally release both keys.

▶ **Checkboxes, radio buttons, tabs.** See Figure 1-2 for a quick visual reference to the onscreen controls you're most often asked to use.

The Right Mouse Button is King

One of the most important features of Windows isn't on the screen—it's under your hand. The standard mouse has two mouse buttons. You use the left one to click buttons, highlight text, and drag things around on the screen.

When you click the right button, however, a *shortcut menu* appears onscreen, like the ones shown in Figure 1-3. Get into the habit of *right-clicking* things—icons, folders, disks, text in your word processor, buttons on your menu bar, pictures on a Web page,

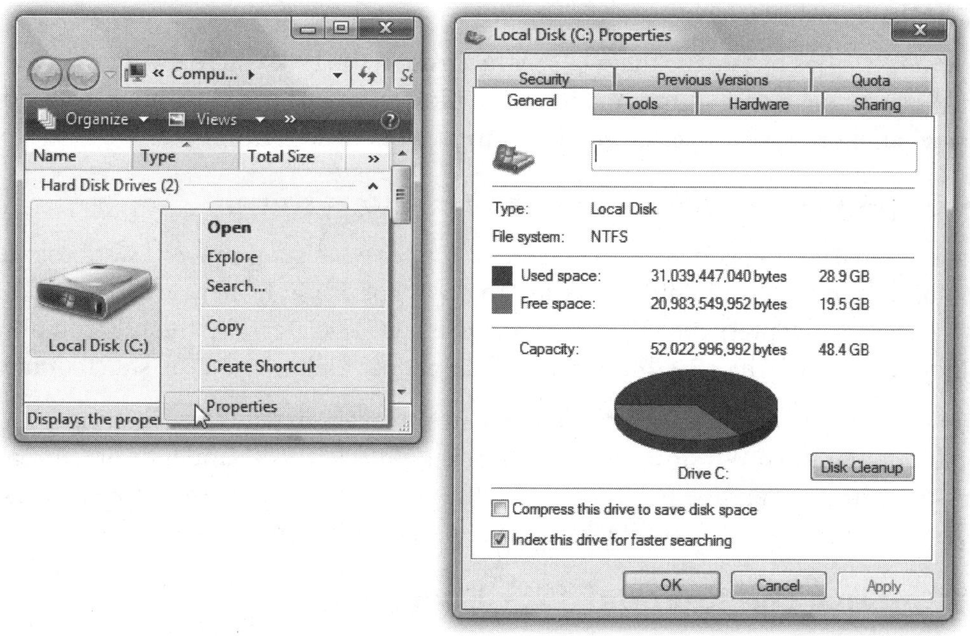

Figure 1-3: One quick way to find out how much space is left on your hard drive is to right-click the corresponding icon, and then choose the Properties command (left). The Properties dialog box appears (right), featuring a handy disk-space graph.

and so on. The commands that appear on the shortcut menu will make you much more productive and lead you to discover handy functions you never knew existed.

This is a big deal: Microsoft's research suggests that nearly 75 percent of Windows users don't use the right mouse button, and therefore miss hundreds of timesaving shortcuts. Part of the rationale behind Windows Vista's redesign is putting these functions out in the open. Even so, many more shortcuts remain hidden under your right mouse button.

___ Tip _____

Microsoft doesn't discriminate against left-handers... much. You can swap the functions of the right and left mouse buttons easily enough.

Choose Start→Control Panel. Click "Classic view." Open the Mouse icon. When the Mouse Properties dialog box opens, click the Buttons tab, and then turn on "Switch primary and secondary buttons." Then click OK. Windows now assumes that you want to use the *left* mouse button as the one that produces shortcut menus.

_____

Wizards = Interviews

A *wizard* is a series of screens that walks you through the task you're trying to complete. Wizards make configuration and installation tasks easier by breaking them down into smaller, more easily digested steps. Figure 1-4 offers an example.

There's More Than One Way to Do Everything

No matter what setting you want to adjust, no matter what program you want to open, Microsoft has provided 165 different ways to do it. For example, here are the various ways to delete a file: press the Delete key; choose File→Delete; drag the file icon onto the Recycle Bin; or right-click the file, and then choose Delete from the shortcut menu.

Pessimists grumble that there are too many paths to every destination, making it much more difficult to learn Windows. Optimists point out that this abundance of approaches means that almost everyone will find, and settle on, a satisfying method for each task. Whenever you find a task irksome, remember you have other options.

You Can Use the Keyboard for Everything

In earlier versions of Windows, underlined letters appeared in the names of menus and dialog boxes. These underlines were clues for people who found it faster to do something by pressing keys than by using the mouse.

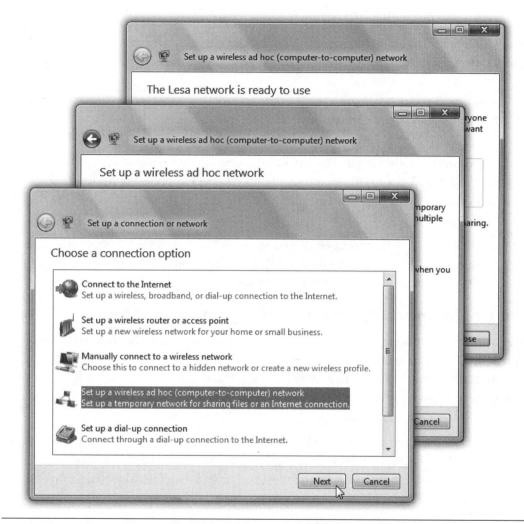

Figure 1-4: Wizards (interview screens) are everywhere in Windows. On each of the screens, you're supposed to answer a question about your computer or your preferences, and then click a Next button. When you click the Finish button on the final screen, Windows whirls into action, automatically completing the installation or setup.

The underlines are hidden in Windows Vista, at least in disk and folder windows. (They may still appear in your individual software programs.) If you miss them, you can make them reappear by pressing the Alt key, Tab key, or an arrow key whenever the menu bar is visible. (When you're operating menus, you can release the Alt key immediately after pressing it.) In this book, in help screens, and computer magazines, you'll see key combinations indicated like this: Alt+S (or Alt+ whatever the letter key is).

___ **Note** _____
    In some Vista programs, in fact, the entire *menu bar* is gone until you press Alt (or F10).
    That includes everyday Explorer windows.
_____

Once the underlines are visible, you can open a menu by pressing the underlined letter (F for the File menu, for example). Once the menu is open, press the underlined letter key that corresponds to the menu command you want. Or press Esc to close the menu without doing anything. (In Windows, the Esc key always means *cancel* or *stop*.)

If choosing a menu command opens a dialog box, you can trigger its options by pressing Alt along with the underlined letters. (Within dialog boxes, you can't press and release Alt; you have to hold it down while typing the underlined letter.)

You Could Spend a Lifetime Changing Properties

You can't write an operating system that's all things to all people, but Microsoft has certainly tried. You can change almost every aspect of the way Windows looks and works. You can replace the gray backdrop of the screen (the *wallpaper*) with your favorite photograph, change the typeface used for the names of your icons, or set up a particular program to launch automatically every time you turn on the PC.

When you want to change some *general* behavior of your PC, like how it connects to the Internet, how soon the screen goes black to save power, or how quickly a letter repeats when you hold down a key, you use the Control Panel window (described in Chapter 6).

Many other times, however, you may want to adjust the settings of only one particular element of the machine, such as the hard drive, the Recycle Bin, or a particular application. In those cases, simply right-click the corresponding icon. In the resulting shortcut menu, you'll often find a command called Properties. When you click it, a dialog box appears, containing settings or information about that object, as shown in Figure 1-4.

___ **Tip** _____
    As a shortcut to the Properties command, just highlight an icon and then press Alt+Enter.
_____

It's also worth getting to know how to operate *tabbed dialog boxes,* like the one shown in Figure 1-2. These are windows that contain so many options, Microsoft has had to split them up into separate panels, or *tabs.* To reveal a new set of options, just click a different tab (called General, Tools, Hardware, Sharing, Security, and Quota in Figure 1-3). These tabs are designed to resemble the tabs at the top of file folders.

___ Tip _____

You can switch tabs without using the mouse by pressing Ctrl+Tab (to "click" the next tab to the right) or Ctrl+Shift+Tab (for the previous tab).

_____

UP TO SPEED

Scrolling: The Missing Manual

These days, PC monitors are bigger than ever—but so are the Web pages and documents that they display.

Scroll bars, of course, are the strips that may appear at the right side and/or bottom of a window. The scroll bar signals you that the window isn't big enough to reveal all of its contents.

Click the arrows at each end of a scroll bar to move slowly through the window, or drag the rectangular handle (the *thumb*) to move faster. (The position of the thumb in the scroll bar reflects your relative position in the entire window or document.) You can quickly move to a specific part of the window by holding the mouse button down on the scroll bar where you want the thumb to be. The scroll bar rapidly scrolls to the desired location and then stops.

Scrolling is such a frequently needed skill, though, that all kinds of other scrolling gadgets have cropped up.

Your mouse probably has a little wheel on the top. You can scroll in most programs just by turning the wheel with your finger, even if your cursor is nowhere near the scroll bar. You can turbo-scroll by dragging the mouse upward or downward while keeping the wheel pressed down inside the window.

Laptops often have some kind of scrolling gizmo, too. Maybe you have an actual roller, or maybe the trackpad offers drag-here-to-scroll strips on the right side and across the bottom.

Of course, keyboard addicts should note that you can scroll without using the mouse at all. Press the Page Up or Page Down keys to scroll the window by one window-full, or use the up and down arrow keys to scroll one line at a time.

Every Piece of Hardware Requires Software

When computer geeks talk about their *drivers,* they're not talking about their chauffeurs (unless they're Bill Gates); they're talking about the controlling software required by every hardware component of a PC.

The driver is the translator between your PC's brain and the equipment attached to it: mouse, keyboard, screen, DVD drive, scanner, digital camera, palmtop, and so on. Without the correct driver software, the corresponding piece of equipment doesn't work at all.

When you buy one of these gadgets, you receive a CD containing the driver software. If the included driver software works fine, then you're all set. If your gadget acts up, however, remember that equipment manufacturers regularly release improved (read: less buggy) versions of these software chunks. (You generally find such updates on the manufacturers' Web sites.)

Fortunately, Windows Vista comes with drivers for over 12,000 components, saving you the trouble of scavenging for them on a disk or on the Internet. This gigantic library is the heart of Microsoft's Plug and Play feature, which lets you connect a new gadget to your PC without even thinking about the driver software (Chapter 12).

It's Not Meant to Be Overwhelming

Windows has an absolutely staggering array of features. You can burrow six levels down, dialog box through dialog box, and never come to the end of it. There are enough programs, commands, and help screens to keep you studying the rest of your life.

It's crucial to remember that Microsoft's programmers created Windows in modules—the digital-photography team here, the networking team there—with different audiences in mind. The idea, of course, was to make sure that no subset of potential customers would find a feature lacking.

But if *you* don't have a digital camera, a network, or whatever, there's absolutely nothing wrong with ignoring everything you encounter on the screen that isn't relevant to your setup and work routine. Not even Microsoft's CEO uses every single feature of Windows Vista.

WELCOME CENTER, DESKTOP, AND THE START MENU

▶ The Welcome Center

▶ The Vista Desktop—Now with Aero!

▶ The Start Menu

▶ What's in the Start Menu

▶ Start→⏻ (Sleep)

▶ Start→🔒 (Lock)

▶ Start→Log Off, Restart, Hibernate, Shut Down

▶ Start→Help and Support

▶ Start→Default Programs, →Control Panel

▶ Start→Connect To

► Start→Network

► Start→Computer

► Start→Recent Items

► Start→Search

► Start→Games

► Start→Music, Pictures

► Start→Documents

► Start→[Your Name]: The Personal Folder

2

It's hard to predict exactly what you see the very first time you turn on your Vista computer. It may be a big welcome screen bearing the logo of Dell or whomever; it may be the Vista Setup Wizard (Appendix A); or it may be the *login* screen, where you're asked to sign in by clicking your name in a list. (Skip to page 365 for details on logging in.)

Eventually, though, you arrive at something that looks like Figure 2-1: the shining majesty of the new Vista Welcome Center.

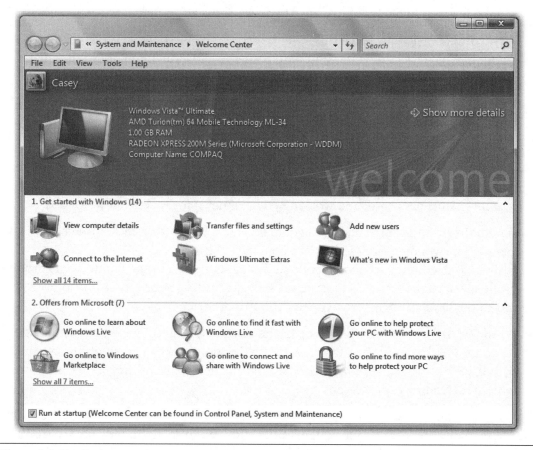

Figure 2-1: The Welcome Center, new in Windows Vista, offers links to various useful corners of the operating system. Most are designed to help you set up a new PC. (Click once to read a description, and then double-click to open the link.)

The Welcome Center

The Welcome Center is supposed to be an antidote to the moment of dizzy disorientation that you'd otherwise feel the first time you fire up Vista. It's basically a window full of links to useful places in the Vista empire. Click a link *once* to read its description in the top part of the window, or *twice* to open up the control panel or program you need to make changes.

Here are a few highlights (you may have to click "Show all 14 items" to see them):

▶ **View computer details.** Click this icon to read, in the top pane of the Welcome Center, the tech specs of your computer: its name, how much memory it has, what processor chip is inside, which graphics card you have, and so on.

▶ **Transfer files and settings.** The Vista program called Windows Easy Transfer is designed to transfer files and settings from an older PC.

▶ **Add new users.** If you're the lord of the manor, the sole user of this computer, you can ignore this little item. But if you and other family members, students, or workers *share* this computer, you'll want to consult Chapter 15 about how to set up a separate *account* (name, password, and working environment) for each person.

▶ **Personalize Windows.** Sure, sure, eventually you'll be plotting rocket trajectories and mapping the genome—but let's not kid ourselves. The first order of business is decorating: choosing your screen saver, replacing the desktop background (wallpaper), choosing a different cursor shape, adjusting your monitor resolution, and so on. Double-click here to open the appropriate control panel.

▶ **Windows Basics.** Double-click to open the electronic help screen whose articles cover the *very* basics of your PC: how to use the mouse, how to turn off the computer, and so on. If you're very new to PCs, close the door, turn off the phone, and spend some time reading these screens.

Below a horizontal line, you'll find another group of icons called Offers from Microsoft. Needless to say, these are various opportunities for you to spend money on Microsoft software and services, or to download Microsoft add-on programs.

At the *very* bottom of the Welcome Center, you'll find an important checkbox called "Run at startup." This is not some kind of warning that you should evacuate every time the computer boots. Instead, it's the on/off switch for the Welcome Center itself. If you turn off the checkbox, the Welcome Center no longer appears each time you turn on the PC. (You can always bring it back by clicking its link in the Control Panel, as described on page 152.)

If you'd rather get rid of the Welcome Center just for now, click its Close box. Or learn to press Alt+F4, the universal Windows keystroke for "Close this window."

UP TO SPEED

The Windows Experience Index

Quick—which computer is better, an AMD Turion 64 ML-34 processor at 1.80 gigahertz but only 512 megs of RAM, or a Core Duo 2.0 gigahertz with 1 gig of RAM but only a Radon Xpress 200M graphics card?

If you know the answer offhand, you shouldn't be reading a book about Vista; you should be writing your own darned book.

The point is, of course, that Vista is an extremely demanding operating system. It craves horsepower, speed, and memory. But Microsoft didn't really expect the average person, or even the average I.T. manager, to know at a glance whether a particular PC is up to the Vista challenge.

That's why Vista analyzes the guts of your computer and boils the results down to a single numerical rating. To find out yours, choose Start→Control Panel. Click "System and Maintenance," and then click "Check your computer's Windows Experience Index base score."

The final score is the lowest of any of the subscores. For example, if your memory,

hard drive, and graphics all get scores over 4, but your processor's score is only 3.1, your overall score is 3.1, which makes it easy to spot the bottleneck.

A score of 5 is the best; it means you'll be able to run all of Vista's features well and fast. (Actually, it's technically possible to get a score *above* 5; if so, all the better.) You need a score of at least 4 to play and edit high-definition video. A 3 is the minimum for running Vista's new Aero look (page 24). A 1 is the worst; Vista will be dog slow unless you turn off some of the eye-candy features, as described on page 340.

True, finding out that the computer you bought last year for $2,800 is now worth only a measly 2 on the Performance scale could deal your ego quite a bruise.

But fortunately, Microsoft also offers the Vista Upgrade Advisor (available through this book's "Missing CD" at *missingmanuals.com*). This free program reveals your PC's report card *before* you install Vista, so at least you can avoid getting a rude surprise.

The Vista Desktop—Now with Aero!

Once you've recovered from the excitement of the Welcome Center, you get your first glimpse of the full Vista desktop.

All of the usual Windows landmarks are here—the Start menu, taskbar, and Recycle Bin—but they've been given a drastic cosmetic overhaul since the last version of Windows (Figure 2-2). For example:

▶ The edges of windows are extra thick (for easier targeting with your mouse). Parts of the Start menu and window edges are transparent. Windows and dialog boxes cast subtle shadows on the background, as though they're floating.

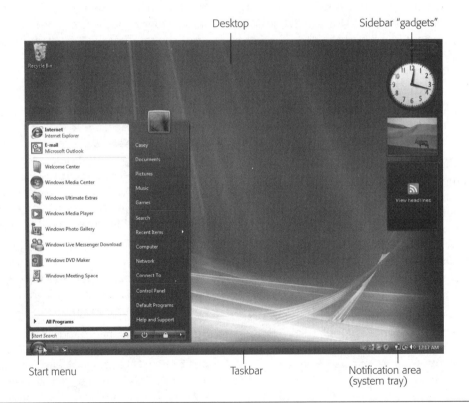

Figure 2-2: There's a new desktop picture in Vista—Microsoft evidently endured one *Teletubbies* joke too many during the Windows XP era—and a glowing, more modern look called Aero. The only truly new element is the Sidebar, the stack of small floating windows that appears at the right side of the screen. (Chapter 6 covers the Sidebar in detail.)

- A new, bigger, more modern font is used for menus and labels.

- When you point to a window button without clicking, the button "lights up." The Minimize and Maximize buttons glow blue; the Close button glows red.

- The *default* button in a dialog box—the one Microsoft thinks you really want, like Save or Print—pulses gently, using fading color intensity to draw your eye.

- Little animations liven up the works, especially when you minimize, maximize, or close a window.

Aero isn't just looks, either—it also includes a couple of features, like Flip 3D and live taskbar icons. You can read about these two useful features in Chapter 3.

What you're seeing is the new face of Windows, known to fans as *Aero*. (It supposedly stands for Authentic, Energetic, Reflective, and Open, but you can't help suspecting that somebody at Microsoft retrofitted those words to fit the initials.)

The Aero design may not actually be Authentic or whatever, but it does look clean and modern. You'll see it, however, *only* if you have a fairly fast, modern PC. Basically, you need a Windows Experience Index score of 3 or higher (page 23), meaning a good amount of memory and a recent graphics card with Vista-specific drivers.

__ Tip _____

The Windows Upgrade Advisor, described on page 23, can tell you in advance if your PC is capable of showing you the Aero goodies.

Furthermore, the Aero features are available only in the more expensive versions of Vista. If you have a slower computer or the Home Basic version of Vista, you'll be able to enjoy all of Vista's features—but they just won't look quite as nice. You'll use them without the transparencies, animations, and other eye candy. The pictures in this book will match the buttons and text you'll see on the screen, but without so much decoration around the edges.

Nobody ever said Microsoft's specialty was making things simple.

The Start Menu

Windows Vista is composed of 50 million lines of computer code, scattered across your hard drive in thousands of files. The vast majority of them are support files, there for behind-the-scenes use by Windows and your applications—they're not for you. They may as well bear a sticker saying, "No user-serviceable parts inside."

That's why the Start menu is so important. It lists every *useful* piece of software on your computer, including commands, programs, and files. Just about everything you do on your PC begins—or can begin—with your Start menu.

In Vista, the *word* Start no longer appears on the Start menu; now the Start menu is just a round, backlit, glass pebble with a Windows logo behind it. But it's still called the Start menu, and it's still the gateway to everything on the PC.

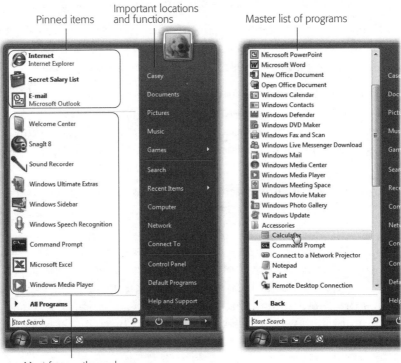

Figure 2-3: Left: The Start menu's top-left section is yours to play with. You can "pin" whatever programs you want here, in whatever order you like. The lower-left section lists programs you use most often. (You can delete individual items here—see page 120—but you can't add things manually or rearrange them.) The right-hand column links to important Windows features and folder locations.

Right: The All Programs menu replaces the left column of the Start menu, listing almost every piece of software you've got. You can rearrange, add to, or delete items from this list.

If you're the type who bills by the hour, you can open the Start menu (Figure 2-3) by clicking it with the mouse. If you're among those who feel that life's too short, however, open it by tapping the ⊞ key on the keyboard instead.

> **Tip**
>
> To find out what something is—something in your Start menu, All Programs menu, or indeed anywhere on your desktop—point to it with your cursor without clicking. A shaded, rectangular Tooltip bar appears, containing a text description. (If the Tooltip doesn't appear, it might be that the window you're pointing to isn't the *active* window on your desktop. Click the window and then try again.)

Anatomy of the Start Menu

The new Start menu is split down the middle into two columns:

▶ **Left side (white).** At the top, above the thin divider line, is the *pinned items list,* which is yours to modify; it lists programs, folders, documents, and anything else you want to open quickly. This list never changes unless you change it.

Below that is the standard Windows *most frequently used programs list. This list is* computed automatically by Windows and may change from day to day.

▶ **Right side (dark).** In general, the right side of the open Start menu is devoted to listing important *places* on the computer: folders like Documents, Pictures, and Music, or special windows like Network, Control Panel, and Computer.

The important new Search command (Chapter 4) appears here, too. And at the bottom, you'll find new buttons that let you turn the PC off or, when you're about to wander away for coffee, lock it so that a password is required to re-enter.

> **Tip**
>
> After 20 years, Microsoft has finally eliminated the prefix My from the important folders of your PC (My Pictures, My Music, My Documents, My Computer, and so on). Maybe it was tired of all the lawsuits from Fisher-Price.
>
> In any case, if you miss that touch of homey personalization, it's easy enough to bring it back; you can rename these special icons just as you would any other icon (page 86). Call it My Computer, call it Your Computer, call it Jar Jar Binks—makes no difference to Vista.

What's in the Start Menu

The following pages take you on a whirlwind tour of the Start menu itself—from the bottom up, left to right, the way your mouse encounters its contents as it moves up from the Start button.

Search Box

This thing is *awesome*.

The instant you pop open the Start menu, your insertion point blinks in the new Start Search box at the bottom of the menu (Figure 2-4). That's your cue that you can begin typing the name of whatever you want to open.

The instant you start to type, you trigger Vista's new, very fast, whole-computer search function. This search finds, among other things, anything *in* the Start menu, making it a very quick way to pull up something without having to click through a bunch of Start menu submenus.

You can read the meaty details about Search in Chapter 4.

All Programs

When you click All Programs, you're presented with an important list indeed: the master catalog of every program on your computer. You can jump directly to your word processor, calendar, or favorite game, for example, just by choosing its name from the Start→All Programs menu.

Rather than covering up the regularly scheduled Start menu (as it did in Windows XP), the All Programs list *replaces* it (or at least the left-side column of it).

You can restore the original left-side column by clicking Back (at the bottom of the list) or pressing the Esc key.

Folders

As you'll quickly discover, the All Programs list in Vista doesn't just list programs. It also houses a number of *folders*. Some of them bear the names of software you've installed; you might see a folder called, for example, Urge (Microsoft's online music-store partner) or Logitech. These generally contain programs, uninstallers, instruction manuals, and other related junk.

___ Tip ___

When you open something that contains *other* things—like a folder listed in the Start menu—you see its contents listed beneath, indented slightly, as shown in **Figure 2-5**. Click the folder name again to collapse the sublisting.

Keyboard freaks should note that you can also open a highlighted folder in the list by pressing the Enter key (or the right arrow key). Close the folder by pressing Enter again (or the left arrow key).

Figure 2-4: As you type, Vista winnows down the list of found items, letter by letter. (You don't have to type the search term and then press Enter.) If the list of results is too long to fit the Start menu, click "See all results" below the list. In any case, Vista highlights the first item in the results. If that's what you want to open, press Enter. If not, you can click what you want to open, or use the arrow keys to walk down the list and then press Enter to open something.

Another set of folders is designed to trim down the Programs menu by consolidating related programs, like Games, Accessories (little single-purpose programs), and Extras and Upgrades. Everything in these folders is described in Chapter 6.

The Startup folder

This folder contains programs that load automatically every time you start Windows Vista. This can be a very useful feature. For instance, if you check your email every morning, you may as well save yourself a few mouse clicks by putting your email program into the Startup folder. If you spend all day long word processing, you may as well put Microsoft Word in there.

Of course, you may be interested in the Startup folder for a different reason: to *stop* some program from launching itself. This is a particularly common syndrome if somebody else set up your PC. Some program seems to launch itself, unbidden, every time you turn the machine on.

Fortunately, it's easy to either add or remove items from the Startup folder:

▶ **Deleting something.** With the Startup folder's listing visible in the All Programs menu, right-click whatever you want to delete. From the shortcut menu, choose Delete. Click Yes to send the icon to the Recycle Bin.

Enjoy your newfound freedom from self-launching software.

▶ **Adding something.** With the All Programs list open, right-click the Startup folder and, from the shortcut menu, choose Open. You've just opened the Startup folder itself.

Once its window is open, navigate to the disk, folder, **application**, or document icon you want to add. (Navigating your files and folders is described in the following chapters.)

Using the right mouse button, drag the icon directly into the Startup window, as shown in Figure 2-5. When you release the button, a shortcut menu appears; from the shortcut menu, choose Create Shortcuts Here.

Close any windows you've opened. From now on, each time you turn on or restart your computer, the program, file, disk, or folder you dragged will open by itself.

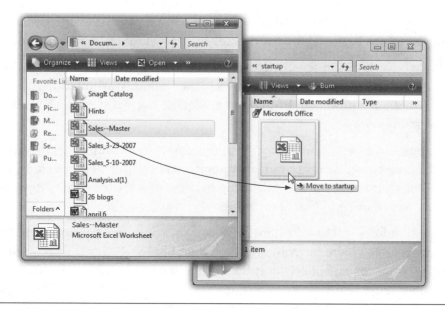

Figure 2-5: It's easy to add a program or document icon to your Startup folder so that it launches automatically every time you turn on the computer. Here, a document from the Documents folder is being added. You may also want to add a shortcut for the Documents folder itself, which ensures that its window will be ready and open each time the computer starts up.

Start→⏻ (Sleep)

The ⏻ button, at the bottom of the Start menu's right column, is the trigger for one of Vista's most useful new features, Sleep mode. Yes, that's right: one of the best things about Vista is how it behaves when you *turn it off*.

Millions of people shut their PCs off every day, but they shouldn't; it's a huge, colossal waste of time on both ends. When you shut down, you have to wait for all your programs to close—and then the next morning, you have to reopen everything, reposition your windows, and get everything back the way you had it.

Millions of other people, therefore, avoid the whole problem by leaving their computers *on* all the time. That, of course, represents a massive waste of electricity and isn't great for the environment.

A new Vista feature called Sleep solves the dilemma neatly. The instant you put the computer to sleep, Vista quietly transfers a copy of everything in memory into an invisible file on the hard drive. But at the same time, it still keeps everything alive in memory, in case you return to the laptop (or desktop) and want to dive back into work.

If you return to work within several hours, starting up is lightning-fast. Everything reappears on the screen faster than you can say, "Redmond, Washington." After you've enjoyed the speed of a power-up from Sleep mode, the normal startup seems interminably, unbearably slow.

But now suppose you *don't* return shortly. In that case, Vista assumes that you're really done for the time being. It cuts power, abandoning what it had memorized. Now your computer is using no power at all. The laptop battery isn't slowly running down; the desktop isn't contributing to global warming.

Fortunately, Windows still has the hard drive copy of your work environment. So *now* when you tap a key to wake the computer, you might have to wait 30 seconds or so—not as fast as two seconds, but certainly better than the five minutes it would take to start up, reopen all your programs, reposition your document windows, and so on.

So here's the bottom line: when you're done working for the moment—or for the day—put your computer to Sleep instead of shutting it down. You save power, you save time, and you risk no data loss.

You can send a laptop to Sleep just by closing the lid. On any kind of computer, you can trigger Sleep by choosing Start→⏻.

Tip _____

Keyboard speed freaks should note that on a desktop *or* a laptop, you can trigger Sleep entirely from the keyboard by pressing ⊞, right arrow, then Enter, in rapid succession.

FREQUENTLY ASKED QUESTION

Start→Stop

Could someone explain why all the variations of Turn Off Computer are in a menu called Start?

The Name-the-Button committee at Microsoft probably thought that you'd interpret Start to mean, "Start here to get some-

thing accomplished."

But you wouldn't be the first person to find it illogical to click Start when you want to stop. Microsoft probably should have named the button "Menu," saving all of us a lot of confusion.

Start→🔒 (Lock)

Also at the bottom of the Start menu's right side, you'll find this little padlock button. Clicking it locks your computer—in essence, it throws a sheet of inch-thick steel over everything you were doing, hiding your screen from view. This is an ideal way to protect your PC from nosy people who happen to wander by your desk while you're away getting coffee or lunch.

All they'll find on your monitor is the standard Logon screen described on page 365. They (and even you) will have to enter your account password to get past it (page 359).

Start→Log Off, Restart, Hibernate, Shut Down

To the right off the little 🔒 icon at the bottom of the Start menu is a small arrow button. As shown in Figure 2-6, it offers a more complete listing of ways to end your work session.

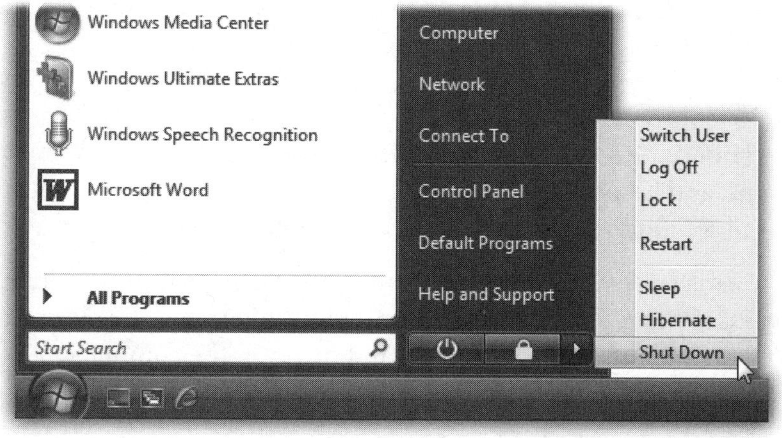

Figure 2-6: It just wouldn't be Microsoft if you didn't have nine different ways to end a work session. Two of them, Sleep and Lock, are duplicated in the form of the ⏻ and 🔒 buttons to the left of the little ▶ button.

Your options include:

▶ **Switch User.** This command refers to Vista's *accounts* feature, in which each person who uses this PC gets to see his own desktop picture, email account, files, and so on. (See Chapter 15.)

When you choose Switch User, somebody else can log into the computer with her own name and password—to do a quick calendar or email check, for example. But whatever *you* had running remains open behind the scenes. After the interloper is finished, you can log in again to find all of your open programs and documents exactly as you left them.

▶ **Log Off.** If you click Log Off, Windows closes all of your open programs and documents (giving you an opportunity to save any unsaved documents first). It then presents a new Welcome screen (page 365) so that the next person can sign in.

▶ **Lock.** When you're going to wander away from your PC for a bit, use this command to protect whatever you were working on, as described above.

▶ **Restart.** This command quits all open programs, then quits and restarts Windows again automatically. The computer doesn't actually turn off. (You might do this to "refresh" your computer when you notice that it's responding sluggishly, for example.)

▶ **Sleep.** You can read about Sleep on page 31.

▶ **Hibernate. Hibernate** mode is a predecessor of Sleep, leftover from previous Windows editions, and it's not nearly as good. (It *doesn't* offer a several-hour period during which the computer will wake up instantly.) Ignore it.

▶ **Shut Down.** This is what most people would call "really, really off." When you shut down your PC, Windows quits all open programs, offers you the opportunity to save any unsaved documents, exits Windows, and turns off the computer.

Start→Help and Support

Choosing Start→Help and Support opens the new, improved Windows Help and Support Center window, which is described in Chapter 14.

Once again, speed fans have an alternative to using the mouse—just press the F1 key to open the Help window. (If that doesn't work, some other program may have Vista's focus. Try it again after clicking the desktop.)

Start→Default Programs, →Control Panel

These commands are just shortcuts to the Default Programs control panel (where you can establish your preferred Web browser, email program, and so on) and the Control Panel window itself (Chapter 6).

Start→Connect To

This command opens the "Connect to a network" dialog box, a simple list of wireless networks that your computer can "see" at the moment. You'll find details on hooking up to a wireless network in Chapter 16.

Start→Network

Choosing Start→Network opens a single, ready-to-use window containing icons of all nearby computers that are on the same network, ready to open and browse for files and folders your comrades have decided to share with you.

Details on networking in Vista are in Chapter 16.

Start→Computer

The Computer command is the trunk lid, the doorway to every single shred of software on your machine. When you choose this command, a window opens to reveal icons that represent each disk drive (or drive partition) in your machine, as shown in Figure 2-7.

For example, by double-clicking your hard drive icon and then the various folders on it, you can eventually see the icons for every single file and folder on your computer. (The Computer icon no longer appears on the desktop—unless you put it there, as described on page 114.)

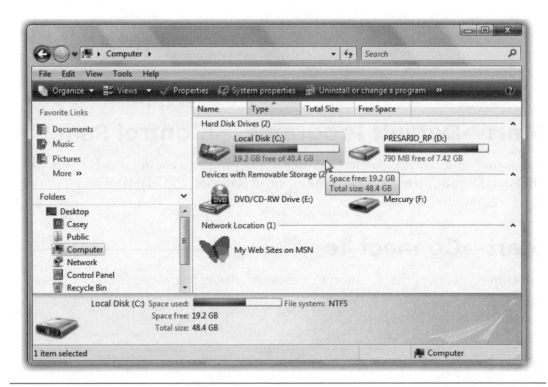

Figure 2-7: The Computer window lists your PC's drives—hard drives, CD drives, USB flash drives, and so on; you may see networked drives listed here, too. This computer has two hard drives, a USB flash drive, and a CD-ROM drive. (If there's a disk in the CD drive, you see its name, not just its drive letter.) When you select a disk icon, the Details pane (if visible) shows its capacity and amount of free space (bottom).

Start→Recent Items

When you click or highlight this command, a submenu sprouts to the right, listing the last 15 documents you've opened. The point, of course, is that you can *re*open one just by clicking its name.

This list can save you time when you want to resume work on something you had open recently, but you're not in the mood to burrow through folders to find its icon.

Note, however, that:

▶ Documents appear on the Recent Items list only if your applications are smart enough to update it. Not all programs do.

▶ The Recent Items list doesn't know when you've deleted a document or moved it to another folder or disk; it continues to list the file even after it's gone. In that event, clicking the document's listing produces only an error message. (At least the message now offers to delete the listing from Recent Items so you don't confuse yourself again the next time.)

By the way, there's another easy way to open a document you've recently worked on. To start, simply open the program you used to create it. Many programs maintain a list of recent documents at the bottom of the File menu; choose one of these names to open the corresponding file.

Secrets of the Personal Folder

Why did Microsoft bury my files in a folder three levels deep?

Vista has been designed from the ground up for *computer sharing.* It's ideal for any situation where different family members, students, or workers share the same PC.

Each person who uses the computer will turn on the machine to find his own separate desktop picture, set of files, Web bookmarks, font collection, and preference settings. (You'll find much more about this feature in Chapter 15.)

If you're the only one who uses this PC, fine—simply ignore the sharing features. But in its little software head, Vista still considers you an account holder, and stands ready to accommodate any others who should come along.

In any case, now you should see the importance of the Users folder in the main hard drive window. Inside are folders—the Personal folders—named for the different people who use this PC. In general, nobody is allowed to touch what's inside anybody else's folder.

If you're the sole proprietor of the machine, of course, there's only one Personal folder in the Users folder—named for you. (You can ignore the Public folder, which is described on page 377.)

This is only the first of many examples in which Vista imposes a fairly rigid folder structure. Still, the approach has its advantages. By keeping such tight control over which files go where, Vista keeps itself pure—and very, very stable. (Other operating systems known for their stability, such as Windows 2000 and Mac OS X, work the same way.)

Furthermore, keeping all of your stuff in a single folder makes it very easy for you to back up your work. It also makes life easier when you try to connect to your machine from elsewhere in the office (over the network), as described in Chapter 16.

Start→Search

This juicy new feature is the new, superfast Search feature; see Chapter 4 for details.

> **Note**
>
> *This* Search command isn't quite the same thing as the Search *box* at the bottom of the Start menu. This one gives you more control. For example, the window that appears when you use *this* Search lets you confine your search to photos, documents, email messages, and so on.

Start→Games

This item is nothing but a shortcut to Vista's folder full of free video games.Good to know when there's time to kill.

Start→Music, Pictures

Microsoft correctly assumes that most people these days use their home computers for managing digital photos and music albums that have been downloaded or copied from CDs. As you can probably guess, the Pictures and Music folders are intended to house your photo and tune collections—and these Start menu commands are quick ways to open them.

In fact, you'll probably find that whatever software came with your digital camera or MP3 player automatically dumps your photos into, and sucks your music files out of, these folders. You'll find much more on these topics in Chapter 7.

Start→Documents

This command opens up your Documents folder, a very important folder indeed. It's designed to store just about all the work you do on your PC—everything except Music, Pictures, and Videos, which get folders of their own.

Of course, you're welcome to file your documents *anywhere* on the hard drive, but most programs propose the Documents folder as the target location for newly created documents.

Sticking with that principle makes a lot of sense, because it makes navigation easy. You never have to wonder where you filed something, since all your stuff is sitting right there in Documents.

Start→[Your Name]: The Personal Folder

As the box on page 37 makes clear, Windows Vista keeps *all* of your stuff—your files, folders, email, pictures, music, bookmarks, even settings and preferences—in one handy, central location: your *Personal folder.* That's a folder bearing your name (or whatever account name you typed when you installed Vista).

Everyone with an account on your PC has a Personal folder—even if you're the only one with an account.

___ **Note** _____

> See Chapter 15 for the full scoop on user accounts.

_____

Technically, your Personal folder lurks inside the C:→Users folder. But that's a lot of burrowing when you just want a view of your entire empire.

That's why your Personal folder is also listed here, at the top of the Start menu's right-side column. Choose this listing to open the folder that you'll eventually fill with new folders, organize, back up, and so on.

FREQUENTLY ASKED QUESTION

On and Off

OK, this is a little embarrassing—but hey, it's supposed to be a beginner's book, right? OK, here goes. How do I turn my PC on and off?

Don't be shy; everybody has to start somewhere.

Somewhere on your PC is an On button. It's usuallymarked by the ⏻ symbol. Pushing it turns your computer on.

Pushing it again, however (or closing the lid, if it's a laptop), just puts the computer to sleep (page 31).

If you're really determined to shut off the PC for real, see page 34.

But truth is, you're better off using Sleep. You're not wasting electricity, yet the computer will snap right to attention the next time you sit down to work, without making you sit through a long startup.

FILES, FOLDERS, AND WINDOWS

▶ Universal Window Controls

▶ Explorer Window Controls

▶ Optional Window Panes

▶ Icon and List Views

▶ Sorting, Grouping, Stacking, and Filtering

▶ Sizing, Moving, and Closing Windows

▶ Windows Flip (Alt+Tab)

▶ Windows Flip 3D

▶ The Taskbar

Windows got its name from the rectangles on the screen—the *windows*—where every computer activity takes place. You look at a Web page in a window, type into a window, read email in a window, and look at lists of files in a window. But as you create more files, stash them in more folders, and open more programs, it's easy to wind up paralyzed before a screen awash with cluttered, overlapping rectangles.

Fortunately, Windows Vista is crawling with icons, buttons, and other inventions to help you keep these windows under control—along with the files and folders inside them.

Universal Window Controls

There are two categories of windows in Windows:

▶ **Explorer windows.** *Windows Explorer* is Microsoft's name for the desktop world of folders and icons. It's the home-base program that greets you when you first turn on the PC. When you double-click a folder or disk icon on your desktop, what opens is an Explorer window. This is where you organize your files and programs.

▶ **Application windows.** These are the windows where you do your work—in Word or Internet Explorer, for example.

All of these windows have certain parts in common (see Figure 3-1).

Here are the controls that appear on almost every window, whether in an application or Explorer:

▶ **Title bar.** The window's *title* no longer appears here (Figure 3-1), as it did in previous versions of Windows. But this big fat top strip is still a giant handle that you can use to drag a window around.

___ Tip ___

If you double-click the title bar area, you *maximize* the window, making it expand to fill your entire screen exactly as though you had clicked the Maximize button described below. Double-click the title bar again to restore the window to its original size.

▶ **Window edges.** Now they're fatter, making them easier to grab with your mouse. You can change the size of a window by dragging any edge except the top. Position your cursor over any border until it turns into a double-headed arrow. Then drag inward or outward to reshape the window. (To resize a full-screen window, click the Restore Down button first.)

You can resize a window in both dimensions at once just by dragging one of its corners. Sometimes diagonally striped ribs appear at the lower-right corner, sometimes not; in either case, all *four* corners work the same way.

▶ **Minimize, Maximize, [Restore Down].** These three window-control buttons, which appear at the top of every Windows window, are much bigger in Vista than before, which is supposed to make them easier to click. These buttons cycle a window among its three modes—minimized, maximized, and restored—as described on page 64.

▶ **Close button.** Click the X button to close the window. *Keyboard shortcut:* Press Alt+F4.

▶ **Scroll bar.** A scroll bar appears on the right side or bottom of the window if the window isn't large enough to show all its contents (as described in the box on page 17).

Figure 3-1: All windows have the same basic ingredients, making it easy to become an expert in window manipulation. This figure shows an Explorer (desktop) window—a disk or folder—but you'll encounter the same elements in application windows.

Explorer Window Controls

When you're working at the desktop—that is, opening Explorer windows—you'll find a few additional controls dotting the edges. Again, they're quite a bit different from the controls of Windows XP and its predecessors.

Address Bar

In a Web browser, the Address bar is where you type the addresses of the Web sites you want to visit. In an Explorer window, the Address bar is more of a "breadcrumbs bar" (a shout out to Hansel and Gretel fans). That is, it now shows the path you've taken—folders you burrowed through—to arrive where you are now (Figure 3-2, top).

There are two especially cool things about the Vista Address bar:

▶ **It's clickable.** You can click any breadcrumb to open the corresponding folder. For example, if you're viewing the Casey ▶ Pictures ▶ Halloween, you can click the *word* Pictures to backtrack to the Pictures folder.

> **Tip**
> If the succession of nested folders' names is too long to fit the window, then a tiny << icon appears at the left end of the address. Click it to reveal a pop-up menu showing, from last to first, the other folders you've had to burrow through to get here.

UP TO SPEED

The Path to Enlightenment about Paths

Windows is too busy to think of a particular file as "that family album program in the Program Files folder, which is in the Programs folder on the C drive." Instead, it uses shorthand to specify each icon's location on your hard drive—a series of disk and folder names separated by backslashes, like this: *C:\program files\pbsoftware\beekeeperpro.exe.*

This kind of location code is that icon's *path.* (Capitalization doesn't matter, even though you may see capital letters in Microsoft's examples.)

You'll encounter file paths when using several important Windows features. The Address bar at the top of every Explorer window is one, although Microsoft has made addresses easier to read by displaying triangle separators in the Address bar instead of slashes. (That is, you now see Users ▶ Casey instead of Users\Casey.)

Windows Vista for Starters: The Missing Manual

▶ **You can edit it.** You can "open" the Address bar for editing in several different ways. (1) Press Alt+D. (2) Click the tiny icon to the left of the address. (3) Click any blank spot. (4) Right-click anywhere in the address; from the shortcut menu, choose Edit Address.

In each case, the Address bar changes to reveal the old-style slash notation (see the box on the facing page), ready for editing (Figure 3-2, bottom).

___ Tip _____

After you've had a good look, press the Esc key to restore the ▸ notation.

_____

Figure 3-2: Top: The notation in the Address bar, Casey ▸ Pictures ▸ Halloween, indicates that you, Casey, opened your Personal folder (page 37); then opened the Pictures folder inside; and finally opened the Halloween folder inside that.

Bottom: If you press Alt+D, the Address bar restores the slash notation of Windows versions gone by, so that you can type in a different address.

Components of the Address bar

On top of all that, the Address bar houses a few additional doodads that make it easy for you to jump around on your hard drive (Figure 3-3):

- **Back, Forward.** Just as in a Web browser, the Back button opens whatever window you opened just before this one. Once you've used the Back button, you can then use the Forward button to return to the window where you started. *Keyboard shortcuts:* Alt+left arrow, Alt+right arrow.

- **Recent pages list.** Click the ▾ (to the left of the address box) to see a list of folders you've had open recently; it's like a multilevel Back button.

- **Recent folders list.** Click the ▾ at the *right* end of the address box to see a pop-up menu listing addresses you've recently typed.

- **Contents list.** This one takes some explaining, but for efficiency nuts, it's a gift from the gods.

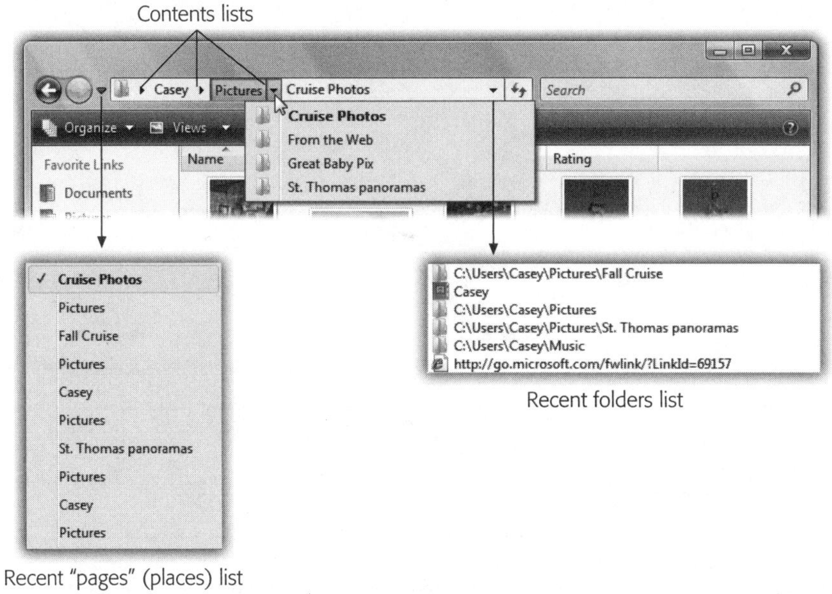

Contents lists

Recent folders list

Recent "pages" (places) list

Figure 3-3: The new Address bar is crawling with useful controls and clickable doodads. It may take you awhile to appreciate the difference between the little ▾ to the left of the Address bar and the one to its right, though. The left-side one shows a list of folders you've had open recently; the right-side one shows addresses you've explicitly typed (and not passed through by clicking).

It turns out that the little ▸ next to each breadcrumb (folder name) is actually a pop-up menu. Click it to see what's *in* the folder name to its left.

How is this useful? Suppose you're viewing the contents of the USA ▸ Florida ▸ Miami folder, but you decide that the folder you're looking for is actually in the USA ▸ California folder. Do you have to click the Back button, retracing your steps to the USA folder, only to then walk back down a different branch of the folder tree? No, you don't. You just click the ▸ that's next to the USA folder's name and choose California from the list.

▸ **Refresh (double swirling arrows button).** If you suspect that the window contents aren't up to date (for example, that maybe somebody has just dropped something new into it from across the network), click this button, or press F5, to make Vista update the display.

▸ **Search box.** Type a search phrase into this box to find what you're looking for *within this window.* Page 79 has the details.

What to type into the Address bar

When you click the tiny folder icon at the left end of the Address bar (or press Alt+D), the triangle ▸ notation changes to the slash\notation, meaning that you can edit the address. At this point, the Address bar is like the little opening that lets you speak to the driver of a New York City taxi; you tell it where you want to go. Here's what you can type there (press Enter afterward):

▸ **A Web address.** You can leave off the *http://* portion. Just type the body of the Web address, such as *www.sony.com,* into this strip. When you press Enter (or click the → button, called the Go button), Internet Explorer opens to the Web page you specified.

> **Tip**
>
> If you press Ctrl+Enter instead of just Enter, you can surround whatever you've just typed into the Address bar with *http://www.* and *.com.* See Chapter 9 for even more address shortcuts along these lines.

▸ **A search phrase.** If you type some text into this strip that isn't obviously a Web address, Windows assumes that you're telling it, "Go online and search for this phrase." From here, it works exactly as though you've used the Internet search feature described on page 230.

▸ **A folder name.** You can also type one of several important folder names into this strip, such as *Computer, Documents, Music,* and so on. When you press Enter, that particular folder window opens.

In each case, as soon as you begin to type, a pop-up list of recently visited Web sites, files, or folders appears below the Address bar. Windows Vista is trying to save you some typing. If you see what you're looking for, click it with the mouse, or press the down arrow key to highlight the one you want and then press Enter.

The Toolbar

See the colored strip (Organize, Views…) that appears just below the Address bar? That's the new *toolbar*. It's something like a menu bar, in that some of the words on it (including Organize and Views) are actually menus, yet also something like the task pane of Windows XP, in that its buttons change from window to window. In a folder that contains pictures, you'll see buttons here like Slide Show and E-mail; in a folder that contains music files, the buttons might say Play All and Burn.

Later in this chapter, you'll meet some of the individual commands in the toolbar.

NOSTALGIA CORNER

Would You Like to See a Menu?

You may have noticed already that in Vista, there's something dramatically different about the menu bar (File, Edit, View and so on): it's gone. Microsoft decided that you'd rather have a little extra space to see your icons.

Fortunately, you can bring it back, in three ways.

Temporarily. Press the Alt key or the F10 key. Presto! The traditional menu bar reappears. You even get to see the classic one-letter underlines that tell you what letter keys you can type to operate the menus without the mouse.

Permanently, all windows. On the Task toolbar, choose Organize→Layout→ Menu Bar. The traditional menu bar appears, right above the task toolbar. There it will stay forever, in all Explorer windows, or at least until you turn it off using the same command.

Permanently, all windows (alternate method). Here's another trick that achieves the same thing. Choose Start→Control Panel. Click Classic View, then Folder Options, then the View tab. Turn on "Always show menus," and then click OK.

Column Headings

Just below the toolbar, every Explorer window also has another horizontal strip you can't hide: a row of column headings like Name, Date Modified, Size, and so on. These, it turns out, are important tools in sorting and grouping the icons, as described on page 58.

Optional Window Panes

Most Explorer windows have some basic informational stuff across the top: the Address bar and the task toolbar, at the very least.

But that's just the beginning. As shown in Figure 3-4, the Organize menu on the task toolbar lets you hide or show as many as four *other* strips of information. Turning them all on at once may make your windows feel a bit claustrophobic, but at least you'll know absolutely everything there is to know about your files and folders.

The trick is to choose a pane name from the Organize→Layout command, as shown in Figure 3-4. Here are the options you'll find there.

___ Tip ___
You can adjust the size of any pane by dragging the dividing line that separates it from the main window. (You'll know when you've got the right spot when your cursor turns into a double-headed arrow.)

Search Pane

As shown in Figure 3-1, the Search pane appears across the top of the window, just below the Address bar. Of course, the Search *box* already appears in every Explorer window, next to the Address bar—so why do you need a Search *pane* as well?

Because the pane gives you a lot more control. It lets you specify more elaborate search criteria, including *where* you want Windows to look. Details are on page 81.

Details Pane

This strip appears at the *bottom* of the window, and it can be extremely useful. It reveals all kinds of information about whatever icon you've clicked in the main part of the window: its size, date, type, and so on. You can even edit some of this information, like the name, "tags" (keywords), and star rating. This is the sort of information that, in the old days, you could see only if you right-clicked and opened the Properties window.

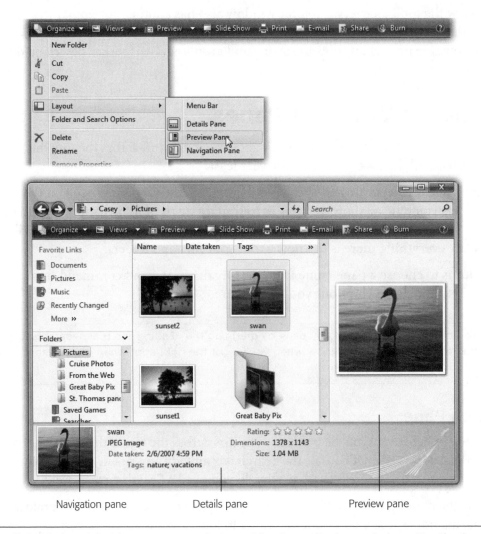

Figure 3-4: Windows Vista has you surrounded—or at least your Explorer windows. Use the Organize menu (top) to summon or dismiss each of the optional panes that can line a window. A subtle outline appears around the icon for each pane you've summoned. Choose the name of a pane once to make it appear, and a second time to hide it.

Preview Pane

The Preview pane appears at the *right* side of the window. That's right: Microsoft has now invented information strips that wrap all four sides of a window.

Anyway, the Preview pane can be handy when you're examining pictures, text files, Office documents, PDF files, sounds, and movies. As you click each icon, you see a miniature version of what's actually *in* that document. As Figure 3-5 demonstrates, a controller lets you play sounds and movies right there in the Explorer window, without having to fire up Windows Media Player. (Cool.)

Figure 3-5: In many windows, the Preview pane can get in the way, because it shrinks the useful window space without giving you much useful information. But when you're browsing movies or sound files, it's awesome; it lets you play the music or the movie right in place, right in the window, without having to open up a playback program.

Navigation Pane

The Navigation pane has two halves: Favorite Links (the top part) and Folders (the bottom part).

Favorite Links list

This area lists *places* to which you want quick access. For example, click the Pictures icon to view the contents of your Pictures folder in the main part of the window (Figure 3-6).

Install your own frequently used folders and disks

Drag to rearrange them

Figure 3-6: The Navigation pane makes navigation very quick, because you can jump back and forth between distant corners of your PC with a single click. Folder and disk icons here work just like normal ones. You can drag a document onto a folder icon to file it there, for example.

The beauty of this parking lot for containers is that it's so easy to set up with *your* favorite places. For example:

▶ **Remove** an icon by dragging it out of the window entirely and onto the Recycle Bin icon; it vanishes from the list. (Of course, you haven't actually removed anything from your *PC*; you've just unhitched its alias from the Navigation pane.)

▶ **Rearrange** the icons by dragging them up or down in the list. Release the mouse when the thick black horizontal line lies in the desired new location.

▶ **Install a new disk or folder icon** by dragging it off of your desktop (or out of a window) into any spot in the list.

▶ **Adjust the width** of the pane by dragging the vertical divider bar right or left.

Folders list

The bottom of the Navigation pane, if you've chosen to view it (Figure 3-7), is a folder "tree" that shows the hierarchy of your entire computer. In essence, this view shows every folder on the machine at once. It lets you burrow very deeply into your hard drive's nest of folders without ever losing your bearings.

Figure 3-7: When you click a disk or folder in the Folders hierarchy, the main window displays its contents, including files and folders. Double-click to expand a disk or folder, opening a new, indented list of what's inside it; double-click again to collapse the folder list again. At deeper levels of indentation, you may not be able to read an icon's full name. Point to it without clicking to see an identifying tooltip.

This hierarchical displays *only* disks and folders; the main window displays the contents (folders *and* files) of whatever disk or folder you click.

When you double-click a folder or disk name (or single-click the flippy triangle next to it), you turn the list view into an outline; the contents of the folder appear in an indented list, as shown in Figure 3-7. Double-click again, or click the flippy triangle again, to collapse the folder listing.

By selectively expanding folders like this, you can, in effect, peer inside two or more folders simultaneously, all within the single Folders list. You can move files around by dragging them onto the tiny folder icons, too.

If you expand folders within folders to a sufficient level, the indentation may push the folder names so far to the right that you can't read them. You can remedy this problem either by making the pane wider (Figure 3-8), or by pointing to a folder whose name is being chopped off. Vista temporarily displays its entire name.

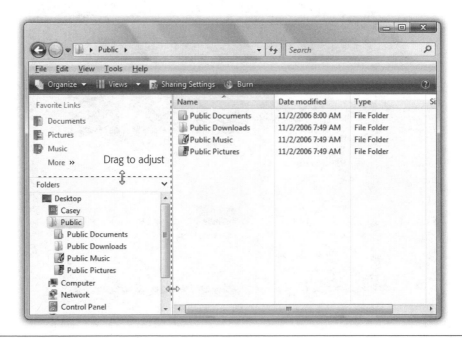

Figure 3-8: If you don't already see the Folders tree, open it by clicking the ^ button at the bottom of the Navigation pane. You can then adjust its height or width by dragging the top or right edges, as shown here.

Icon and List Views

Windows' windows look just fine straight from the factory; the edges are straight, and the text is perfectly legible. Still, if you're going to stare at this computer screen for half of your waking hours, you may as well investigate some of the ways these windows can be enhanced for better looks and greater efficiency.

For starters, you can view the files and folders in an Explorer window in either of two ways: as icons (of any size) or as a list. Figure 3-9 shows some of your options.

Every window remembers its view settings independently. You might prefer to look over your Documents folder in list view (because it's crammed with files and folders), but you may prefer to view the Pictures folder in icon view, where the icons depict miniatures of the actual photos.

To switch a window from one view to another, you have three options, all of which involve the Views pop-up menu shown in Figure 3-9:

▶ **Click the Views button.** With each click, the window switches to the next view in this sequence: List, Details, Tiles, Large Icons.

▶ **Use the Views pop-up menu.** If you click the ▾ triangle next to the word Views, the menu opens, listing Extra Large Icons, Large Icons, Small Icons, List, and so on. Choose the option you want. (They're described below.)

▶ **Use the slider.** The Views menu, once opened, also contains a strange little slider down the left side. It's designed to let Vista's graphics software show off a little. The slider makes the icons shrink or grow freely, scaling them to sizes that fall *between* the canned Extra Large, Large, Medium, and Small choices.

What's so strange about the slider is that part way down its track, it stops adjusting icon sizes and turns into a selector switch for the last three options in the menu: List, Details, or Tiles. Try it—you'll see.

▶ **Icon View.** In an icon view, every file, folder, and disk is represented by a small picture—an *icon*. This humble image, a visual representation of electronic bits and bytes, is the cornerstone of the entire Windows religion. (Maybe that's why it's called an icon.)

What's especially cool is that if you make your icons big enough, *folder* icons appear turned 90 degrees. Now, in real life, setting filing folders onto a desk that way would be idiotic; everything inside would tumble out in a chaotic mess. But in Windows-land, the icons within a folder remain exactly where they are. Better yet, they peek out just enough so that you can see them. In the Music folder, for example, a singer's

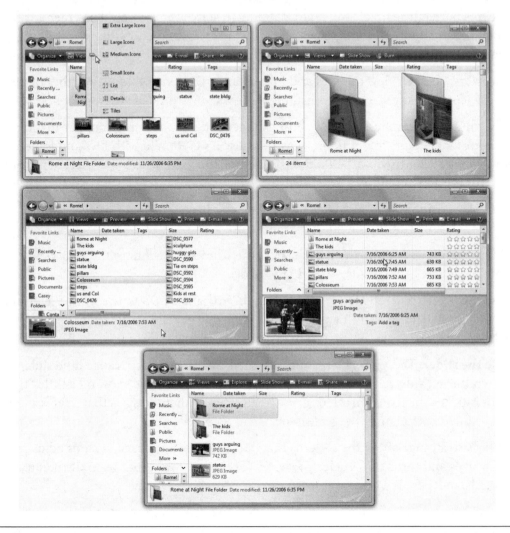

Figure 3-9: The Views pop-up menu is a little weird; it actually has two columns. At right, it displays the preset view options for the files and folders in a window. At left, a slider adjusts icon sizes to any incremental degree of scaling—at least until it reaches the bottom part of its track.

In any case, here's a survey of the window views in Vista. From top left: Icon view (small), Icon view (large), List view, Details view, and Tiles view. List and Details views are great for windows with lots of files.

folder shows the first album cover within; a folder full of PowerPoint presentations shows the first slide or two; and so on. (You can see the effect in Figure 3-9.)

▶ **Tiles view.** Your icons appear at standard size, with name and file details just to the *right*.

▶ **List view** packs, by far, the most files into the space of a window; each file has a tiny icon to its left, and the list of files wraps around into as many columns as necessary to maximize the window's available space.

▶ **Details view** is the same as List view, except that it presents only a single column. It's a table, really; additional columns reveal the size, icon type, modification date, rating, and other information.

Sorting, Grouping, Stacking, and Filtering

Until Vista came along, you could sort the files in a window into an alphabetical or chronological list. But that is *so* 2005.

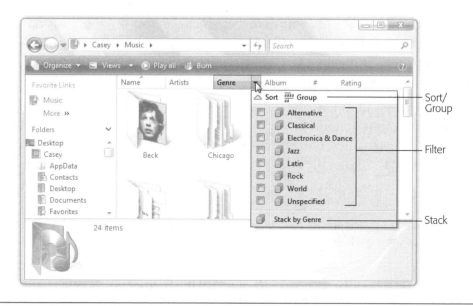

Figure 3-10: This menu looks simple, but is actually complicated. Or maybe the other way around. In any case, this is the menu that sprouts out of each column heading (Name, Size, and so on). In the following pages, you can read about these controls; the top-to-bottom structure (sort/group at the top, filtering controls in the middle, then the Stack command) is always the same.

In Windows Vista, sorting is only one way to impose order on your teeming icons. Now there's *grouping, stacking, and filtering*—new approaches to organizing the stuff in a window.

All of this may get confusing, because every new feature means new controls and new window clutter. But in the end, mastering the stacking-and-grouping bit can pay off in time savings.

As Figure 3-10 shows, the key to sorting, grouping, stacking, and filtering is the pop-up menus hiding within the column headings.

Sorting Files

See the column headings at the top of every Explorer window (Name, Date modified, and so on)?

In Details view, they make perfect sense; they're labels for the columns of information. But what the heck are they doing there in Icon view and List view? Your files and folders aren't even lined up beneath those headings!

It turns out that these headings are far more important in Windows Vista than they were before. They're now your controls for sorting the icons—even in icon view. These headings aren't just signposts; they're also buttons. Click Name for alphabetical order, "Date modified" for chronological order, Size to view largest files at the top, and so on (Figure 3-11).

It's especially important to note the tiny, dark triangle in the heading you've most recently clicked. It shows you *which way* the list is being sorted. When the triangle points upward, oldest files, smallest files, or files whose names begin with numbers (or the letter A) appear at the top of the list, depending on which sorting criterion you have selected.

___ Tip _____

It may help you to remember that when the *smallest* portion of the triangle is at the top, the *smallest* files are listed first when viewed in size order.

_____

To reverse the sorting order, just click the column heading a second time. Now newest files, largest files, or files whose names start with the letter Z appear at the top of the list. The tiny triangle turns upside-down.

Within each window, Windows groups *folders* separately from *files.* They get sorted, too, but within their own little folder ghetto.

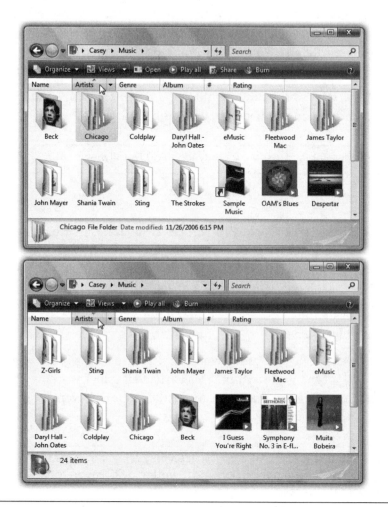

Figure 3-11: Top: You control the sorting order of a list view by clicking the column headings.

Bottom: Click a second time to reverse the sorting order.

The tiny triangle is a reminder. It shows you which way you've sorted the window: in ascending order (for example, A to Z) or descending order (Z to A).

Grouping

When you *group* the icons in a window, they clump together by type, like kids in a high-school cafeteria. In this case, though, the clumping criteria is up to you. You can view your documents grouped by size, your photos grouped by the date they were taken, your music files grouped by band, and so on. As Figure 3-12 shows, Windows identifies each group with its own headline, making the window look like an index. It's an inspired tool that makes it easier to hunt down specific icons in crowded folders.

To group a window, start by opening the pop-up menu next to the *column heading* that represents the criterion you want: size, date, album, author, whatever (Figure 3-12).

> **Note**
>
> Grouping isn't available in List view—only Icon and Detail views.

Stacking

Stacking's a lot like grouping. The big difference: in stacking, all the members of a particular group are represented by a *single* icon (Figure 3-13). It's designed to look like a crazy stack of icons, all piled on top of each other. Since a single stack icon now represents 10 or 100 or 1,000 icons, you save a *lot* of space in the window.

You create stacks using the "Stack by" command in each column heading's pop-up menu, as shown in Figure 3-13.

When you double-click one of these stacks, a special Explorer window opens, showing the "exploded view" of the icons within. This isn't a real folder window, of course; it's a phantom folder, created just so that you can see the icons that were in its stack. Click the Back button to return to the stacked window.

> **Tip**
>
> What's cool about stacks is that a certain icon may appear in more than one. If you've stacked by author, for example, a document written by collaborators Casey and Robin appears in *both* the Casey stack *and* the Robin stack.

Filtering

Filtering means *hiding*. When you turn on filtering, a bunch of the icons in a window *disappear*, which can make filtering a little confusing.

Figure 3-12: Top: This folder might look like chaos. Wouldn't it be nice to see all these icons organized into groups with similar characteristics? Suppose, for example, that you want to see all the songs by each band—no matter what album—grouped together.

So you click ▾ next to the Artists column heading; in the pop-up menu, click Group.

Bottom: Windows adds headlines to separate the different groups and sorts the files alphabetically within each group. At this point, you can group a different way by clicking a different heading. (To return to ordinary sorting, open a column-heading pop-up menu again, but this time click Sort.)

In case you one day think that you've lost a bunch of important files, look for the check-mark next to a column heading, as shown in **Figure 3-14**. That's your clue filtering is turned on, that Windows is deliberately hiding something from you.

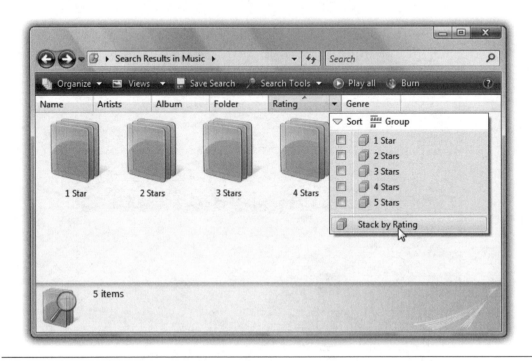

Figure 3-13: To stack the icons in a window, click the pop-up menu in the appropriate column head-ing. For example, to stack these photos by star rating, open the Rating pop-up menu and, at the bot-tom of the pop-up menu, choose "Stack by Rating."

On the positive side, filtering means screening out stuff you don't care about. When you're looking for a document you know you worked on last week, you can tell Windows to show you *only* the documents that were edited last week.

Once again, you turn on filtering by opening the pop-up menu next to the column heading you want. For instance, if you want to see only your five-star photos in the Pictures folder, open the Rating pop-up menu (Figure 3-14, top).

Sometimes, you'll see a whole long list of checkboxes in one of these pop-up menus (Figure 3-14, bottom). For example, if you want to see only the songs in your Music folder by the Beatles, turn on the Beatles checkmark.

___ Tip _____

You can turn on more than one checkbox. To see music by the Beatles *and* U2, turn on both checkboxes.

_____

Figure 3-14: Top: There are actually hundreds of photos in this folder. So where are they all? They've been filtered out (hidden). You've asked Windows to show you only your five-star photos.

Bottom: The filtering options may be very few or extensive.

Filtering, by the way, can be turned on *with* sorting or grouping/stacking.

To stop filtering, open the heading pop-up menu again and turn off the Filter checkbox.

Sizing, Moving, and Closing Windows

Any Windows window can cycle among three altered states:

▶ **Maximized** means that the window fills the screen; its edges are glued to the boundaries of your monitor, and you can't see anything behind it. It gets that way when you click its Maximize button (see Figure 3-1)—an ideal arrangement when you're surfing the Web or working on a document for hours at a stretch, since the largest possible window means the least possible scrolling.

At this point, the Maximize button has changed into a Restore Down button (whose icon shows two overlapping squares); click this to return the window to its previous size.

___ Tip _____

Double-clicking the title bar—the big, fat top edge of a window—alternates a window between its maximized (full-screen) and restored conditions.

_____

▶ When you click a window's **Minimize** button (Figure 3-1), the window gets out of your way. It shrinks down into the form of a button on your taskbar, at the bottom of the screen. Minimizing a window is a great tactic when you want to see what's in the window behind it.

You can bring the window back by clicking this taskbar button, which bears the window's name. On Aero machines (page 24), this button also displays a handy thumbnail miniature when you point to it without clicking, to remind you of what was in the original window.

▶ A **restored** window is neither maximized nor minimized; it's a loose cannon, floating around on your screen as an independent rectangle. Because its edges aren't attached to the walls of your monitor, you can make it any size you like by dragging its borders.

Moving a Window

Moving a window is easy—just drag the big, fat top edge.

Most of the time, you move a window to get it out of the way when you're trying to see what's *behind* it. However, moving windows around is also handy if you're moving or copying data between programs, or moving or copying files between drives or folders.

Closing a Window

Microsoft wants to make absolutely sure that you're never without some method of closing a window. Here are just a few ways to do it:

▶ Click the Close button (the X in the upper-right corner).

▶ Press Alt+F4. (This one's worth memorizing. You'll use it everywhere in Windows.)

▶ Double-click the window's upper-left corner.

Be careful. In many programs, including Internet Explorer, closing the window also quits the program entirely.

Layering Windows

When you have multiple windows open on your screen, only one window is *active,* which means that:

▶ It's in the foreground, *in front* of all other windows.

▶ It's the window that "hears" your keystrokes and mouse clicks.

▶ Its Close button glows red. (Background windows' Close buttons are transparent.)

As you would assume, clicking a background window brings it to the front. And what if it's so far back that you can't even see it? Read on.

___ Tip _____

For quick access to the desktop, clear the screen by clicking the Desktop button on the Quick Launch toolbar—its icon looks like an old desk blotter—or just press ⊞+D. Pressing that keystroke again brings all the windows back to the screen exactly as they were.

_____

Windows Flip (Alt+Tab)

In its day, the concept of overlapping windows on the screen was brilliant, innovative, and extremely effective. In that era before digital cameras, MP3 files, and the Web, managing your windows was easy this way; after all, you had only about three of them.

These days, however, managing all the open windows in all your open programs can be like herding cats. Off you go, burrowing through the microscopic pop-up menus of your taskbar buttons, trying to find the window you want. And heaven help you if you need to duck back to the desktop—to find a newly downloaded file, for example, or eject a disk. You'll have to fight your way through 50,000 other windows on your way to the bottom of the "deck."

In Windows Vista, the same window-shuffling tricks are available that were available in previous editions:

▶ **Use the Taskbar.** Clicking a button on the taskbar (page 68) makes the corresponding program pop to the front, along with any of its floating toolbars, palettes, and so on.

▶ **Click the window.** You can also bring any window forward by clicking any visible part of it.

▶ **Alt+Tab.** For years, this keyboard shortcut has offered a quick way to bring a different window to the front without using the mouse. If you press Tab while holding

Figure 3-15: Alt+Tab highlights successive icons; add Shift to move *backward*. (Add the Ctrl key to lock the display, so you don't have to keep Alt down. Tab to the icon you want, then press Space or Enter.)

down the Alt key, a floating palette displays the icons of all running programs, as shown at the top in Figure 3-15. Each time you press Tab again (still keeping the Alt key down), you highlight the next icon; when you release the keys, the highlighted program jumps to the front, as though in a high-tech game of duck-duck-goose.

This feature has been gorgeous-ized in Windows Vista, as shown in Figure 3-15. It's been renamed, too; it's now called Windows Flip.

___ Tip _____

If you just *tap* Alt+Tab without *holding down* the Alt key, you get an effect that's often even more useful: you jump back and forth between the *last two* windows you've had open. It's great when, for example, you're copying sections of a Web page into a Word document.

_____

Windows Flip 3D

If your PC is capable of running Aero (page 24), Microsoft has something much slicker for this purpose: Flip 3D, a sort of holographic alternative to the Alt+Tab trick.

The concept is delicious. With the press of a keystroke, Vista shrinks *all windows in all programs* so that they all fit on the screen (Figure 3-16), stacked like the exploded view of a deck of cards. You flip through them to find the one you want, and you're there. It's fast, efficient, animated, and a lot of fun.

___ Tip _____

You even see, among the other 3D "cards," a picture of the desktop itself. If you choose it, Vista minimizes all open windows and takes you to the desktop for quick access to whatever is there.

_____

Here's how you use it, in slow motion. First, press ⊞+Tab. If you keep your thumb on the ⊞ key, you see something like Figure 3-16.

Keep your thumb on the ⊞ key. At this point, you can shuffle through the "deck" of windows using any of these techniques:

▶ Tap the Tab key repeatedly. (Add the Shift key to move backward through the stack.)

▶ Press the down arrow key or the right arrow key. (Use the up or left arrow key to move backward.)

▶ Turn your mouse's scroll wheel toward you. (Roll it away to move backward.)

When the window you want is in front, release the key. The 3-D stack vanishes, and the lucky window appears before you at full size.

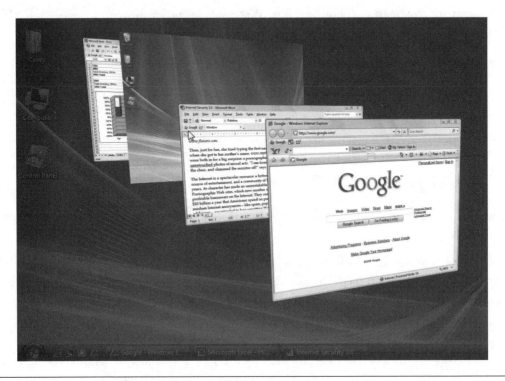

Figure 3-16: These window miniatures aren't snapshots; they're "live." That is, if anything is changing inside a window (a movie is playing, for example), you'll see it right on the 3D miniature.

By the way: Don't miss the cool slow-mo trick described in Appendix B.

The Taskbar

The dark, translucent stripe across the bottom of your screen is the *taskbar*, one of the most prominent and important elements of the Windows interface (Figure 3-17).

The taskbar has several segments, each dedicated to an important function. Its right end, the *notification area* (or *system tray*, as old-timers call it), contains tiny status icons.

They let you know the time, whether or not you're online, whether or not your laptop's plugged in, and so on.

The main portion of the taskbar helps you keep your open windows and programs under control. You can even dress up your taskbar with additional little segments called toolbars, as described in the following pages. This section covers each of these features in turn.

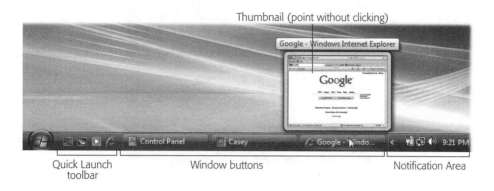

Figure 3-17: On the left is the Quick Launch toolbar; drag favorite icons here for easy launching. In the middle are buttons for every program you're running (and every desktop window). When you see nothing but microscopic icons, point without clicking to view a thumbnail.

The Notification Area (System Tray)

The notification area gives you quick access to little status indicators and pop-up menus that control various functions of your PC. Many a software installer inserts its own little icon into this area: fax software, virus software, palmtop synchronization software, and so on.

Here's your system-tray crash course:

▶ To figure out what an icon represents, point to it without clicking so that a tooltip balloon appears. To access the controls that accompany it, try both left-clicking and right-clicking the tiny icon. Often, each kind of click produces a different pop-up menu filled with useful controls.

▶ See the time display at the lower-right corner of your screen? If you point to the time without clicking, a tooltip appears to tell you the day of the week and today's date. If you single-click, you get a handy date-and-time-changing panel. And if you right-click, you get a pop-up menu that lets you visit the Date & Time Control Panel applet.

▶ If you don't use a tray icon for a couple of weeks, Vista may summarily hide it. See Figure 3-18 for details.

Figure 3-18: Top: If you see a < button, Windows is telling you that it has hidden some of your notification-area icons.

Bottom: Click this button to expand the notification area, bringing all of the hidden icons into view.

Taskbar Buttons—Now with Thumbnails!

Every time you open a window, whether at the desktop or in one of your programs, the taskbar sprouts a button bearing that window's name and icon. Buttons make it easy to switch between open programs and windows. Just click one to bring its associated window into the foreground, even if it has been minimized.

On PCs that are fast enough to run Aero, in fact, the taskbar does more than display each window's name. If you point to a window button without clicking, you actually see a thumbnail image of *the window itself.* Figure 3-19 shows the effect.

Button Groups

The taskbar is the antidote for COWS (cluttered, overlapping window syndrome), thanks in large part to taskbar button *groups.*

Figure 3-19: Top: Pointing to a taskbar button without clicking produces these "live" thumbnail previews of the windows themselves, which can be a huge help. After all, you're much more likely to recognize the image of the brochure you're designing than some truncated text button label.

Bottom: If a taskbar button is grouped, then you see only one thumbnail (representing whichever window you opened first in that program). But if you click the button to open its pop-up menu, you can point to each listed window in turn to see its own preview.

In the old days, opening a lot of windows might produce a relatively useless display of truncated buttons. Not only were the buttons too narrow to read the names of the windows, but the buttons appeared in chronological order, not software-program order.

Nowadays, though, when conditions become crowded, the taskbar automatically groups the names of open windows into a single menu that sprouts from the corresponding program button, as shown at bottom in Figure 3-19. Click the taskbar button bearing the program's name to produce a pop-up menu of the window names; now you can jump directly to the one you want.

Second, even when there is plenty of room, Windows aligns the buttons into horizontal groups *by program*. All the Word-document buttons appear, followed by all the Excel-document buttons, and so on.

Despite these improvements (which appeared in Windows XP), most of the following time-honored basics still apply:

▶ To bring a window to the foreground, making it the active window, click its button on the taskbar. (If clicking a button doesn't bring a window forward, it's because Windows has combined several open windows into a single button. Just click the corresponding program's button as though it's a menu, and then choose the specific window you want from the resulting list, as shown at bottom in Figure 3-19.)

▶ To *hide* the frontmost window, click its taskbar button—a great feature that a lot of PC fans miss. (To hide a *background* window, click its taskbar button *twice:* once to bring the window forward, then a pause, then again to hide it.)

▶ To minimize, maximize, restore, or close a window, even if you can't see it on the screen, right-click its button on the taskbar and choose from the shortcut menu (Figure 3-20).

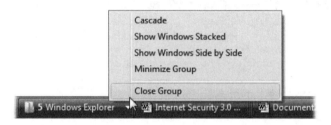

Figure 3-20: The number on a button (like "5 Windows Explorer") indicates that several windows are open in that program; the ▾ is another cue that you must click to see a list of windows. Right-clicking one of these buttons lets you perform certain tasks on all the hidden windows together, such as closing them all at once.

▶ Windows can make all open windows visible at once, either by *cascading* them, *stacking* them, or displaying them in side-by-side vertical slices. To create this effect, right-click a blank spot on the taskbar and choose Cascade Windows from the shortcut menu.

▶ If you change your mind, the taskbar shortcut menu always includes an Undo command for the last taskbar command you invoked. (Its wording changes to reflect your most recent action—"Undo Minimize All," for example.)

The Quick Launch Toolbar

At the left end of the taskbar—that is, just to the right of the Start button—is a handful of tiny, unlabeled icons (Figure 3-21). This is the Quick Launch toolbar, one of the most useful features in Windows.

It contains icons for functions that Microsoft assumes you'll use most often. They include:

Figure 3-21: You can add any kind of icon to the Quick Launch toolbar by dragging it there (top); a vertical bar shows you where it'll appear.

▶ **Desktop**, a one-click way to minimize (hide) *all* the windows on your screen to make your desktop visible. Don't forget about this button the next time you need to burrow through some folders, put something in the Recycle Bin, or perform some other activity in your desktop folders. *Keyboard shortcut:* ⊞+D.

▶ **Switch between windows**, a one-click trigger for the Flip 3D effect described on page 67.

▶ **Launch Internet Explorer Browser**, for one-click access to the Web browser included with Windows.

But what makes this toolbar great is how easy it is to add your *own* icons—particularly those you use frequently. There's no faster or easier way to open them, even when your screen is otherwise filled with clutter.

To add an icon to this toolbar, simply drag it there, as shown in Figure 3-21. To remove an icon, just drag it off the toolbar—directly onto the Recycle Bin, if you like. (You're not actually removing any software from your computer.) If you think you'll somehow survive without using Internet Explorer each day, for example, remove it from the Quick Launch toolbar.

SEARCHING AND ORGANIZING YOUR FILES

- ▶ Meet Vista Search
- ▶ Search from the Start Menu
- ▶ Explorer-Window Searches
- ▶ The Folders of Windows Vista
- ▶ Life with Icons
- ▶ Selecting Icons
- ▶ Copying and Moving Folders and Files
- ▶ The Recycle Bin
- ▶ Shortcut Icons
- ▶ Burning CDs and DVDs from the Desktop

Every disk, folder, file, application, printer, and networked computer is represented on your screen by an icon. To avoid spraying your screen with thousands of overlapping icons seething like snakes in a pit, Windows organizes icons into folders, puts those folders into *other* folders, and so on. This folder-in-a-folder-in-a-folder scheme works beautifully at reducing screen clutter, but it means that you've got some hunting to do whenever you want to open a particular icon.

Helping you find, navigate, and manage your files, folders, and disks with less stress and greater speed was one of the primary design goals of Windows Vista—and of this chapter. The following pages cover Vista Search, plus icon-management life skills like selecting them, renaming them, moving them, copying them, making shortcuts of them, assigning them to keystrokes, deleting them, and burning them to CD or DVD.

Tip

To create a new folder to hold your icons, right-click where you want the folder to appear (on the desktop, or in any desktop window except Computer), and choose New→Folder from the shortcut menu. The new folder appears with its temporary "New Folder" name highlighted. Type a new name for the folder and then press Enter.

Meet Vista Search

Every computer offers a way to find files. And every system offers several different ways to open them. But Search, a star feature of Vista, combines these two functions in a way that's so fast, so efficient, and so spectacular, it reduces much of what you've read in the previous chapters to irrelevance.

It's important to note, though, that you can search for files on your PC using the super-fast Search box in two different places:

▶ **The Start menu.** The Start Search box at the bottom of the Start menu searches *everywhere* on your computer (see Figure 4-1).

▶ **Explorer windows.** The Search box at the top of every desktop window searches only *that window* (including folders within it). You can expand it, too, into something called the Search *pane*—a way to limit the scope of your search to certain file types or date ranges, for example.

Search boxes also appear in the Control Panel window, Internet Explorer, Windows Mail, Windows Media Player, and other spots where it's useful to perform small-time, limited searches. The following pages, however, cover the two main Search boxes, the ones that hunt down files and folders.

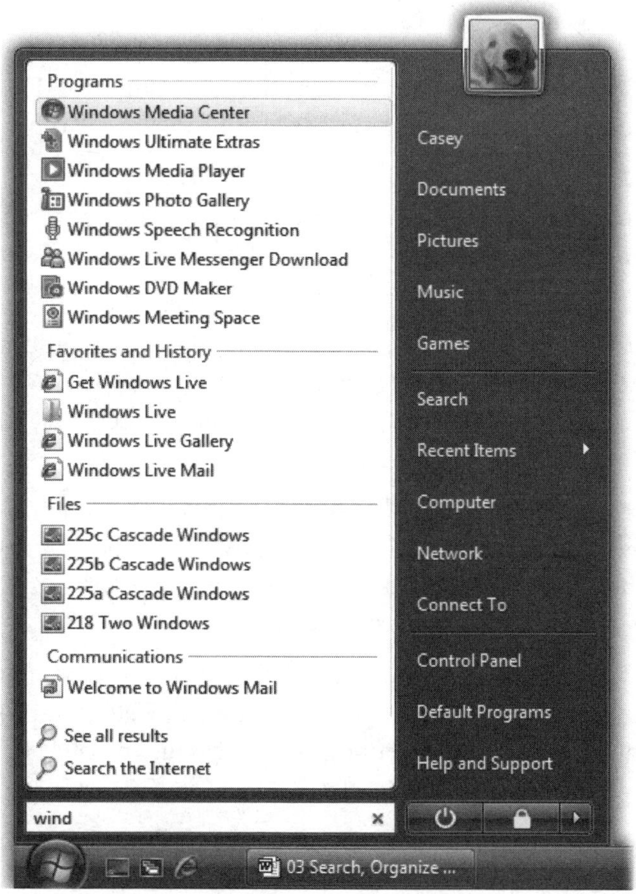

Figure 4-1: Press ⊞, or click the Start-menu icon, to see the Search box. As you type, Vista builds the list of every match it can find, neatly arranged in four categories: Programs, Favorites and History, Files, and Communications (which means email and chat transcripts).

You don't have to type an entire word. Typing kumq will find documents containing the word "kumquat." However, it's worth noting that Vista recognizes only the beginnings of words. Typing umquat won't find a document containing—or even named—Kumquat.

Press the up/down arrow keys to walk through the list one item at a time.

Search from the Start Menu

Start by opening the Start menu, either by clicking the Start button or by pressing the ⊞ key.

The Start Search text box appears at the bottom of the Start menu; you can immediately begin typing to identify what you want to find and open (Figure 4-1). For example, if you're trying to find a file called "Pokémon Fantasy League.doc," typing just *pok* or *leag* will probably work.

As you type, the familiar Start menu items disappear, and are soon replaced by search results. This is a live, interactive search; Vista modifies the menu of search results as you type—don't press Enter after entering your search phrase.

The results menu lists every file, folder, program, email message, address book entry, calendar appointment, picture, movie, PDF document, music file, Web bookmark, and Microsoft Office document (Word, PowerPoint, and Excel) that contains what you typed, regardless of its name or folder location.

Vista isn't just searching icon *names*. It's also searching their contents—the words inside your documents—as well as all your files' properties. (That's descriptive text information, usually invisible, about what's in a file, like its height, width, size, creator, copyright holder, title, editor, created date, and last modification date.)

If you see the icon you were hoping to dig up, double-click it to open it. If you choose a program (programs are listed first in the results menu), well, that program pops onto the screen. Selecting an email message opens that message in your email program. And so on.

As you'll soon learn, Vista Search is an enhancement that's so deep, convenient, and powerful, it threatens to make all that folders-in-folders business nearly pointless. Why burrow around in folders when you can open any file or program with a couple of keystrokes?

Results Menu Tips

It should be no surprise that a feature as important as Vista Search comes loaded with options, tips, and tricks. Here it is—the official, unexpurgated Search Tip-O-Rama:

▶ You can open anything in the results menu by highlighting it and then pressing Enter to open it.

It's incredibly convenient to open a *program* using this technique, because the whole thing happens very quickly and you never have to take your hands off the keyboard. That is, you might hit ⊞ to open the Start menu, type *cale* (to search for Windows Calendar), and press Enter.

Why does pressing Enter open Windows Calendar? Because it's the first item in the list of results, and its name is highlighted.

▶ Vista's menu shows you only 20 of the most likely suspects. They appear grouped into four categories: **Programs** (including Control Panel applets), **Favorites and History** (that is, Web sites), **Files** (which includes documents, folders, and shortcuts), and **Communications** (email and chat transcripts).

To see the complete list, you have to open the Search results *window* by clicking "See all results" (Figure 4-2).

▶ The Esc key (top left corner of your keyboard) is a quick "back out of this" keystroke. Tap it to close the results menu and restore the Start menu to its original form.

▶ To clear the Search box—either to try a different search, or just to get the regularly scheduled Start menu back—click the little x at the right end of the Search box.

▶ If you point to an item in the results menu without clicking, a little tooltip box appears. It tells you the item's actual name and its folder path (that is, where it is on your hard drive).

▶ You can drag the name of a found item *directly out of the menu* and onto the desktop, into a folder or window, or—what the heck—into the Recycle Bin.

▶ At the bottom of the results menu, the "Search the Internet," of course, opens up your Web browser and searches the *Web* for your search term, using Google or whatever search site you've designated as your favorite.

Explorer-Window Searches

See the Search text box at the top of every Explorer window? This, too, is a piece of the Vista Search empire. But there's a big difference: The Search box in the Start menu searches *your entire computer.* The Search box in an Explorer window searches *only this window* (and folders within it).

As you type, the window changes to show search results *as* you type into the Search box, much the way the Start menu changes. Once the results appear, you can sort, filter, group, and stack them just like the icons in any other Explorer window.

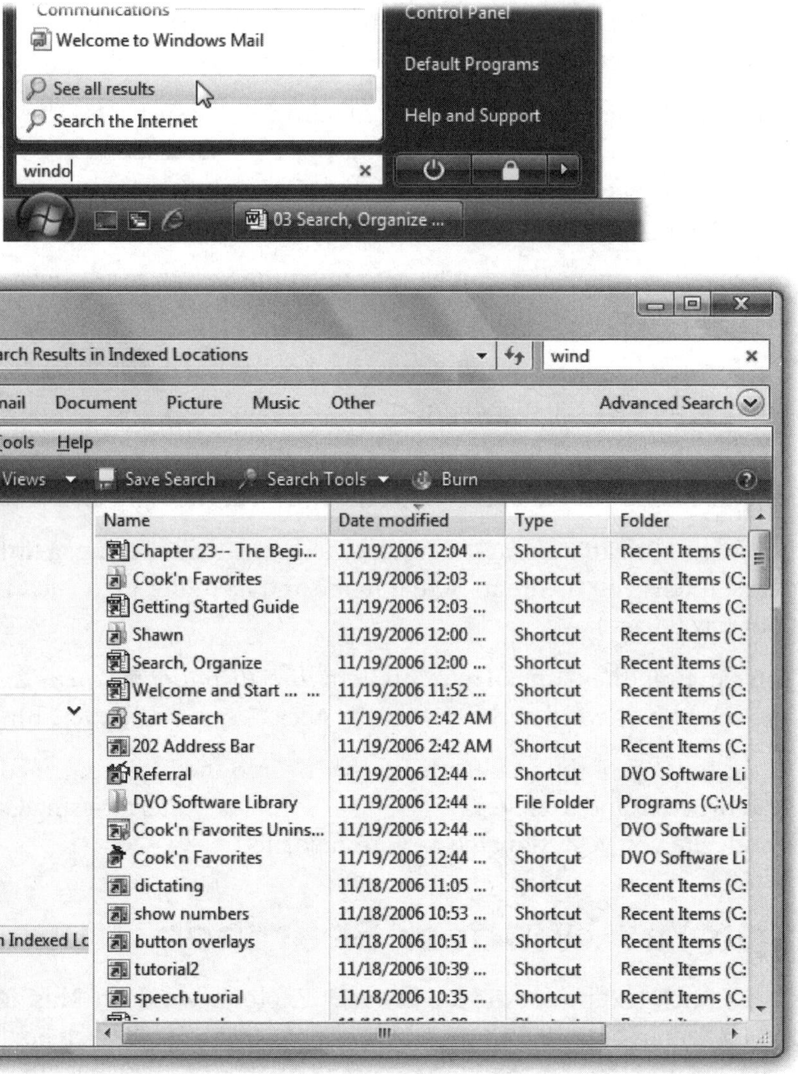

Figure 4-2: You can open this window (bottom) by clicking "See all results" in the Start menu's results list (top). (If Vista found no matches for your search, you don't get a "See all results" link—instead, you get a "Search Everywhere" link that expands the scope of your search.)

The Search Pane

As described in Chapter 3, you can adorn every Explorer window with up to four different *panes*—inch-wide strips at the left, right, top, and bottom of a window. One of them is the Search pane.

You can get to it in several ways:

▶ Press ⊞+F, which is the keyboard shortcut for the Search window (for *find,* get it?).

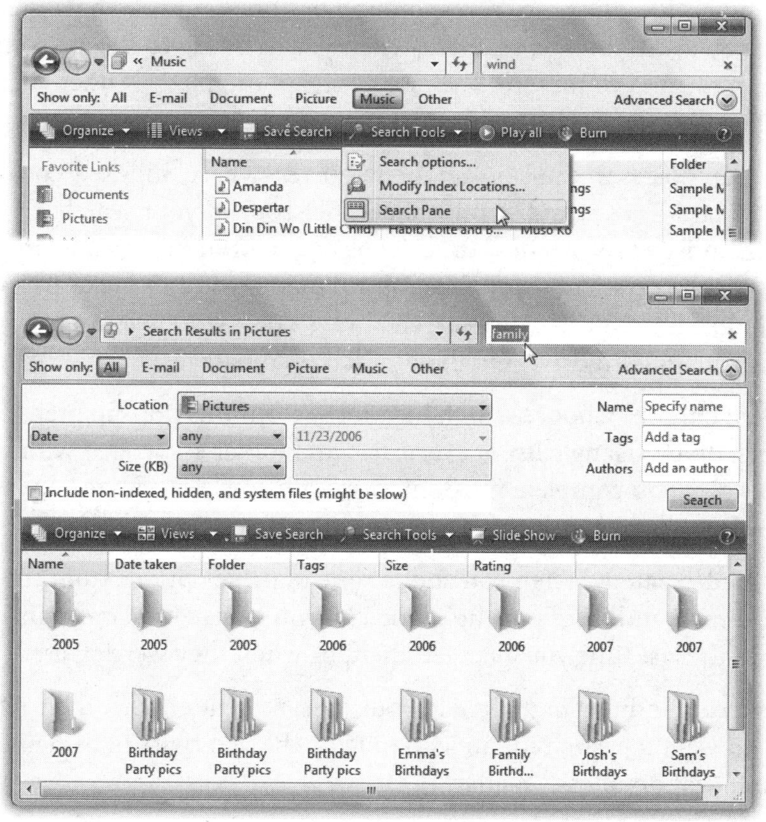

Figure 4-3: You can gain much more control over the search process using the Search pane. Top: One way to make it appear is to choose "Search pane" from the Search Tools menu, which appears after you perform a regular Explorer-window search.

Bottom: At that point, you can click Advanced to open a much more powerful, expanded version of the Search strip.

▶ After a regular Explorer-window search, open the Search Tools menu that now appears in the task toolbar. Choose Search Pane.

▶ After a regular Explorer-window search, click Advanced Search at the bottom of the results list (Figure 4-3).

As you can see in Figure 4-3, the Search pane lets you fine-tune the search by adding controls like these:

▶ **Show only.** If you know what you're looking for is an email message, document, picture, or music file, click the corresponding button. Your search will reveal only the kind of file you asked for. For example, when you're trying to free up some space on your drive, you could round up all your gigantic photo files. ("Other," here, means everything *except* email, documents, pictures, or music.)

▶ **Location.** The choices in this pop-up menu—Everywhere, Indexed Locations, Computer, Local Hard Drives, and so on—affect the scope of your search. Ordinarily, searching in an Explorer window finds icons *only* within the open window, including what's in its subfolders. But using this pop-up menu, you can make an Explorer-window search do what a Start-menu search always does: search your *entire* computer. Or only your main hard drive. Or all hard drives. Whatever.

In fact, if you choose "Choose search locations" from this pop-up menu, you get a collapsible, flippy-triangle list of *every* disk and folder associated with your PC). Checkboxes give you complete freedom to specify any crazy, mixed-up assortment of random folders you'd like to search at once.

▶ **Date modified/created.** When you choose one of these options from the first pop-up menu, the second and third pop-up menus let you isolate files, programs, and folders according to the last time you changed them or when they were created.

▶ **Name.** Vista can find text *anywhere* in your files, no matter what their *names* are. But when you do want to search for an icon only by the text that's in its name, this is your ticket. Capitalization doesn't matter.

▶ **Tags.** If you're in the practice of assigning *tags* (keywords) to your documents, using the Properties dialog box or the Details pane (page 49), you can use the tag search feature to round up all icons that have a certain tag. They might be all files pertaining to a certain project, for example, or that you wrote during your dry spell of '06.

▶ **Size.** Using this control, and its "equals/is less than/is greater than" pop-up menu, you can restrict your search to files of a certain size. Use the text box to specify the file's size, in kilobytes. If you want to round up files larger than 5 gigabytes, for example, you'll have to type *5242880*, or, if "close enough" is close enough, *5000000*.

Tip

If you're not handy with kilobyte/megabyte/gigabyte conversions—or even area, weight, mass, volume, or other conversions—Google can help you. Type this right into Google's main search box: *kilobytes in 5 gigabytes* or whatever. When you hit Enter, Google displays the answer.

A key feature of the Advanced Search pane is that it lets you *combine* criteria. Using these controls, you can set up a search for email messages created last week with file sizes over 200 K, for example, or pictures under 500K that are at least two months old and bear the tag *Detroit Coffee-Table Book Project.*

The Search Window

If you've slogged through this chapter up to this point, you're probably under the impression that searching *all* your stuff (not just one window) requires using the Start menu.

Technically, however, that's not quite true. Vista also offers a Search *window,* a sort of hybrid of the Search and Explorer methods. Figure 4-4 explains; for now, just note that you can open the Search window by pressing F3 or ⊞+F.

Figure 4-4: Like the Start menu Search box, the Search window searches your entire PC. But like Explorer searches, file-type filters (and, if you like, the Advanced Search pane) are available at the top. The results list works just like an Explorer-window search.

The Folders of Windows Vista

The top-level, all-encompassing, mother-ship window of your PC is the Computer window. From within this window, you have access to every disk, folder, and file on your computer. Its slogan might well be, "If it's not in here, it's not on your PC."

To see it, choose Start→Computer, or double-click its icon on the desktop, if you've put it there (page 114).

No matter how you open the Computer window (Figure 4-5), you wind up face-to-face with the icons of every storage gizmo connected to your PC: hard drives, CD and DVD drives, USB flash drives, digital cameras, and so on.

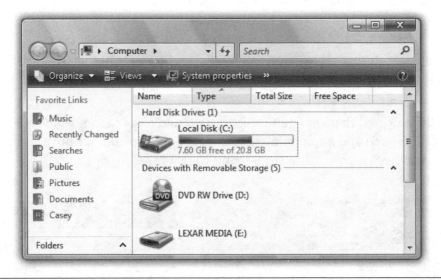

Figure 4-5: The Computer window is the starting point for any and all folder-digging. It shows the "top-level" folders: the disk drives of your PC. If you double-click the icon of a removable-disk drive (such as your CD or DVD drive), you receive only a "Please insert a disk" message, unless there's actually a disk in the drive.

Most people, most of the time, are most concerned with the Local Disk (C:), which represents the internal hard drive preinstalled in your computer. (You're welcome to rename this icon, by the way, just as you would any icon.)

The drive letters, such as C: for your main hard drive, are an ancient convention that doesn't offer much relevance these days. (Back at the dawn of computing, the A: and B: drives were floppy drives, which is why you rarely see them any more.)

What's in the Local Disk (C:) Window

If you double-click the Local Disk (C:) icon in Computer—that is, your primary hard drive—you'll find these standard folders:

Users

Windows' *accounts* feature is ideal for situations where different family members, students, or workers use the same machine at different times (Chapter 15.)

That's the importance of the Users folder. Inside are folders—the *Personal folders*, described in a moment—named for the different people who use this PC. In general, *standard* account holders (page 355) aren't allowed to open anybody else's folder.

Program Files

This folder contains all of your applications—Word, Excel, Internet Explorer, your games, and so on.

Windows

Here's a folder that Microsoft hopes you'll simply ignore. This most hallowed folder contains Windows itself, the thousands of little files that make Windows, well, Windows. Most of these folders and files have cryptic names that appeal to cryptic people.

In general, the healthiest PC is one whose Windows folder has been left alone. (One exception: the Fonts folder contains the icons that represent the various typefaces installed on your machine. You're free to add or remove icons from this folder.)

Your Personal Folder

Everything that makes your Vista experience your own sits inside the Users→[your name] folder. This is your *Personal* folder, where Windows stores your preferences, documents, email, address book, pictures, music, Web favorites, and so on. You can get to it more directly by choosing your name from the top right of the Start menu.

Life with Icons

Windows Explorer, the program that runs automatically when you turn on your PC, has only one purpose in life: to help you manage your file, folder, and disk *icons*. You could spend your entire workday just mastering the techniques of naming, copying, moving, and deleting these icons—and plenty of people do.

Here's the crash course.

Renaming Your Icons

To rename a file, folder, printer, or disk icon, you need to open up its "renaming rectangle." You can do so with any of the following methods:

▶ Highlight the icon and then press the F2 key at the top of your keyboard.

▶ Click carefully, just once, on a previously highlighted icon's name.

▶ Right-click the icon and choose Rename from the shortcut menu.

In any case, once the renaming rectangle has appeared around the current name, simply type the new name you want, and then press Enter. Feel free to use all the standard text-editing tricks while you're typing: Press Backspace to fix a typo, press the left and right arrow keys to position the insertion point, and so on. When you're finished editing the name, press Enter to make it stick. (If another icon in the folder has the same name, Windows beeps and makes you choose another name.)

___ Tip _____

If you highlight a bunch of icons at once and then open the renaming rectangle for any *one* of them, you wind up renaming *all* of them. For example, if you've highlighted folders called Cats, Dogs, and Fish, renaming one of them *Animals* changes the original set of names to Animals (1), Animals (2), and Animals (3).

If that's not what you want, press Ctrl+Z repeatedly (that's the keystroke for Undo) until you've restored all the original names.

_____

Windows doesn't let you use any of these symbols in a file name: \ / : * ? " < > |

You can give more than one file or folder the same name, as long as they're not in the same folder.

Icon Properties

Properties are a big deal in Windows. Properties are preference settings that you can change independently for every icon on your machine.

To view the properties for an icon, choose from these techniques—the first three open the Properties dialog box:

▶ Right-click the icon; choose Properties from the shortcut menu.

▶ While pressing Alt, double-click the icon.

▶ Highlight the icon; press Alt+Enter.

▶ Open the Details pane (page 49), and then click an icon.

--- Tip ---

You can also see some basic info about any icon (type, size, and so on) by pointing to it without clicking. A little info balloon pops up, saving you the trouble of opening the Properties box or even the Details pane.

These settings aren't the same for every kind of icon, however. Here's what you can expect when opening the Properties dialog boxes of various icons (Figure 4-6).

Computer

There are about 500 different ways to open the Properties dialog box for your Computer icon. The quickest is to right-click the word Computer *right in the Start menu.*

The System Properties window is packed with useful information about your machine: what kind of processor is inside, how much memory (RAM) your PC has, its overall "Experience Index" (horsepower score), and what version of Windows you've got.

Disks

In a disk's Properties dialog box, you can see all kinds of information about the disk itself, like its name (which you can change), its capacity (which you can't change), and how much of it is full.

Data files and Folders

The Properties for plain old documents and folders may vary. You always see a General tab, but other tabs may also appear (especially for Microsoft Office files). These tabs show things like a file's name, size, modification date, author name, and so on.

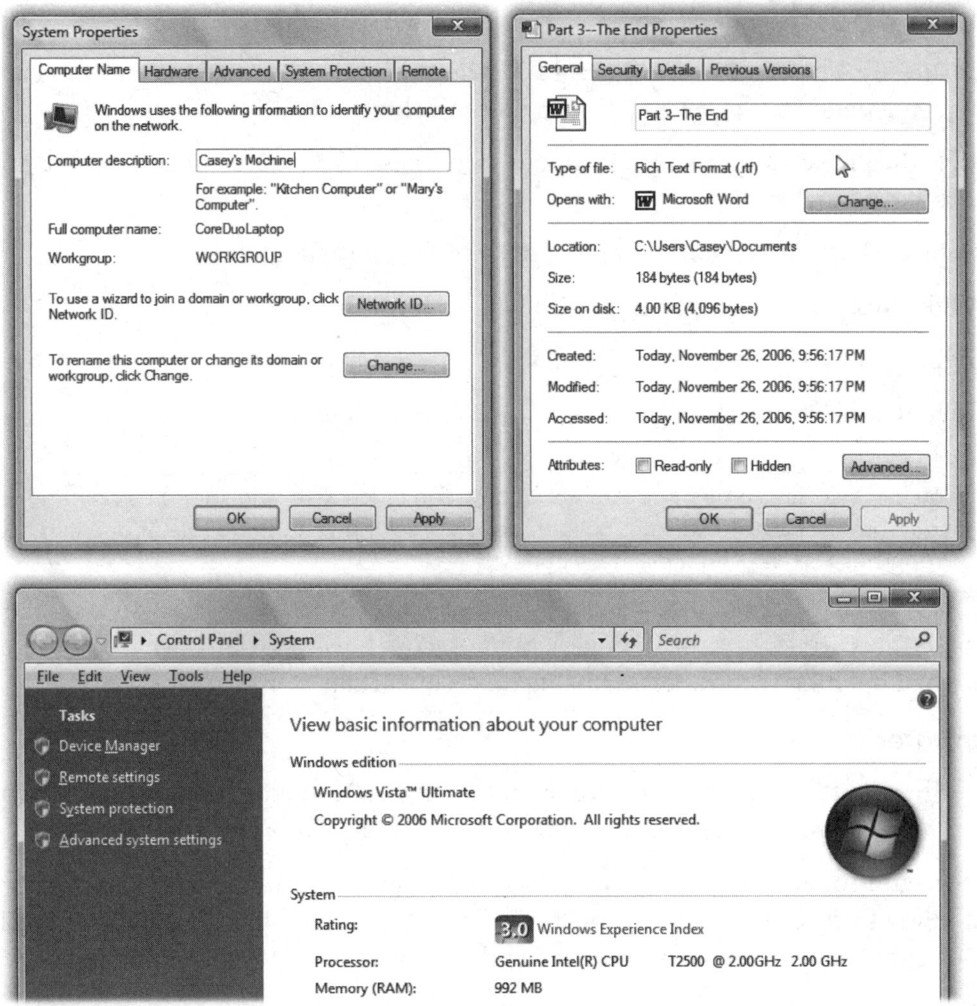

Figure 4-6: The Properties dialog boxes are different for every kind of icon. In the months and years to come, you may find many occasions when adjusting the behavior of some icon has big benefits in simplicity and productivity.

Top left: The old System Properties dialog box, which opens when you click some of the links on the left side of the new dialog box (bottom).

Top right: The Properties dialog box for a Word document.

Selecting Icons

Before you can delete, rename, move, copy, or otherwise tamper with any icon, you have to be able to *select* it somehow. By highlighting it, you're essentially telling Windows what you want to operate on.

Use the Mouse

To select one icon, just click it once. To select *multiple* icons at once—in preparation for moving, copying, renaming, or deleting them en masse, for example—use one of these techniques:

▶ **Select all.** Highlight all of the icons in a window by choosing Organize→Select All. (Or press Ctrl+A, its keyboard equivalent.)

▶ **Highlight several consecutive icons.** Start with your cursor above and to one side of the icons, and then drag diagonally. As you drag, you create a temporary dotted-line rectangle. Any icon that falls within this rectangle darkens to indicate that it's been selected.

Alternatively, click the first icon you want to highlight, and then Shift-click the last file. All the files in between are automatically selected, along with the two icons you clicked. (These techniques work in any folder view: Details, Icon, Thumbnails, or whatever.)

> **Tip**
>
> If you include a particular icon in your diagonally-dragged group by mistake, Ctrl-click it to remove it from the selected cluster.

▶ **Highlight non-consecutive icons.** Suppose you want to highlight only the first, third, and seventh icons in the list. Start by clicking icon No. 1; then Ctrl-click each of the others. (If you Ctrl-click a selected icon *again*, you *de*select it. A good time to use this trick is when you highlight an icon by accident.)

> **Tip**
>
> The Ctrl key trick is especially handy if you want to select *almost* all the icons in a window. Press Ctrl+A to select everything in the folder, then Ctrl-click any unwanted subfolders to deselect them.

Use the Keyboard

You can also highlight one icon, plucking it out of a sea of pretenders, by typing the first couple letters of its name. Type *nak,* for example, to select an icon called "Naked Chef Broadcast Schedule."

Checkbox Selection

It's great that you can select random icons by holding down a key and clicking—if you can remember *which* key must be pressed.

Fortunately, there's an easier way: checkbox mode. In this mode, any icon you point to temporarily sprouts a little checkbox that you can click to select (Figure 4-7).

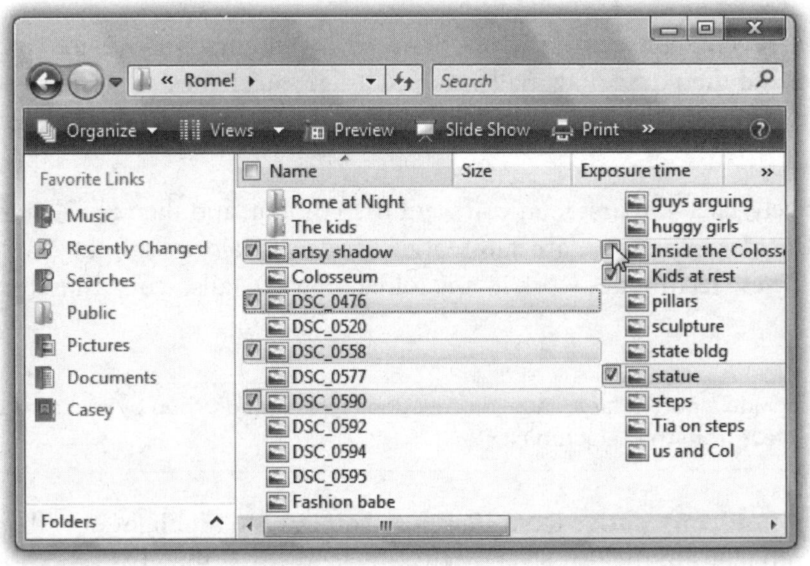

Figure 4-7: Each time you point to an icon, a clickable checkbox appears. Once you turn it on, the checkbox remains visible, making it easy to select several icons at once. What's cool about the new checkboxes feature is that it doesn't preclude your using the old click-to-select method; if you click an icon's name, you deselect all checkboxes except that one.

To turn this feature on, open any Explorer window, and then choose Organize→Folder and Search Options. Click the View tab, scroll down in the list of settings, and then turn on "Use check boxes to select items." Click OK.

With the checkboxes visible, no secret keystrokes are necessary; it's painfully obvious how you're supposed to choose only a few icons out of a gaggle.

Copying and Moving Folders and Files

Windows offers two different techniques for moving files and folders from one place to another: dragging them, and using the Copy and Paste commands.

Whichever method you choose, you must start by showing Windows which icons you want to copy or move—by highlighting them, as described on the previous pages. Then proceed as follows.

Copying by Dragging Icons

You can drag icons from one folder to another, from one drive to another, from a drive to a folder on another drive, and so on. (When you've selected several icons, drag any *one* of them and the others will go along for the ride.)

Here's what happens when you drag icons in the usual way (using the left mouse button):

▶ Dragging to another folder on the same disk *moves* the folder or file.

▶ Dragging from one disk to another *copies* the folder or file.

▶ Holding down the Ctrl key while dragging to another folder on the same disk *copies* the icon. (If you do so within a single window, a duplicate of the file called "[File name] - Copy" is created.)

▶ Pressing Shift while dragging from one disk to another *moves* the folder or file (without leaving a copy behind).

___ Tip _____
   You can move or copy icons by dragging them either into an open window or directly
   onto a disk or folder *icon*.
_____

The right mouse button trick

Think you'll remember all of those possibilities every time you drag an icon? Probably not. Fortunately, you never have to. One of the most important tricks you can learn is to use the *right* mouse button as you drag. When you release the button, the menu shown in Figure 4-8 appears, letting you either copy or move the selected icons.

___ Tip _____

Press the Esc key to cancel a dragging operation at any time.

Figure 4-8: Thanks to this shortcut menu, right-dragging icons is much easier and safer than left-dragging when you want to move or copy something. New in Vista: the handy numeric "badge" on your cursor, which reminds you how many things you're about to move or copy.

Dragging icons into the Navigation pane

You may find it easier to copy or move icons using the Navigation pane (page 51), since the two-pane display format makes it easier to see where your files are and where they're going.

Just expand the flippy triangles of the Navigation pane until you can see the destination folder. Then locate the icon you want to move in the right pane and drag it to the appropriate folder in the left pane (Figure 4-9). Windows copies the icon.

Copying with Copy and Paste

Dragging icons to copy or move them feels good because it's so direct; you actually see your arrow cursor pushing the icons into the new location.

But you also pay a price for this satisfying illusion. That is, you may have to spend a moment or two fiddling with your windows, or clicking in the Explorer folder hierarchy, so that you have a clear "line of drag" between the icon to be moved and the destination folder.

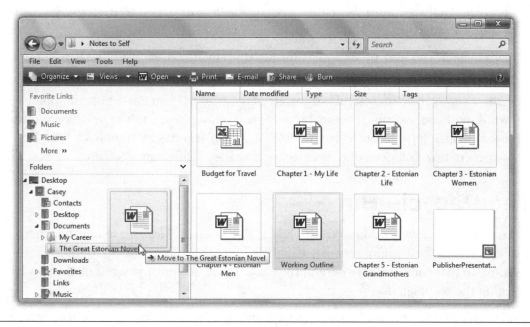

Figure 4-9: The file Working Outline is being dragged to the folder named The Great Estonian Novel (in the Documents folder). As the cursor passes each folder in the left pane, the folder's name darkens. Release the mouse when it's pointing to the correct folder or disk.

Fortunately, there's a better way. You can use the Cut, Copy, and Paste commands to move icons from one window into another. The routine goes like this:

1. **Highlight the icon or icons you want to move.**

    Use any of the tricks described on page 89.

2. **Right-click one of the icons. From the shortcut menu, choose Cut or Copy.**

    Alternatively, you can choose Organize→Cut or Organize→Copy, using the task toolbar at the top of the window. (Eventually, you may want to learn the keyboard shortcuts for these commands: Ctrl+C for Copy, Ctrl+X for Cut.)

The Cut command makes the highlighted icons appear dimmed; you've now stashed them on the invisible Windows Clipboard. (They don't actually disappear from their original nesting place until you paste them somewhere else.)

Copy also puts copies of the files on the Clipboard without disturbing the originals.

3. **Right-click the window, folder icon, or disk icon where you want to put the icons. Choose Paste from the shortcut menu.**

   Once again, you may prefer to use the appropriate menu bar option, Organize→Paste. *Keyboard equivalent:* Ctrl+V.

   Either way, you've successfully transferred the icons. If you pasted into an open window, the icons appear there. If you pasted onto a closed folder or disk icon, you need to open its window to see the results. And if you pasted right back into the same window, you get a duplicate of the file called "[File name] - Copy."

The Recycle Bin

The Recycle Bin is your desktop trash basket. This is where files and folders go when they've outlived their usefulness. Basically, the Recycle Bin is a waiting room for data oblivion, in that your files stay here until you *empty* it—or until you rescue the files by dragging them out again.

While you can certainly drag files or folders onto the Recycle Bin icon, it's usually faster to highlight them and then perform one of the following options:

▶ Press the Delete key.

▶ Choose File→Delete.

▶ Right-click a highlighted icon and choose Delete from the shortcut menu.

Windows asks if you're sure you want to send the item to the Recycle Bin. (You don't lose much by clicking Yes, since it's easy enough to change your mind, as noted below.) Now the Recycle Bin icon looks like it's brimming over with paper.

___ Tip _____

To turn off the "Are you sure?" message that appears when you send something Bin-ward, right-click the Recycle Bin. From the shortcut menu, choose Properties, and turn off "Display delete confirmation dialog." Turning off the warning isn't much of a safety risk; after all, files aren't really being removed from your drive when you put them in the Recycle Bin.

_____

You can put unwanted files and folders into the Recycle Bin from any folder window or even inside the Open File dialog box of many applications (see Chapter 6).

Restoring Deleted Files and Folders

If you change your mind about sending something to the software graveyard, simply open the Recycle Bin by double-clicking. A window like the one in Figure 4-10 opens.

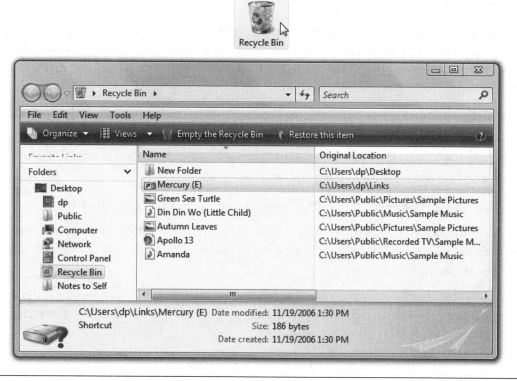

Figure 4-10: When you double-click the Recycle Bin (top), its window (bottom) displays information about each folder and file that it holds. To sort its contents, making it easier to find a deleted icon, click the gray column heading for the type of sort you need.

To restore a selected file or a folder—or a bunch of them—click the "Restore this item" link on the task toolbar. Or right-click any one of the selected icons and choose Restore from the shortcut menu.

Restored means returned to the folder from whence it came—wherever it was on your hard drive when deleted. If you restore an icon whose original folder has been deleted in the meantime, Windows even recreates that folder to hold the restored file(s).

Tip

You don't have to put icons back into their original folders. By *dragging* them out of the Recycle Bin window, you can put them back into any folder you like.

Emptying the Recycle Bin

While there's an advantage to the Recycle Bin (you get to undo your mistakes), there's also a downside: the files in the Recycle Bin occupy as much disk space as they did when they were stored in folders. Deleting files doesn't gain you additional disk space until you *empty* the Recycle Bin.

That's why most people, sooner or later, follow up an icon's journey to the Recycle Bin with one of these cleanup operations:

▶ Right-click the Recycle Bin icon, or a blank spot in the Recycle Bin window, and choose Empty Recycle Bin from the shortcut menu.

▶ Click "Empty the Recycle Bin" on the toolbar in the Recycle Bin window.

▶ In the Recycle Bin window, highlight only the icons you want to eliminate, and then press the Delete key. (Use this method when you want to nuke only *some* of the Recycle Bin's contents.)

▶ Wait. When the Recycle Bin accumulates so much stuff that it occupies a significant percentage of your hard drive space, Windows empties it automatically, as described in the next section.

The first three of these procedures produce an "Are you sure?" message.

Shortcut Icons

A *shortcut* is a link to a file, folder, disk, or program (see Figure 4-11). You might think of it as a duplicate of the thing's icon—but not a duplicate of the thing itself. (A shortcut occupies almost no disk space.) When you double-click the shortcut icon, the original folder, disk, program, or document opens. You can also set up a keystroke for a shortcut icon, so that you can open any program or document just by pressing a certain key combination.

Shortcuts provide quick access to the items you use most often. And because you can make as many shortcuts of a file as you want, and put them anywhere on your PC, you can, in effect, keep an important program or document in more than one folder. Just create a shortcut of each to leave on the desktop in plain sight, or drag their icons onto the Start button or the Quick Launch toolbar. In fact, everything listed in the Start→All Programs menu *is* a shortcut. So is every link in the top part of your Navigation pane.

___ Tip _____

Don't confuse the term *shortcut,* which refers to one of these duplicate-icon pointers, with *shortcut menu,* the context-sensitive menu that appears when you right-click almost anything in Windows. The shortcut *menu* has nothing to do with the shortcut icons feature; maybe that's why it's sometimes called the *context* menu.

_____

Figure 4-11: You can distinguish a desktop shortcut (left) from its original in two ways. First, the tiny arrow "badge" identifies it as a shortcut; second, its name contains the word "shortcut." Right: The Properties dialog box for a shortcut indicates which actual file or folder this one "points" to. The Run drop-down menu (shown open) lets you control how the window opens when you double-click the shortcut icon.

Creating and Deleting Shortcuts

To create a shortcut, right-drag an icon from its current location to the desktop. When you release the mouse button, choose Create Shortcuts Here from the menu that appears.

You can delete a shortcut the same as any icon, as described in the Recycle Bin discussion earlier in this chapter. (Of course, deleting a shortcut *doesn't* delete the file it points to.)

Burning CDs and DVDs from the Desktop

Burning a CD or DVD is great for backing stuff up, transferring stuff to another computer, mailing to somebody, or archiving older files to free up hard drive space. These days, you can buy blank CDs and DVDs very inexpensively in bulk via the Web or discount store.

In ancient times—you know, like 2002—every PC came with a CD-ROM drive. Nowadays, new PCs come with either a *combo drive* (a drive that can burn blank CDs *and* play DVDs) or a drive that burns *both* CDs and DVDs.

Before you dig in, however, here's a brief chalk talk about CD data formats.

A Tale of Two Formats

Turns out Windows Vista can burn blank CDs and DVDs using your choice of *two* formats.

▶ **Mastered.** This is what most of the world is used to. It's what everybody burned before Windows Vista came along.

You insert the blank disc and then drag files and folders into its window. Then you burn all the files and folders at once.

The Mastered format's virtue is compatibility. These discs play in just about any computer, including Macs and older PCs.

▶ **Live File System.** This newer, more modern format—Vista's new factory setting—is light-years more convenient. It lets you use a blank CD or DVD exactly as though it's a floppy disk or USB flash drive. You can drag files and folders onto it, move icons around on it, rename them, and so on. There's no momentous Moment of Burn; files are copied to the CD in real time, whenever you put them there. You can leave a disc in your drive, dragging stuff onto it throughout the week as it's convenient—without every having to click a Burn button.

What's more, you can the eject the CD, store it or share it—and then, later, put it back into your PC and *burn more stuff onto it.* That's right—you can burn a single CD as many times as you like. And we're talking regular, cheapie CD-R discs, not the CD-RW (rewritable) kind.

The downside is that discs you burn this way generally work only in *Windows XP and Windows Vista* computers.

Burning, Step by Step

Now that, with luck, you understand the difference between the two formats, you're ready to proceed.

1. **Insert a blank disc into your PC.**

   The AutoPlay dialog box appears, asking whether you intend for this CD or DVD to hold computer files or music (Figure 4-12, top left). If you want to burn a music CD, skip ahead to Chapter 7. Otherwise, continue to step 2.

2. **Click the "Burn files to disc" link.**

   Windows asks you to name the CD or DVD.

3. **Type a name for the disc.**

   But don't click Next yet. This crucial moment is your only chance to change the disc's format.

   If you're OK with burning in the delicious, newfangled UDF format described above, never mind; skip to step 4.

   If you want this disc to be usable by a Macintosh, a CD or DVD player, or somebody using a version of Windows before Windows XP, though, take this moment to change the format. Figure 4-12 shows the full life cycle of a disk you're burning.

   Once that's done, you can go on to step 4.

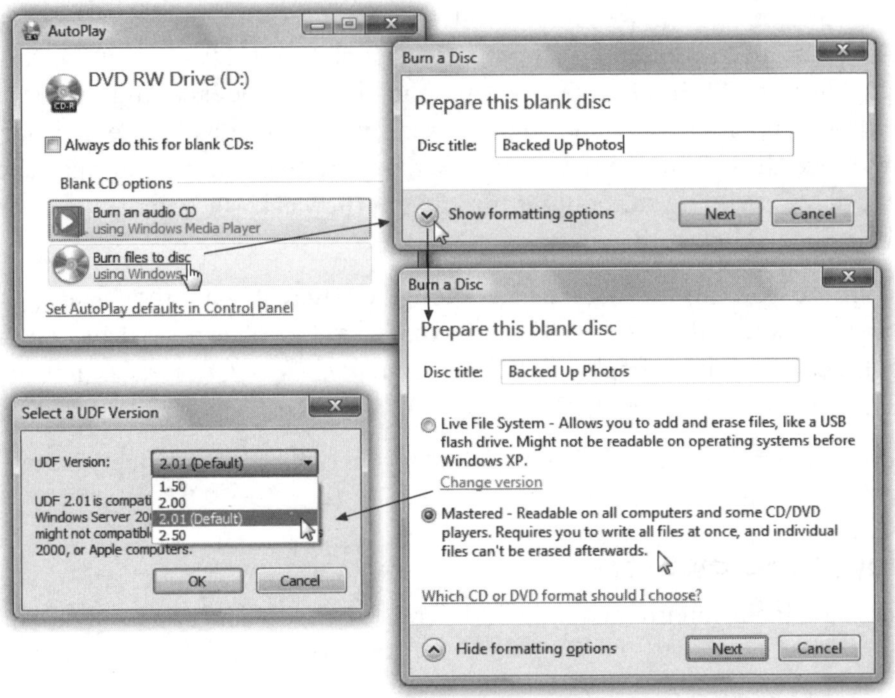

Figure 4-12: Top: First, you're asked what you want to do with the blank. Click "Burn files to disc."

Top right: Name your disc. If you want to change the burn format, click "Show formatting options."

Lower right: Your Big Two options: the new, super-convenient Live File System format (UDF), and the older, highly compatible Mastered format (ISO). If you click Change Version (lower left), you can even specify a version of UDF.

4. **Click Next.**

   Your PC takes a moment—a long one—to format the blank disc.

   When it's finished, it opens a special disc-burning window, which will be the temporary waiting room for files that you want to copy. (If you can't find the window, choose Start→Computer and double-click the name of your CD/DVD drive.)

5. **Begin putting files and folders into the disc's window.**

   You can use any combination of these three methods:

   First, you can scurry about your hard drive, locating the files and folders you want on the CD. Drag their icons into the open CD/DVD window, or onto the disc burner's icon in the Computer window.

Second, you can highlight the files and folders you want burned onto the CD. Choose Organize→Copy. Click in the CD or DVD's window, and then choose Organize→Paste to copy the material there.

Finally, you can explore your hard drive. Whenever you find a file or folder you'd like backed up, right-click it. From the shortcut menu, choose Send To→DVD/CD-RW Drive (or whatever your burner's name is).

To finish the job, see "The final steps," below, for the kind of disc you're burning.

— Tip ——————————————————————————————————————
The Details pane at the bottom of the window gives you a running tally of the disk space you've filled up so far. (It may say, for example, "223.2 MB of 702.8 used on disc.") At last, you have an effortless way to exploit the blank disc's capacity with precision.

The final steps: Mastered format

When you put files and folders into the disc's window, Windows actually *copies* them into a temporary, invisible holding-tank folder. In other words, you need plenty of disk space before you begin burning a CD—at least double the size of the CD files themselves.

— Tip ——————————————————————————————————————
Remember that a standard CD can hold only about 650 MB of files. To ensure that your files and folders will fit, periodically highlight all the icons in the Computer→CD window (choose Organize→Select All). Then inspect the Details pane to confirm that the size is within the legal limit.

What you see in the disc's window, meanwhile, is nothing but shortcuts (denoted by the downward arrows on their icons). The little down arrows mean, "This icon hasn't been burned to the disc yet. I'm just waiting my turn."

At last, when everything looks ready to go, click the "Burn to disc" link in the task toolbar. Or right-click the burner's icon, or any blank spot in its window, and, from the shortcut menu, choose "Burn to disc."

The CD Writing Wizard appears, to guide you through the process of naming and burning the disc. The PC's laser proceeds to record the CD or DVD, which can take some time. Feel free to switch into another program and continue working.

When the burning is over, the disc pops out, and you have a freshly minted CD or DVD, whose files and folders you can open on any PC or even Macintosh.

The final steps: Live File System format

If you've been dragging files and folders into the window of a Live File System-formatted disc, the truth is, you can stop here. You can keep that CD or DVD in your drive, or eject it and store it—whatever. Whenever you put it back into your PC, you can pick up right where you left off, adding and erasing files as though it's a big flash drive.

To eject the disc, right-click your burner's icon; from the shortcut menu, choose Eject.

Final Notes

Here are a few final notes on burning CDs and DVDs at the desktop:

▶ Not sure what kinds of disks your PC can burn? Choose Start→Computer. Study the name of the burner. There it is, plain as day: a list of the formats your machine can read and write (that is, burn). If you have a combo drive (can burn and play CDs, but can only play DVDs), for example, you'll see something like: "DVD/CD-RW Drive." If your burner can *both* play and record *both* CDs and DVDs, it will say "DVD-RW/ CD-RW Drive."

▶ To erase a –RW type disc (rewritable, like CD-RW or DVD-RW), open your Computer window. Right-click the burner's icon; from the shortcut menu, choose Format. Authenticate yourself (page 127), if necessary, change the file-system format if you like, and then turn on Quick Format. Finally, click Start to erase the disc.

___ Tip _____

> Of course, you don't have to erase the disc completely. You can always select and delete individual icons from it using the Delete key.

_____

▶ If you do a lot of disc burning, a full-fledged burning program like Nero adds myriad additional options. Only with a commercial CD-burning program can you burn MP3 music CDs, create *mixed-mode* CDs (containing both music and files), create Video CDs (low-quality video discs that play on DVD players), and so on.

INTERIOR DECORATING VISTA

5

- ▶ Aero or Not
- ▶ Desktop Background (Wallpaper)
- ▶ Screen Savers
- ▶ Sounds
- ▶ Mouse Makeover
- ▶ Customizing the Start Menu

In designing Windows Vista, Microsoft had three giant goals. First, beef up Windows's security. Second, modernize its features. Third, give it a makeover. That last part was especially important; it drove Microsoft nuts that little old Apple, with its five-percent market share, was getting all the raves for the good looks and modern lines of its Macintosh operating system.

Without a doubt, Vista looks a heck of a lot better than previous versions of Windows. And it's every bit as tweakable as previous versions of Windows. You can turn off the new Aero look, or just selected parts of it. You can change the picture on your desktop. You can bump up the text size or the cursor size for better reading by over-40 eyeballs. As Microsoft might say, "Where do you want to redesign today?"

Aero or Not

If you ask Microsoft, the whole Aero thing (the look and the features) is a key benefit of Vista. Indeed, those glassy surfaces and see-through window edges are, in large part, where Vista got its name and its breathless marketing slogan ("Bring clarity to your world").

But there's certain to be someone, somewhere, who doesn't care for the new look. You can not only change Vista's color scheme, you can also completely turn off the Aero look and features, if you so desire (Figure 5-1).

> **Tip**
>
> Aero Glass uses up some of your PC's horsepower, 24 hours a day. Changing your scheme from Aero to Basic (or simply turning off transparency) can give your computer a speed boost, because it no longer has to compute and draw fuzzy images of whatever is behind your window title bars.

Microsoft figures that's not something you'll want to do often, so the controls are a bit buried. But here they are, just in case you're a believer in opaque window edges:

1. **Right-click a blank spot on the desktop. From the shortcut menu, choose Personalize.**

   The Personalization control panel opens.

2. **Click the first link, "Window Color and Appearance."**

   If you've been using the Aero design, you now arrive at the dialog box shown in Figure 5-2. Here's where you can choose a different accent color for your windows,

Windows Aero

Vista Basic

Windows
Standard

Figure 5-1: Most people with fast enough computers use the Aero Glass look. But your computer may look different, especially if you've deliberately turned on one of the other styles.

Your choices are: Vista Basic (middle), which looks a lot like Aero—the window edges are still rounded, but the window edges aren't transparent. You lose taskbar thumbnails (page 70) and Flip 3D, too (page 67). With Windows Standard (bottom) and the slightly darker Windows Classic, you lose all semblance of 3-D window elements; windows have sharp, square corners, and the Start menu is solidly gray. You're in a weird cross between Windows Vista and Windows Me.

or adjust (or turn off) the degree of window-edge transparency, which will make your PC slightly faster.

If you've been using one of the other themes, you go directly to the dialog box shown in Figure 5-2; skip to step 4.

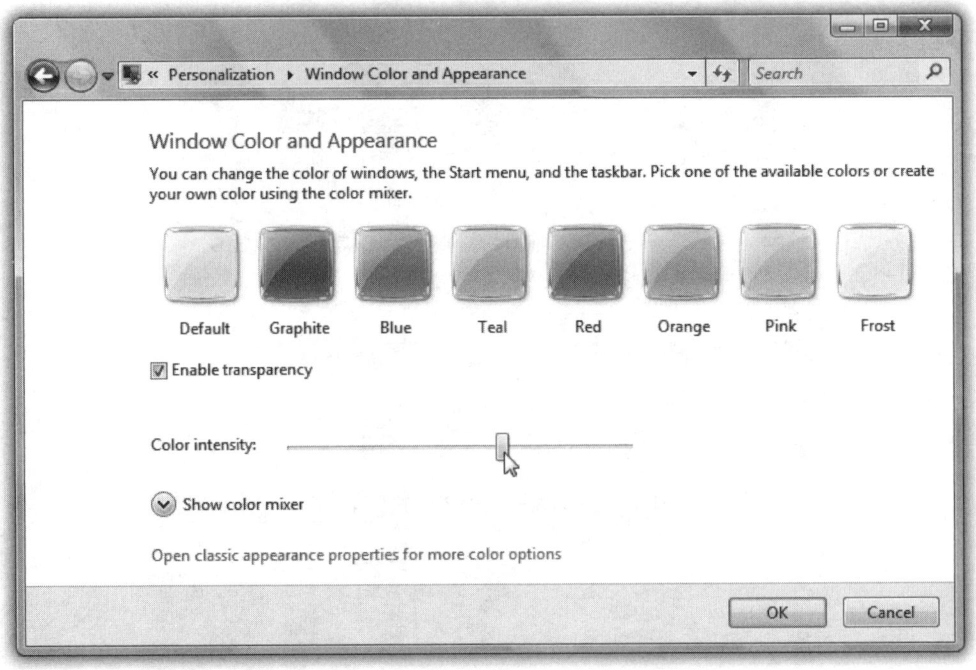

Figure 5-2: This dialog box, new in Vista, is offered only if Windows deems your computer worthy to run the Aero cosmetic scheme (page 22). Here's where you can adjust the color tint, change (or turn off) the transparency effect, or open the Appearance Settings dialog box (Figure 5-3).

3. **Click "Open classic appearance properties…" at the bottom of the window.**

   The Appearance Settings dialog box opens.

4. **In the Color Scheme list, click the Windows design look you prefer: Windows Vista Aero, Windows Vista Basic, Windows Standard, or Windows Classic.**

   With each click, you see a sample at the top of the dialog box. (Figure 5-3 shows the samples more clearly.)

5. **Once you find a design you like, click OK.**

   The screen flickers, thunder rolls somewhere, and your screen changes.

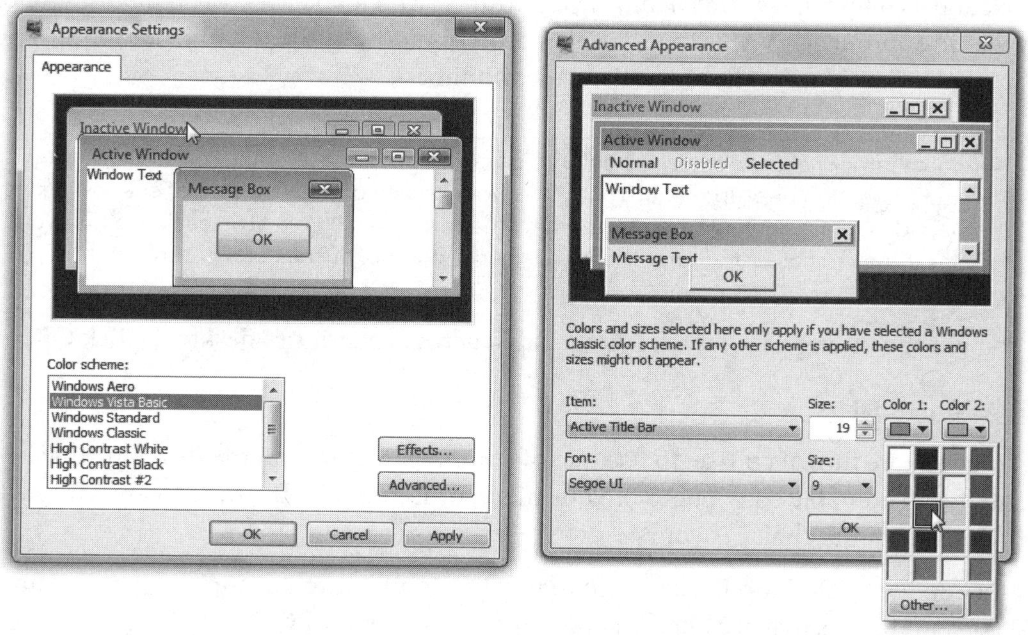

Figure 5-3: Left: This box lists canned designs, but for real fun, click Advanced.

Right: Click a part of the view pane (Desktop, Scrollbar, and so on). Then use the menus to choose colors and type sizes for the chosen interface element.

Desktop Background (Wallpaper)

Vista has a whole new host of desktop pictures, patterns, and colors for your viewing pleasure. You want widescreen images for your new flat-panel monitor? No problem, Vista's got 'em. Want something gritty, artsy, in black and white? They're there, too. And you can still use any picture you'd like as your background as well.

To change yours, right-click the desktop. From the shortcut menu, choose Personalize. In the Personalization dialog box, click Desktop Background.

Use a Microsoft Photo

Now you're looking at the box shown in Figure 5-4. It starts you off examining the Microsoft-supplied photos that come with Vista. They're organized into categories like Black and White, Light Auras, Paintings, Textures (which take well to being *tiled*—more on that in a moment), Vistas (panoramic nature shots—yes, there had to be some), and Widescreen (designed to fit especially wide monitors).

Tip

If you'd rather have a plain, solid-colored background, choose Solid Colors from the Picture Location pop-up menu. You'll have your choice of a full palette of shades. It's not a bad idea, actually; you'll gain a little bit of speed, and it'll be a little easier to find your icons if they're not lost among the weeds and mountain bushes of a nature photo.

If you see something you like, click it to slap it across your entire desktop. Click OK.

Use Your Photo

It's much more fun, of course, to use one of your *own* pictures on the desktop. That might be an adorable baby photo of your niece, or it might be Britney Spears with half her clothes off; the choice is yours.

At the top of the Desktop Background dialog box is a Picture Location pop-up menu. It lists several folders that are likely to contain photos on your PC:

▶ **Pictures** points to your Pictures folder, so it conveniently shows you all of the pictures saved there—up for grabs for your desktop.

▶ **Sample Pictures** contains even more great pictures for the desktop. They've been supplied by Microsoft so that, immediately upon installing Vista, you'll have some pix to fool around with.

▶ **Public Pictures** is a subfolder of the Public folder (page 377). It's expected to be the place you share your pictures with others who have access to your computer. (Ironically, the Public Pictures folder *contains* the Sample Pictures folder.)

Beneath the thumbnails, by the way, Microsoft asks a very good question: "How should the picture be positioned?" What it means, actually, is, "How should the picture be positioned *if* it's too small to fill your screen?"

Your choices are (as represented by the mini-pictures):

▶ **Fit to screen.** Stretch the picture to fit the desktop, even if distortion may result.

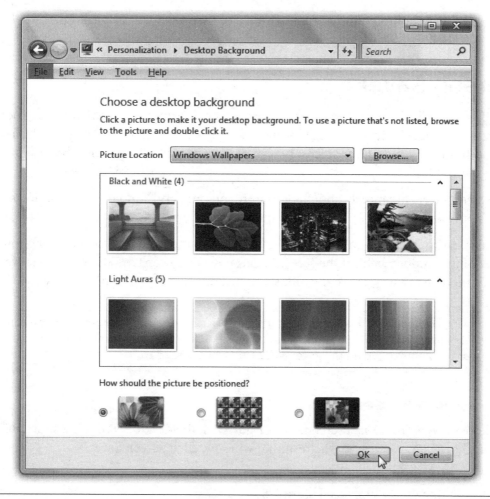

Figure 5-4: Desktop Backgrounds have come a long way since Windows 3.1. Because of Windows Vista's name, most of the desktop images Desktop Backgrounds points to are, well, vistas—beautiful, expansive, nature images. There are many more to choose from, so feel free to look around.

▶ **Tile.** Place the picture in the upper-left corner of the desktop, and repeat it over and over until the entire desktop is covered.

▶ **Center.** Plop the picture in the middle of the desktop. If the picture is smaller than the desktop, a colored border fills in the gaps. (You can change the border color by clicking the little "Change background color" link that appears when you choose the Center option.)

Once you have chosen your desktop picture, and the way it will be positioned, apply your new desktop by clicking OK.

Screen Savers

You don't technically *need* a screen saver to protect your monitor from burn-in. Today's energy-efficient monitors wouldn't burn an image into the screen unless you left them on continuously, unused, for at least two years, according to the people who design and build them.

No, screen savers are mostly about entertainment, pure and simple—and Windows Vista's built-in screen saver is certainly entertaining.

The idea is simple: A few minutes after you leave your computer, whatever work you were doing is hidden behind the screen saver; passers-by can't see what's on the screen. To exit the screen saver, move the mouse, click a mouse button, or press a key.

Tip

Moving the mouse is the best way to get rid of a screen saver. A mouse click or a key press could trigger an action you didn't intend—such as clicking some button in one of your programs or typing the letter whose key you pressed.

Choosing a Screen Saver

To choose a Windows Vista screen saver, right-click the desktop. From the shortcut menu, choose Personalize. In the resulting window, click Screen Saver.

Now use the Screen Saver drop-down list. A miniature preview appears in the preview monitor on the dialog box (see Figure 5-5).

To see a *full-screen* preview, click the Preview button. The screen saver display fills your screen and remains there until you move your mouse, click a mouse button, or press a key.

The Wait box determines how long the screen saver waits before kicking in, after the last time you move the mouse or type. Click the Settings button to play with the chosen screen saver module's look and behavior. For example, you may be able to change its colors, texture, or animation style.

At the bottom of this tab, click "Change power settings" to open the Power Options window described on page 161.

— Tip

If you keep graphics files in your Pictures folder, try selecting the Photos screen saver. Then click the Settings button and choose the pictures you want to see. When the screen saver kicks in, Vista puts on a spectacular slide show of your photos, bringing each to the screen with a special effect (flying in from the side, fading in, and so on).

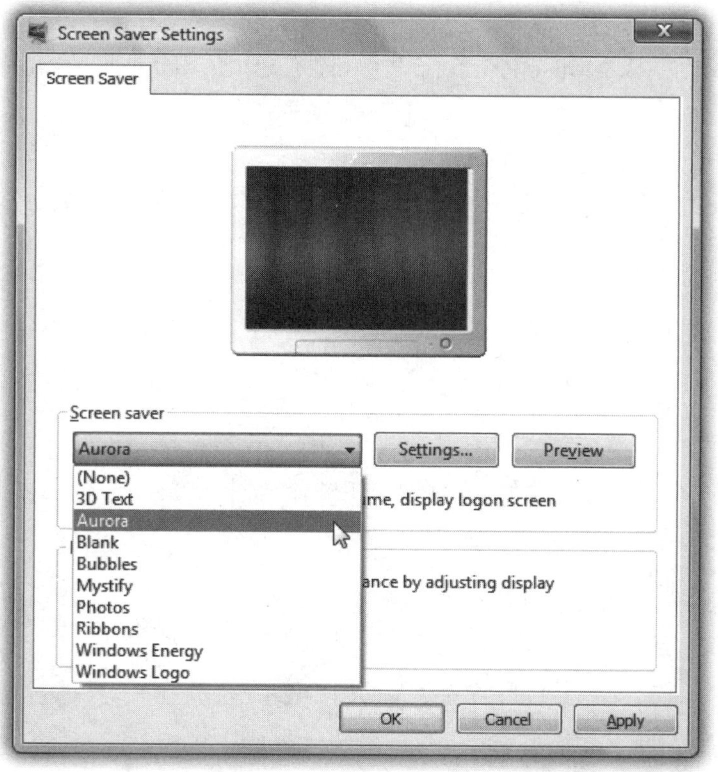

Figure 5-5: Some screen savers don't work unless you have an Aero-capable PC (page 22): Windows Energy, Ribbons, Mystify, Bubbles, Aurora, and 3D Text. If you don't have an Aero machine, you're left with slim pickings. Of course, the photo sample pictures are nice. (If you have an Aero-capable PC but you've turned off the Aero look, the fancy screen savers are still available.)

Sounds

Windows plays beeps and bloops to celebrate various occasions: closing a program, yanking out a USB drive, logging in or out, getting a new fax, and so on. You can turn these sounds on or off, or choose new sounds for these events; see page 164.

Mouse Makeover

If your fondness for the standard Windows arrow cursor begins to wane, you can assert your individuality by choosing a different pointer shape. For starters, you might want to choose a *bigger* arrow cursor—a great solution on today's tinier-pixel, shrunken-cursor monitors.

Begin by right-clicking the desktop and, from the shortcut menu, choosing Personalize. In the dialog box, click Mouse Pointers. You arrive at the dialog box shown in Figure 5-6.

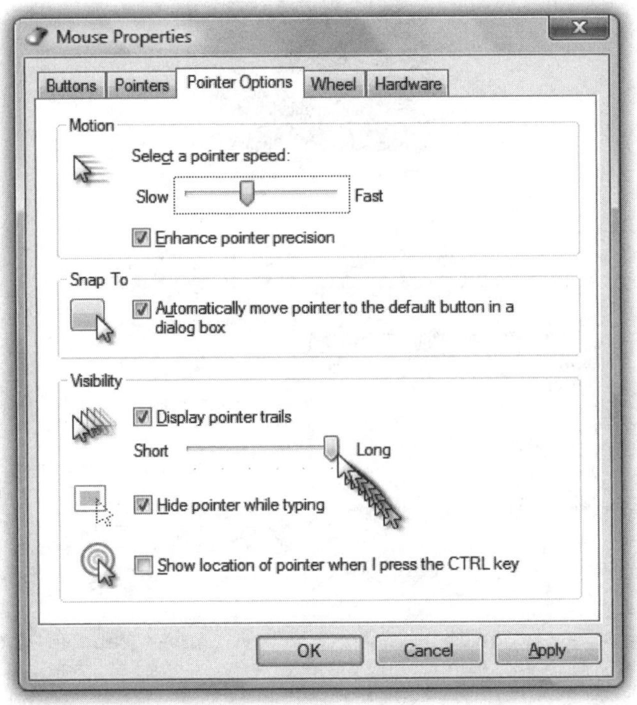

Figure 5-6: Ever lose your mouse pointer while working on a laptop with a dim screen? Maybe pointer trails could help. Or have you ever worked on a desktop computer with a mouse pointer that seems to take forever to move across the desktop? Try increasing the pointer speed.

At this point, you can proceed in any of three ways:

► **Scheme.** Windows has many more cursors than the arrow pointer. At various times, you may also see the spinning circular cursor (which means, "Wait; I'm thinking," or "Wait; I've crashed"), the I-beam cursor (which appears when you're editing text), the little pointing-finger hand made famous by Microsoft's advertising (which appears when you point to a Web page link), and so on.

All of these cursors come prepackaged into design-coordinated sets called *schemes*. To look over the cursor shapes in a different scheme, use the Scheme drop-down list; the corresponding pointer collection appears in the Customize list box. Some are cute: Dinosaur, for example, displays an animated marching cartoon dinosaur instead of the hourglass cursor. Some are functional: the ones whose names include

The Solution to Tiny Type

OK, fine—I can adjust things like the standard Windows type size, but only if I choose the old Windows Classic design scheme. Look, I'm over 40, my new laptop has tiny, tiny pixels, and I want to bump up the point size! Isn't there anything I can do without having to give up the new Vista look?

The people have spoken, and they've said, "We want our screens to show more!" The manufacturers have responded, and they've said, "OK, fine—we'll just make the pixels smaller." These days, text on PC screens (especially laptops) is practically unreadable for over-40 eyes.

Yes, there *is* a way to bump up the standard Windows point size. Right-click the desktop; from the shortcut menu, choose Personalize. Then click the "Adjust font size dpi" link at the left side of the dialog box.

After you authenticate yourself (page 127), you arrive at the DPI Scaling dialog box, where you can scale up the size of the text, at least in programs (like Windows itself) that are modern enough to respond to this control. (The dialog box offers only two choices: default size, or one size bigger. To choose something larger, click the Custom DPI button.)

"large" offer jumbo, magnified cursors ideal for very large screens or failing eyesight. When you find one that seems like an improvement over the Windows Aero (system scheme) set, click OK.

► **Select individual pointers.** You don't have to change to a completely different scheme; you can also replace just one cursor. To do so, click the pointer you want to change, and then click the Browse button. You're shown the vast array of cursor-replacement icons (which are in the Local Disk (C:)→Windows→Cursors folder). Click one to see what it looks like; double-click to select it.

NOSTALGIA CORNER

Restoring the Desktop Icons

The Vista desktop, like the XP desktop before it, is a victim of Microsoft's clean-freak tendencies. It's awfully pretty—but awfully barren. Windows veterans may miss the handy desktop icons that once provided quick access to important locations on your PC, like My Computer, My Documents, My Network Places, and Internet Explorer.

You can still get to these locations— they're listed in your Start menu—but opening them requires two mouse clicks (including one to open the Start menu)—an egregious expenditure of caloric effort.

However, if you miss the older arrangement, it's easy enough to put these icons back on the desktop. To do so, right-click a blank spot on the desktop; from the shortcut menu, choose Personalize.

Now the Personalization dialog box appears. In the Tasks pane on the left side, click "Change desktop icons."

As shown here, checkboxes for the common desktop icons await your summons: Computer, Network, Internet Explorer, Control Panel, and User's Files (that is, your Personal folder—see page 37).

Turn on the ones you'd like to install onto the desktop and then click OK. Your old favorite icons are now back where they once belonged.

► **Create your own pointer scheme.** Once you've replaced a cursor shape, you've also changed the scheme to which it belongs. At this point, either click OK to activate your change and get back to work, or save the new, improved scheme under its own name, so you can switch back to the original when nostalgia calls. To do so, click the Save As button, name the scheme, and then click OK.

Customizing the Start Menu

It's possible to live a long and happy life without ever tampering with the Start menu. In fact, for many people, the idea of making it look or work differently comes dangerously close to nerd territory.

Still, knowing how to manipulate the Start menu listings may come in handy someday, and provides an interesting glimpse into the way Windows works. And tweaking it to reflect your way of doing things can pay off in efficiency down the road.

Note

Thanks to the User Accounts feature described in Chapter 15, any changes you make to the Start menu apply only to *you*. Each person with an account on this PC has an independent, customized Start menu. When you sign onto the machine using your name and password, Windows Vista loads *your* customized Start menu.

Start Menu Settings

Microsoft offers a fascinating set of customization options for the Start menu. It's hard to tell whether these options were selected by a scientific usability study or by a dartboard, but you're likely to find something that suits you.

To view and change the basic options, right-click the Start menu; from the shortcut menu, choose Properties. Now the Taskbar and Start Menu Properties dialog box opens, as seen in Figure 5-7.

When you click the Customize button, you see the dialog box shown at right in Figure 5-7. Here you're offered a random assortment of Start-menu tweaks, neatly listed in alphabetical order; they affect the Start menu in some fairly simple yet profound ways. Here, among other things, is where you'll find the show/hide switches for commands on the *right side* of the Start menu—Computer, Control Panel, Documents, Games, Music, Personal folder, and so on.

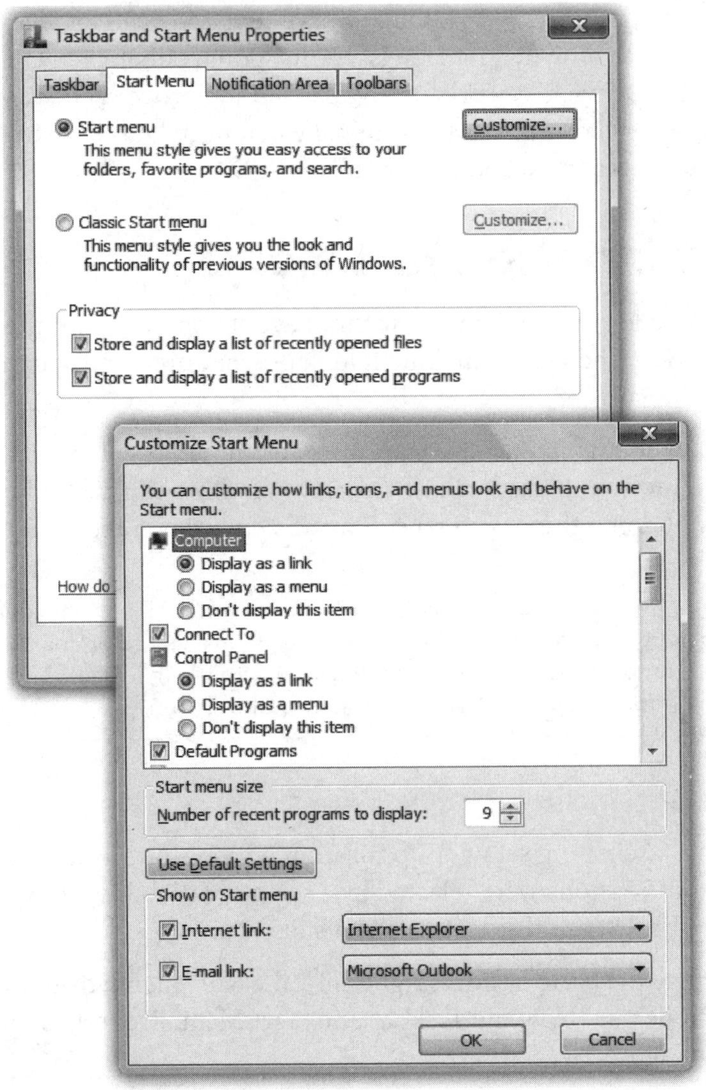

Figure 5-7: Top: On this first screen, you can turn off the new, improved Vista two-column Start menu design to return to the single-column Classic Start menu design of Windows versions gone by. Click Customize to get to the good stuff. (The Privacy checkboxes refer to the lower-left section of the Start menu, which lists the programs you use most often, and the Recent Items submenu, which lists documents you've had open. Turn these off if you don't want to risk your supervisor coming by while you're up getting coffee, and noticing that your most recently used programs are Tetris Max, Myst IV, Tomb Raider, and Quake.)

Bottom: Here's the Customize Start Menu dialog box.

Beneath each of these headings, you'll find three options. The middle one, "Display as a menu," is extremely useful. It means that instead of simply listing the name of a folder (which is what "Display as a link" means), your Start menu sprouts a submenu listing the *contents* of that folder, as shown at bottom in Figure 5-8.

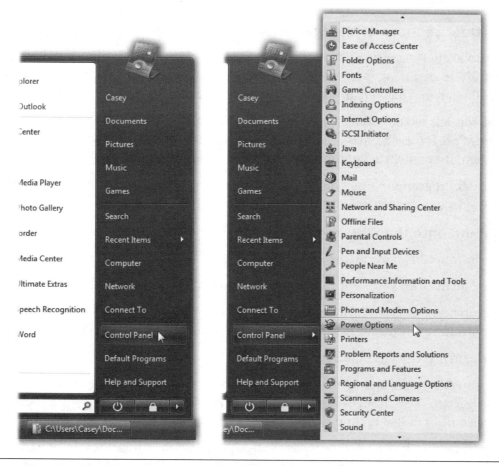

Figure 5-8: Left: When "Display as a link" is selected for Control Panel, you can't open a particular Control Panel program directly. Instead, you must choose Start→Control Panel, which opens the Control Panel window; now it's up to you to open the program you want.

Right: Turning on "Display as a menu" saves you a step; you now get a submenu that lists each Control Panel program. By clicking one, you can open it directly. This feature saves you the trouble of opening a folder window (such as Control Panel or Documents), double-clicking an icon inside it, and then closing the window again.

Adding Icons to the Start Menu

Usually, when you install a new program, its installer automatically inserts the program's name and icon in your Start→All Programs menu. There may be times, however, when you want to add something to the Start menu yourself, such as a folder, document, or even a disk.

The "free" sections of the Start menu

In the following pages, you'll read several references to the "free" portions of the Start menu. These are the two areas that you, the lowly human, are allowed to modify freely—adding, removing, renaming, or sorting as you see fit:

▶ **The top-left section of the Start menu.** This little area lists what Microsoft calls *pinned* programs and files—things you use often enough that you want a fairly permanent list of them at your fingertips.

▶ **The All Programs menu.** This, of course, is the master list of programs (and anything else—documents, folders, disks—you want to see listed).

Dragging onto the Start menu

Here's how to add an icon to one of the free areas:

1. **Locate the icon you want to add to your Start menu.**

    It can be an application, a document, a folder you frequently access, one of the programs in your Control Panel's folder, or even your hard drive or CD-drive icon.

2. **Drag it directly onto the Start button.**

    If you release the mouse now, Windows adds the name of the icon you've just dragged to the bottom of the "pinned items" list (Figure 5-9, right). You're now welcome to drag it up or down within this list.

    Alternatively, if you *keep the mouse button pressed* as you drag onto the Start button, the Start menu itself opens. As long as the button is still pressed, you can drag the new icon wherever you want among the items listed in the top-left section of the menu (Figure 5-9, left).

    Similarly, if you drag to the Start button and then onto the All Programs command without releasing the mouse, you can place it exactly where you want in the Start→All Programs menu.

--- Tip ---

If "Sort All Programs menu by name" is *not* turned on, your All Programs list may gradu-ally become something of a mess.

If you want to restore some order to it—specifically, alphabetical—just right-click any-where on the open All Programs menu and choose Sort by Name from the shortcut menu.

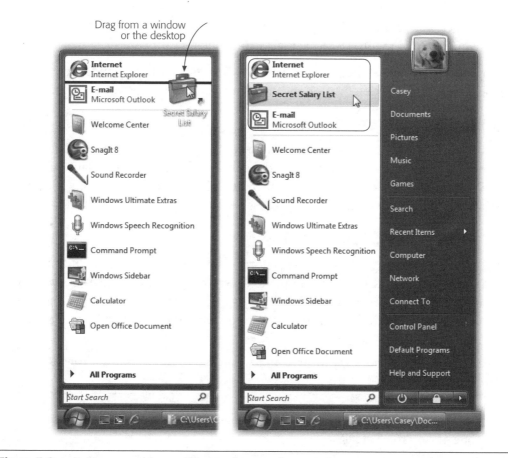

Figure 5-9: Left: You can add something to the top of your Start menu by dragging it (from whatever folder it's in) onto the Start button to open the Start menu, and then dragging it directly into posi-tion. (Once the Start menu is open, you can also drag it onto the All Programs link—and once *that* menu is open, drag it anywhere in *that* list.)

Right: When you release the mouse, you'll find that the item is happily ensconced where you dropped it. Remember, too, that you're always free to drag anything up or down in the "free" areas of the menu: the circled area shown here, and the All Programs list.

Removing Icons from the Start Menu

When it comes time to prune an overgrown Start menu, there are three different sets of instructions, depending on which section of the Start menu needs purging.

▶ **The left-side column and All Programs list.** Right-click the item you've targeted for extinction, and then, from the shortcut menu, choose either "Remove from this list" or "Delete."

In both cases, you're only deleting the *shortcut* that appears on the menu. Deleting items from the Start menu doesn't actually uninstall any software.

▶ **The right-side column.** Open the Properties→Customize dialog box for the Start menu (page 115), and then turn off the checkboxes for the items you want expunged.

Renaming Start-Menu Items

Although few people realize it, you can rename anything in the Start menu's left side. Click the Start menu to open it, right-click the command you want to rename, and choose Rename from the shortcut menu. The name of the command sprouts a little editing box. Type the new name and then press Enter.

Reorganizing the Start Menu

To change the order of listings in the "free" portions of the Start menu, including the All Programs list, just drag the commands up and down the lists as you see fit. As you drag an item, a black line appears to show you the resulting location of your dragging action. Release the mouse when the black line is where you want the relocated icon to appear.

___ Tip _____

If you change your mind while you're dragging, press the Esc key to leave everything as it was.

_____

You can drag program names from the lower-left section of the Start menu, too—but only into one of the "free" areas.

PART TWO: THE PIECES OF VISTA

PROGRAMS, DOCUMENTS, AND GADGETS

▶ Opening Programs

▶ Exiting Programs

▶ When Programs Die: The Task Manager

▶ Saving Documents

▶ Closing Documents

▶ The Open Dialog Box

▶ Moving Data Between Documents

▶ The Sidebar

▶ Filename Extensions and File Associations

▶ Installing Software

▶ Uninstalling Software

▶ The Control Panel

When you get right down to it, an operating system like Windows is nothing more than a home base from which to launch *applications* (programs). And you, as a Windows person, are particularly fortunate, since more programs are available for Windows than for any other operating system on earth.

But when you launch a program, you're no longer necessarily in the world Microsoft designed for you. Programs from other software companies work a bit differently, and there's a lot to learn about how Windows handles programs that were born before it was.

This chapter covers everything you need to know about installing, removing, launching, and managing programs; using programs to generate documents; understanding how documents, programs, and Windows communicate with each other; and exploiting Vista's great new hybrid document/program entity, the Sidebar gadget.

Opening Programs

Windows lets you launch (open) programs in many different ways:

▶ Choose a program's name from the Start→All Programs menu.

▶ Click a program's icon on the Quick Launch toolbar (page 73).

▶ Find a program using the Start menu's Search box (page 47).

▶ Open a document using any of the above techniques; its "parent" program opens automatically. For example, if you used Microsoft Word to write a file called Last Will and Testament.doc, double-clicking the document's icon launches Word and automatically opens that file.

What happens next depends on the program you're using (and whether or not you opened a document). Most present you with a new, blank, untitled document. Some, such as FileMaker and Microsoft PowerPoint, welcome you instead with a question: do you want to open an existing document or create a new one?

Exiting Programs

When you exit, or quit, an application, the memory it was using is returned to the Windows pot for use by other programs.

If you use a particular program several times a day, like a word processor or calendar, you'll save time in the long run by keeping it open all day long. (You can always minimize its window to get it out of the way when you're not using it.)

But if you're done using a program for the day, exit it, especially if it's a memory-hungry one like, say, Photoshop. Do so using one of these techniques:

▶ Choose File→Exit.

▶ Click the program window's Close box, or double-click the upper-left corner of the window.

▶ Right-click the program's taskbar button; from the shortcut menu, choose Close or Close Group.

▶ Press Alt+F4 to close the window you're in. (If it's a program that disappears entirely when its last document window closes, you're home.)

After offering you a chance to save any changes you've made to your document, the program's windows, menus, and toolbars disappear, and you "fall down a layer" into the window that was behind it.

When Programs Die: The Task Manager

Windows Vista may be a revolution in stability (at least if you're used to, say, Windows Me), but that doesn't mean that *programs* never crash or freeze. They crash, all right— it's just that you rarely have to restart the computer as a result.

When something goes horribly wrong with a program, your primary interest is usually exiting it. But when a program locks up (the cursor moves, but menus and tool palettes don't respond) or when a dialog box tells you that a program has "failed to respond," exiting may not be so easy. After all, how do you choose File→Exit if the File menu itself doesn't open?

The solution is to invoke the "three-fingered salute": Ctrl+Alt+Delete.

In Vista, however, Ctrl+Alt+Delete no longer opens the fabled Task Manager. Instead, it opens the new Windows Security screen (Figure 6-1).

From *here* you can get to the Task Manager—by clicking Start Task Manager (Figure 6-1, top). Now you see a list of every open program. The Status column should make clear what you already know: that one of your programs is ignoring you.

As shown in Figure 6-1, shutting down the troublesome program is fairly easy; just click its name and then click the End Task button. (If yet another dialog box appears, telling you that "This program is not responding," click the End Now button.)

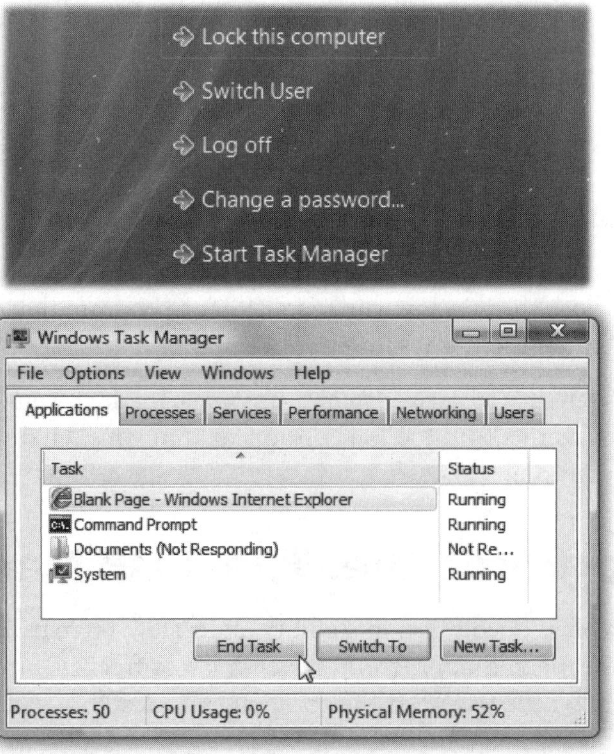

Figure 6-1: Top: Click the Task Manager button on the Windows Security dialog box to check on the status of a troublesome program.

Bottom: As if you didn't know, one of these programs is "not responding." Highlight its name and then click End Task to slap it out of its misery. Once the program disappears from the list, close the Task Manager and get on with your life. You can even restart the same program right away—no harm done.

When you jettison a recalcitrant program this way, Windows generally shuts down the troublemaker gracefully, even offering you the chance to save unsaved changes to your documents.

Authentication: User Account Control

You can't work in Windows Vista very long before encountering the dialog box shown here. It appears any time you install a new program or try to change an important setting on your PC. (Throughout Vista, a tiny colorful shield icon next to a button or link indicates a change that will produce this message box.)

Why do these so-called User Account Control (UAC) boxes pop up? In the olden days before Vista, nasties like spyware and viruses could install themselves invisibly, behind your back.

In Vista, on the other hand, whenever somebody or some program wants to make a big change to your system, the UAC box alerts you.

Most of the time, *you* are the one making the changes, which can make the UAC box a bit annoying. But if that UAC dialog box ever appears *by itself,* you'll know something evil is afoot on your PC, and you'll have the chance to shut it down.

How you get past the UAC box—how you *authenticate yourself*—depends on the kind of account you have (Chapter 15): *standard* or *administrator.*

If you're an administrator, just click Con-

tinue to proceed. If you're a Standard account holder, the UAC dialog box requires the name and password *of* an administrator. You're supposed to call an administrator over to your desk to indicate his permission to proceed by entering his own name and password.

Questions? Yes, you in the back?

Can I turn off these UAC interruptions?

Yes. In your Control Panel, click Classic View, and double-click User Accounts. Click "Turn User Account Control on or off," authenticate yourself (page 127), and then turn off "Use User Account Control (UAC) to help protect your computer." Click OK.

This really, truly isn't a good idea, though. Really it's not. You're sending your PC right back to the days of Windows XP, when any sneaky old malware could install itself or change your system settings without your knowledge. Do this only on a PC that's not connected to a network or the Internet, for example, or maybe when you, the all-knowing system administrator, are trying to troubleshoot and the UAC interruptions are slowing you down.

If even this treatment fails to close the program, you might have to slam the door the hard way. Click the Processes tab, click the name of the program that's giving you grief, and then click the End Process button. (The Processes list includes dozens of programs, including many that Windows runs behind the scenes. Finding the abbreviated name of the program may be the hardest part of this process.)

Using this method, you'll lose any unsaved changes to your documents—but at least the frozen program is finally closed.

___ Tip ___

If you click a program's taskbar button but its window doesn't appear, the program may be frozen. In that case, try right-clicking the taskbar button; from the shortcut menu, choose Restore.

Saving Documents

In a few programs, such as the Calculator or Solitaire, you don't actually create any documents; when you close the window, no trace of your work remains.

Most programs, however, are designed to create *documents*—files that you can reopen for further editing, send to other people, back up on another disk, and so on.

That's why these programs offer File→Save and File→Open commands, which let you preserve the work you've done, saving it onto the hard drive as a new file icon so that you can return to it later.

The Save Dialog Box

When you choose File→Save for the first time, you're asked where you want the new document stored on your hard drive (Figure 6-2). In Windows Vista, this Save As dialog box is crystal-clear; in fact, for the first time in Windows history it's now a *full Explorer window*, complete with taskbar, Navigation pane, Search box, Views menu, and Organize menu. All of the skills you've picked up working at the desktop come into play here; you can even delete a file or folder right from within the Save or Open box. (The Delete command is in the Organize menu.)

To give it a try, launch any Windows program that has a Save or Export command— WordPad , for example. (Not all programs from other software companies have updated their Save dialog boxes yet.) Type a couple of words and then choose File→Save. The Save As dialog box appears (Figure 6-2).

Figure 6-2: When the Save box first opens, it may appear in the collapsed form shown at top. Click the Browse Folders button to expand it into the full-blown dialog box shown at bottom. Type a name, choose a folder location, and specify the format for the file you're saving.

Saving into Your Documents Folder

The first time you use the File→Save command to save a file, Windows suggests putting your newly created document in your Documents folder.

For many people, this is an excellent suggestion. First, it means that your file won't accidentally fall into some deeply nested folder where you'll never see it again. Instead, it will be waiting in the Documents folder, which is very difficult to lose.

Second, the Documents folder is also what Windows displays whenever you use a program's File→*Open* command. In other words, the Documents folder saves you time both when *creating* a new file and when *retrieving* it.

__ Tip _____

If the Documents folder becomes cluttered, feel free to make subfolders inside it to hold your various projects. You could even create a different default folder in Documents for each program.

Saving into Other Folders

Still, the now-familiar Navigation pane (page 51) also appears in the Save dialog box. (At least it does in the Save box's expanded form; see Figure 6-2.) So do the Address bar (page 44) and the Search box. You always have direct access to other places where you might want to save a newly created file.

All the usual keyboard shortcuts apply: Alt+up arrow, for example, to open the folder that *contains* the current one. There's even a New Folder button on the toolbar, **so you can generate a new, empty** folder in the current list of files and folders. Windows asks you to name it.

The File Format Drop-Down Menu

The Save As dialog box in many programs offers a menu of file formats (usually referred to as file *types*) below or next to the "File name" text box. Use this drop-down menu when preparing a document for use by somebody whose computer doesn't have the same software.

For example, if you've typed something in Microsoft Word, you can use this menu to generate a Web page document or a Rich Text Format document that you can open with almost any standard word processor or page-layout program.

Closing Documents

You close a document window just as you'd close any window, as described in Chapter 3: by clicking the close box (marked by an X) in the upper-right corner of the window, by double-clicking the Control menu spot just to the left of the File menu, or by pressing Alt+F4. If you've done any work to the document since the last time you saved it, Windows offers a "Save changes?" dialog box as a reminder.

Sending an Error Report to Microsoft

Whenever Windows detects that a program has exited, shall we say, *eccentrically*—for example, it froze and you had to terminate it—your PC quietly sends a report back to Microsoft, the mother ship, via the Internet. It provides the company with the technical details about whatever was going on at the moment of the freeze, crash, or premature termination.

The information includes the name and version number of the program, the date and time, and other details. Microsoft swears that it doesn't collect any information about *you.*

Microsoft says that it has two interests in getting this information. First, it collates the data into gigantic electronic databases, which it then analyzes using special software tools. The idea, of course, is to find trends that emerge from studying hundreds of thousands of such reports. "Oh, my goodness, it looks like people who own both Speak-it Pro 5 and Beekeeper Plus who right-click a document that's currently being printed experience a system lockup," an engineer might announce one day. By analyzing the system glitches of its customers en masse, the company hopes to pinpoint problems and devise software patches with much greater efficiency than

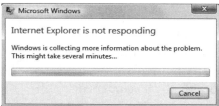

before.

Second, Microsoft's computers may also react to the information on the spot and send you a dialog box that lets you know about an available fix.

Windows XP did this report-sending, too, but it asked you *each time* a program crashed. In Vista, the report-sending feature is either turned *on* all the time or *off* all the time.

To adjust the settings, choose Start→ Control Panel; click Classic View; open the Problem Reports and Solutions applet. On the left-side task pane, click "Change settings." In the resulting dialog box, click "Advanced settings." There, before you, is the On/Off switch (where it says, "For my programs, problem reporting is:").

This dialog box offers various other privacy controls. For example, you can create a Block list—programs whose crashes won't be reported. (This means you, owners of Music Piracy Plus 4.0.) You can also specify whether crashes are *always* reported, *never* reported, or left to the discretion of each account holder.

Finally, you can see a list of the reports it's sent so far; click "View problem history."

Sometimes closing the window also exits the application, and sometimes the application remains running, even with no document windows open. And in a few *really* bizarre cases, it's possible to exit an application (like Windows Mail) while a document window (an email message) remains open on the screen, lingering and abandoned!

The Open Dialog Box

To reopen a document you've already saved and named, you can pursue any of these avenues:

▶ Open your Documents folder (or whichever folder contains the saved file). Double-click the file's icon.

▶ If you've opened the document recently, choose its name from the Start→Recent Items menu.

▶ If you're already in the program that created the document, choose File→Open. (Or check the bottom of the File menu, where many programs add a list of recently opened files.)

▶ Type the document's path and name into the Address bar. (You can also browse for it.)

The Open dialog box looks almost identical to the Save As dialog box. Once again, you start out by perusing the contents of your Documents folder; once again, the dialog box otherwise behaves exactly like an Explorer window. For example, you can press Backspace to back *out* of a folder that you've opened.

When you've finally located the file you want to open, double-click it or highlight it (from the keyboard, if you like), and then press Enter.

In general, most people don't encounter the Open dialog box nearly as often as the Save As dialog box. That's because Windows offers many more convenient ways to *open* a file (double-clicking its icon, choosing its name from the Start→Documents command, and so on), but only a single way to *save* a new file.

Moving Data Between Documents

You can't paste a picture into your Web browser, and you can't paste MIDI music into your word processor. But you can put graphics into your word processor, paste movies into your database, insert text into Photoshop, and combine a surprising variety of seemingly dissimilar kinds of data. And you can transfer text from Web pages, email messages, and word processing documents to other email and word processing files; in fact, that's one of the most frequently performed tasks in all of computing.

Cut, Copy, and Paste

Most experienced PC users have learned to quickly trigger the Cut, Copy, and Paste commands from the keyboard—without even thinking. Figure 6-3 provides a recap.

Bear in mind that you can cut and copy highlighted material in any of three ways. First, you can use the Cut and Copy commands in the Edit menu; second, you can press

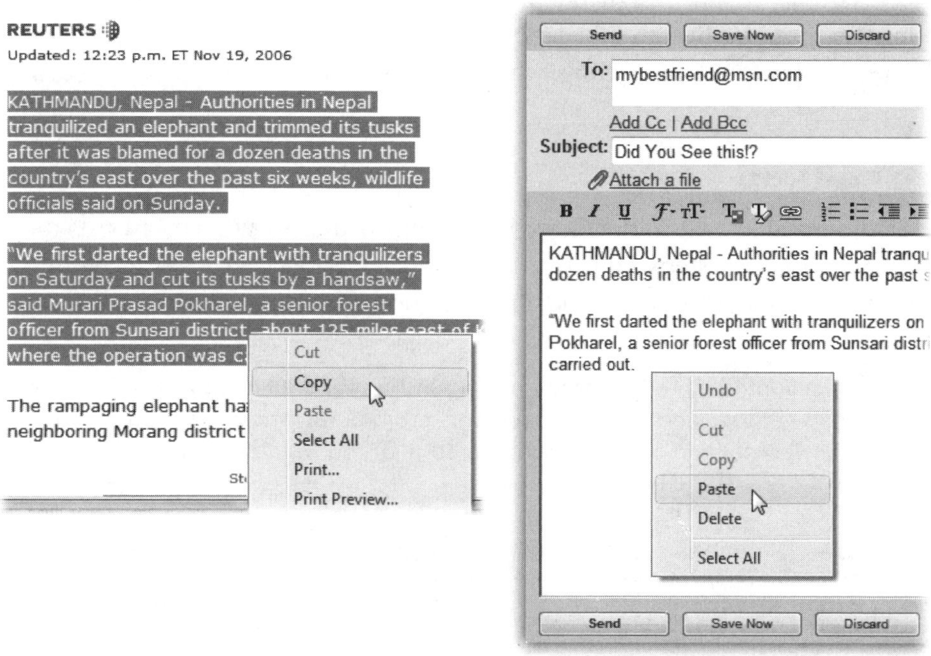

Figure 6-3: Suppose you want to email some text from a Web page to a friend.

Left: Start by dragging through it and then choosing Copy from the shortcut menu (or choosing Edit→Copy).

Right: Now switch to your email program and paste it into an outgoing message.

Ctrl+X (for Cut) or Ctrl+C (for Copy); and third, you can right-click the highlighted material and, from the shortcut menu, choose Cut or Copy.

When you do so, Windows memorizes the highlighted material, stashing it on an invisible Clipboard. If you choose Copy, nothing visible happens; if you choose Cut, the highlighted material disappears from the original document.

Pasting copied or cut material, once again, is something you can do either from a menu (choose Edit→Paste), from the shortcut menu (right-click and choose Paste), or from the keyboard (press Ctrl+V).

The most recently cut or copied material remains on your Clipboard even after you paste, making it possible to paste the same blob repeatedly. Such a trick can be useful when, for example, you've designed a business card in your drawing program and want to duplicate it enough times to fill a letter-sized printout. On the other hand, whenever you next copy or cut something, whatever was previously on the Clipboard is lost forever.

Drag-and-Drop

As useful and popular as it is, the Copy/Paste routine doesn't win any awards for speed; after all, it requires four steps. In many cases, you can replace that routine with the far more direct (and enjoyable) drag-and-drop method. Figure 6-4 illustrates how it works.

___ Tip _____

> To drag highlighted material offscreen, drag the cursor until it approaches the top or bottom edge of the window. The document scrolls automatically; as you approach the destination, jerk the mouse away from the edge of the window to stop the scrolling.

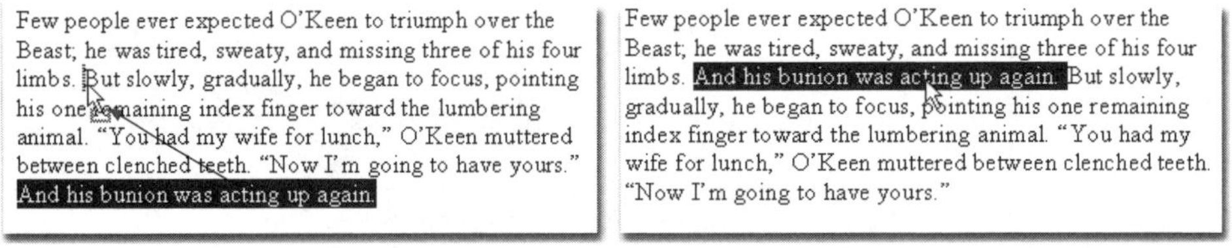

_____

> Few people ever expected O'Keen to triumph over the Beast; he was tired, sweaty, and missing three of his four limbs. But slowly, gradually, he began to focus, pointing his one remaining index finger toward the lumbering animal. "You had my wife for lunch," O'Keen muttered between clenched teeth. "Now I'm going to have yours." And his bunion was acting up again.

> Few people ever expected O'Keen to triumph over the Beast; he was tired, sweaty, and missing three of his four limbs. And his bunion was acting up again. But slowly, gradually, he began to focus, pointing his one remaining index finger toward the lumbering animal. "You had my wife for lunch," O'Keen muttered between clenched teeth. "Now I'm going to have yours."

Figure 6-4: You can drag highlighted text (left) to another place in the document—or a different window or program (right).

Several of the built-in Windows programs work with the drag-and-drop technique, including WordPad and Mail. Most popular commercial programs offer the drag-and-drop feature, too, including email programs and word processors, AOL, Microsoft Office programs, and so on.

As illustrated in Figure 6-4, drag-and-drop is ideal for transferring material between windows or between programs. It's especially useful when you've already copied something valuable to your Clipboard, since drag-and-drop doesn't involve (and doesn't erase) the Clipboard.

Its most popular use, however, is rearranging the text in a single document. In, say, Word or WordPad, you can rearrange entire sections, paragraphs, sentences, or even individual letters, just by dragging them—a terrific editing technique.

___ Tip _____
  Using drag-and-drop to move highlighted text within a document also deletes the text
  from its original location. By pressing Ctrl as you drag, however, you make a *copy* of the
  highlighted text.

Export/Import

When it comes to transferring large chunks of information from one program to another—especially address books, spreadsheet cells, and database records—none of the data-transfer methods described so far in this chapter does the trick. For such purposes, use the Export and Import commands found in the File menu of almost every database, spreadsheet, email, and address-book program.

These Export/Import commands aren't part of Windows, so the manuals or help screens of the applications in question should be your source for instructions. For now, however, the power and convenience of this feature are worth noting. Because of these commands, your four years' worth of collected names and addresses in, say, an old address-book program can find its way into a newer program, such as Palm Desktop, in a matter of minutes.

The Sidebar

As you know, the essence of using Windows is running *programs,* which often produce *documents.* In Vista, however, there's a third category: a set of weird hybrid entities that Microsoft calls *gadgets.* They appear, all at once, floating in front of your other windows, at the right side of the screen. They're there when you first fire up Vista, or whenever you press ⊞+Space bar. (You can also open them by choosing Start→All Programs→Accessories→Windows Sidebar.)

Welcome to the new world of the Sidebar (Figure 6-5).

What are these weird hybrid entities, anyway? They're not really programs, because they don't create documents or have listings in the All Programs menu. They're cer-

Figure 6-5: When you summon the Sidebar, you get a fleet of floating miniprograms that convey or convert all kinds of useful information. They appear and disappear all at once, on a tinted translucent sheet.

tainly not documents, because you can't name or save them. What they *most* resemble, actually, is little Web pages. They're meant to display information, much of it from the Internet, and they're written using Web programming languages like DHTML, Javascript, VBScript, and XML.

Vista's starter gadgets include a calculator, current weather reporter, stock ticker, clock, and so on. Mastering the basics of Sidebar won't take you long at all:

▶ To move a gadget, drag it around the screen. It doesn't have to stay in the Sidebar area.

In fact, you can drag *all* of the gadgets off the Sidebar, if you like, and park them anywhere on the screen. You could even close the now-empty Sidebar—right-click a blank spot and, from the shortcut menu, choose Close Sidebar—and leave the gadgets themselves stranded, floating in place. (If they look too lonely, you can reopen the Sidebar by right-clicking the tiny Windows Sidebar icon in your notification area and, from the shortcut menu, choosing Open.)

___ Tip _____

If the gadget doesn't seem to want to move when you drag it, you're probably grabbing it by a clickable portion. Try to find a purely graphical spot—the spiral binding of the calendar, for example.

And if all else fails, right-click the gadget. From the shortcut menu, choose Detach from Sidebar.

_____

▶ To close a gadget, point to it. You'll see the square X button appear at the gadget's top-left corner; click it. (You can also right-click a gadget and choose Close Gadget from its shortcut menu.)

▶ To add a gadget to the Sidebar, click the + button at the top of the screen (Figure 6-5), or right-click any gadget (or the Sidebar notification-area icon) and choose Add Gadget from the Sidebar.

You've just opened the Gadget Gallery, a semi-transparent catalog of all your gadgets, even the ones that aren't currently on the screen (Figure 6-6). Open one by double-clicking its icon, or by dragging it to a blank spot on your Sidebar.

If you add more gadgets than can fit on the Sidebar, a tiny ▶ appears at the top of the Sidebar. Click it to bring the next "page" full of gadgets into view.

▶ To rearrange your gadgets within the Sidebar, just drag them up or down, using any blank spot as a handle. The other gadgets slide out of the way.

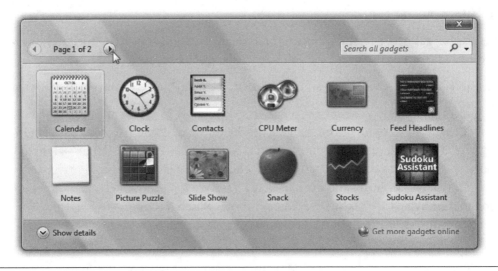

Figure 6-6: You may have to scroll the Gadget Gallery to see all the gadgets, by clicking the Page arrows at the top left of the window. When you're finished opening new gadgets, close the Gadget Gallery by clicking its X button.

Losing the Sidebar

To get rid of the Sidebar, you have several options.

▶ Hide it by right-clicking a blank spot on the Sidebar. From the shortcut menu, choose Close Sidebar.

This technique just hides the actual Sidebar rectangle. It doesn't close any gadgets that you've moved onto your screen, and it's still technically running, using memory.

▶ Quit it completely, so it's not using up memory or distracting you, by right-clicking the Windows Sidebar notification-area icon. From the shortcut menu, choose Exit.

▶ Make it stop auto-starting along with Windows by opening the Windows Sidebar Properties control panel. (Quickest way: Right-click the Windows Sidebar icon in your notification area. From the shortcut menu, choose Properties.) Turn off "Start Sidebar when Windows starts." Click OK.

Sidebar Tips

Like most new Vista features, Sidebar is crawling with tips and tricks. Here are a few of the biggies:

▶ You can open more than one copy of the same gadget. Just double-click its icon more than once in the Gadget Bar. You wind up with multiple copies of it on your screen: three Clocks, two Weather trackers, or whatever. That's a useful trick when, for example, you want to track the time or weather in more than one city, or when you maintain two different stock portfolios.

▶ If you point to a gadget without clicking, two or three tiny icons appear to its right. One is the X (Close button), which you've already met. The one that looks like a tiny wrench opens the gadget's Settings dialog box, where, for example, you can specify which stocks you want to track, or which town's weather you want to see. The third one, a tiny grid, is a "grip strip" that lets you drag the gadget to a new spot on the screen.

▶ Many of the gadgets require an Internet connection, preferably an always-on connection like a cable modem.

Gadget Catalog

Here's a rundown of the standard gadgets that come preinstalled in Vista. True, they look awfully simple, but some of them harbor a few secrets.

___ Tip _____

If you right-click an individual gadget, the shortcut menu offers, among other commands, an Opacity control. That is, you can make any individual gadget more or less see-through—something that makes more sense for the clock than for, say, the photo slideshow.

_____

Calendar

Sure, you can always find out today's date by pointing to the clock on your taskbar. And this gadget isn't much of a calendar. It doesn't show your appointments, and it doesn't hook into Windows Calendar.

But it's much nicer looking than the taskbar one. And besides, you can use this calendar to look ahead or back. (Navigate to a different month by clicking ˉ or ˘ buttons. Change the year by clicking the current year digits at the top of the month view.) Click the red peeking corner to return to the month-view calendar.

Clock

Sure, this clock shows the current time, but your taskbar does that. The neat part is that you can open up several of these clocks—double-click Clock in the Gadget Gallery repeatedly—and set each one up to show the time in a different city. The result looks like the row of clocks in a hotel lobby, making you look Swiss and precise.

Contacts

The concept behind this gadget is, of course, to give you faster access to your own address book.

___ **Tip** _____

This gadget is easier to understand if you drag it off of the Sidebar. Once free on your screen, it appears as a *two*-page binder, with the master list of contacts on the left side of the binding, and the individual Rolodex "page" on the right.

CPU Meter

A power user's dream—now you can watch your PC wheeze and gasp under its load in real time, with statistical accuracy.

Currency

This one's for you, world travelers (or global investors). This little gadget can convert dollars to euros, or shillings to francs, or whatever to whatever.

From the upper pop-up menu, choose the currency type you want to convert *from:* U.S. Dollars, Norwegian Krone, or whatever. Into the text box, type how *many* of those you want to convert.

Use the lower pop-up menu to specify which units you want to convert *to.*

You don't have to click anything or press any key; the conversion is performed for you instantly and automatically as you type. (Never let it be said that technology isn't marching forward.)

___ **Note** _____

This gadget actually does its homework. It goes online to download up-to-the-minute currency rates to ensure that the conversion is accurate.

Notes

Notes is a virtual Post-it note that lets you type out random scraps of text—a phone number, a Web address, a grocery list, or whatever.

▶ Edit the note by typing away. Right-click to access Cut, Copy, and Paste commands.

▶ Add another page by clicking the + button (lower right); delete the current page by clicking the X button (lower left). Once you have more than a single page, use the ¯ or ˘ buttons to move among them.

▶ Change the paper color, font, or size by clicking the Options button (tiny wrench) at the right side of the gadget. Font and Size controls appear there; click the ¯ or ˘ buttons to see the different pastel paper colors available.

Stocks

This gadget lets you build a stock portfolio and watch it rise and fall throughout the day.

It contains your list of stocks, their current prices (well, current as of 20 minutes ago), and the amount they've changed—green if they're up, red if they're down. Click a stock's name to see its chart and other details in a Web page.

To set up your portfolio, proceed like this:

▶ Add a stock by clicking the + button below the list, typing its name or stock abbreviation into the box at the top, and pressing Enter. If there's only one possible match—Microsoft, for example—the gadget adds it to the list instantly. If there's some question about what you typed, or several possible matches, you'll see a pop-up menu listing the alternatives, so you can click the one you want.

Collapse the "Add a stock" dialog box by clicking the + button again, or simply by clicking anywhere else on your screen.

▶ Scroll the list by clicking the ▲ or ▼ buttons.

▶ Remove a stock from the list by clicking the little X button that appears when you point to its name.

▶ See company names instead of abbreviations by clicking the Options (wrench) button and then turning on "Display company name in place of symbol."

Picture Puzzle

The idea is to click the tiles of the puzzle, using logic to rearrange them back into the original sequence, so that they eventually slide together into the put-together photograph.

▶ Change the photo by clicking the Options (wrench) button.

▶ Pause the timer (upper-left corner) by clicking the tiny clock.

▶ See the finished photo, so you know what the goal is, by holding the cursor down on the little ? button.

▶ Give up by clicking the double-arrow button in the upper-right corner of the puzzle window. (The same button rescrambles the puzzle.)

Weather

This gadget shows a handy current-conditions display for your city (or any other city), and, at your option, even offers a three-day forecast.

Before you get started, the most important step is to click the Options (wrench) button. In the Options dialog box, you'll see where you can specify your city and state or Zip code. Type it in and press Enter; the gadget goes online to retrieve the latest Weather.com info. You can also specify whether you prefer degrees Celsius or degrees Fahrenheit. Click OK.

Now the front of the gadget displays the name of your town, general conditions, and current temperature.

Slide Show

So you've got a digital camera and a hard drive crammed with pictures. What are you gonna do with 'em all?

Slide Show presents one photo at a time for a few seconds each. Think of it as an electronic version of the little spouse 'n' kids photo that cubicle dwellers prop up on their desks—except that the picture changes every 15 seconds.

The buttons in the tiny translucent control bar at the bottom of picture correspond to Previous Photo, Pause/Resume, Next Photo, and View (which opens up the picture—much larger now—in Windows Photo Gallery).

▶ **Substitute your own photos.** When you first install Vista, this gadget presents Microsoft's favorite nature photos. Once you're sick of them, click the Options (wrench) button. In the dialog box, use the Folder controls to choose a folder full of your own pictures.

▶ **Set up the show timing.** Fifteen seconds is an awfully long time to stare at one photo, of course. Then again, if the pix change too often, they'll be distracting, and you won't get any work done. Nonetheless, the Options dialog box lets you keep each slide on the screen for as little as 5 seconds or as long as 5 minutes.

The Options box also lets you create a crossfade effect as one slide morphs into the next. And the Shuffle checkbox, of course, makes Slide Show present your pix in a random order, rather than their alphabetical order in the folder.

__ **Tip** _____

If you drag this gadget off the Sidebar itself, you get to see your photos at a larger, more pleasant size.

_____

FREQUENTLY ASKED QUESTION

The Disappearing Notes, Stocks, or Weather

Hey! I filled my Notes gadget with grocery lists and Web addresses, and now they're gone!

Hey! I set up my home city in the Weather gadget, and now it's showing Redmond, Washington!

Hey! I painstakingly typed in all my stocks, and now it's forgotten them all!

Welcome to gadget hell, buddy.

Remember, gadgets are not actually programs. They don't, therefore, have their own preference files stashed away on the

hard drive.

And so—here's the bad news—any time you close a gadget, you *lose all the data you had typed into it.* When you reopen Weather, it always shows Redmond, Washington (Microsoft's home town); when you reopen Stocks, it always shows the NASDAQ and S&P indexes; when you reopen Notes, the sticky notes are always empty; and so on.

And so, a word to the wise: don't click that X button unless you really mean it!

More Gadgets

The gadgets that come with Vista are meant to be only examples—a starter collection. The real beauty of gadgets is that people can write their own new ones for the whole world to enjoy: gadgets that show your local movie listings, regional gas prices, your email Inbox, upcoming Outlook appointments, and so on.

To see the current list of goodies that have been vetted by Microsoft, click "Get more gadgets online" in the Gadget Gallery described above. That takes you to the Microsoft Gadgets Gallery downloads page. (Alternatively, go straight to *http://gallery.microsoft.com.*)

You should have no problem finding gadgets that tell you local traffic conditions, let you know if your flight will be on time, help you track FedEx packages, provide a word (or joke, or comic strip) of the day, and so on.

Installing a gadget

Downloading and installing a gadget isn't hard, but there are a number of steps. Here's what you'll see if you use Internet Explorer (page 226), for example:

▶ A warning that you're installing software not written by Microsoft (click OK).

▶ The File Download dialog box (click Save).

▶ The Save As dialog box, asking where to store the download (click Save).

Unless you interfere, Internet Explorer drops the new gadget into your Personal→ Downloads folder. Open that folder, and then double-click the new gadget to install it.

Uninstalling a gadget

If you decide you don't want a gadget, you can just close it (right-click it; from the shortcut menu, choose Close Gadget). That leaves it on your PC, but dormant.

If, on the other hand, you really doubt you'll ever need it again, open your Gadget Gallery. Right-click the offending gadget; from the shortcut menu, choose Uninstall.

Now it's really, truly gone.

Filename Extensions and File Associations

Every operating system needs a mechanism to associate documents with the applications that created them. When you double-click a Microsoft Word document icon, for example, Word launches and opens the document.

In Windows, every document comes complete with a normally invisible *filename extension* (or just *file extension*)—a period followed by a suffix that's usually three letters long.

Table 6-1 shows some common examples.

Table 6-1. Filename Extensions

When you double-click this icon...	...this program opens it
Fishing trip**.doc**	Microsoft Word
Quarterly results**.xls**	Microsoft Excel
Home page**.htm**	Internet Explorer
Agenda**.wpd**	Corel WordPerfect
A home movie**.avi**	Windows Media Player
Sudoku**.gadget**	Sidebar gadget
Animation**.dir**	Macromedia Director

___ Tip _____

For an exhaustive list of every file extension on the planet, visit *www.whatis.com*; click the link for "Every File Format in the World."

_____

Behind the scenes, Windows maintains a massive table that lists every extension and the program that "owns" it. More on this in a moment.

Displaying Filename Extensions

It's possible to live a long and happy life without knowing much about these extensions. Because file extensions don't feel very user-friendly, Microsoft designed Windows to *hide* the suffixes on most icons (Figure 6-7). If you're new to Windows, you may never have even seen them.

Some people appreciate the way Windows hides the extensions, because the screen becomes less cluttered and less technical-looking. Others make a good argument for the Windows 3.1 days, when every icon appeared with its suffix.

For example, in a single Explorer window, suppose one day you discover that three icons all seem to have exactly the same name: PieThrower. Only by making filename extensions appear would you discover the answer to the mystery: that one of them is called PieThrower.ini, another is an Internet-based software updater called PieThrower. upd, and the third is the actual PieThrower program, PieThrower.exe.

If you'd rather have Windows reveal the file suffixes on *all* icons, open an Explorer window. Choose Organize→Folder and Search Options. In the Folder Options dialog box, click the View tab. Turn off "Hide extensions for known file types," and then click OK.

Now the filename extensions for all icons appear (Figure 6-7).

Figure 6-7: As a rule, Windows shows filename extensions only on files whose extensions it doesn't recognize. The JPEG graphics at left, for example, don't show their suffixes. Right: You can ask Windows to display all extensions, all the time.

Installing Software

As you probably know, Microsoft doesn't actually sell PCs (yet). Therefore, you bought your machine from a different company, which probably installed Windows on it before you took delivery.

Many PC companies sweeten the pot by preinstalling other programs, such as Quicken, Microsoft Works, Microsoft Office, more games, educational software, and so on. The great thing about preloaded programs is that they don't need installing. Just double-click their desktop icons, or choose their names from the Start→All Programs menu, and you're off and working.

Sooner or later, though, you'll probably want to exploit the massive library of Windows software and add to your collection. Today, almost all new software comes to your PC from one of two sources: a disc (CD or DVD) or the Internet.

An installer program generally transfers the software files to the correct places on your hard drive. The installer also adds the new program's name to the Start→All Programs menu and tells Windows about the kinds of files (file extensions) it can open.

The Preinstallation Checklist

You can often get away with blindly installing some new program without heeding the checklist below. But for the healthiest PC and the least time on hold with tech support, answer these questions before you install anything:

▶ **Are you an administrator?** Windows derives part of its security and stability by handling new software installations with suspicion. For example, you can't install most programs unless you have an *administrator account* (see page 355).

▶ **Does it run in Windows Vista?** If the software or its Web site specifically says it's compatible with Vista, great. Install away. Otherwise, consult the Microsoft Web site, which includes a list—not a complete one, but a long one—of all Vista-compatible programs.

▶ **Is the coast clear?** Exit all your open programs. (One quick way is to right-click the buttons on the taskbar, one at a time, and choose Close or Close Group from the shortcut menu.) You should also turn off your virus-scanning software, which may take the arrival of your new software the wrong way.

Installing Software from a CD

Most commercial software these days comes on a CD or DVD. On each one is a program called Setup.exe, which, on most installation discs, runs automatically when you insert the disc into the machine. You're witnessing the *AutoPlay* feature at work.

If AutoPlay is working, a few seconds after you insert the disc, the "wait" cursor appears. A few seconds later, the Welcome screen for your new software appears, and you may be asked to answer a few onscreen questions (for example, to specify the folder into which you want the new program installed). Along the way, the program may ask you to type in a serial number, which is usually on a sticker on the CD envelope or the registration card.

When the installation is over—and sometimes after restarting the PC—the words All Programs appear with orange highlighting in the Start menu. If you click, the new program's name also appears highlighted in orange, and your Start→All Programs menu is now ready for action.

Installing Downloaded Software

The files you download from the Internet (see Figure 6-8) usually aren't ready-to-use, double-clickable applications. Instead, almost all of them arrive on your PC in the form of a *compressed* file, with all the software pieces crammed together into a single, easily downloaded icon. The first step in savoring your downloaded delights is restoring this compressed file to its natural state.

Nthat that it's much work; most Zip files unzip themselves. If you get one that doesn't, just double-click it. You'll usually find, among the resulting pieces, an installer, just like the ones described in the previous section.

Installing Windows Components

The Windows installer may have dumped over a gigabyte of software onto your hard drive, but it was only warming up. Plenty of second-tier programs and features came on the Vista DVD—stuff that Microsoft didn't want to burden you with right off the bat, but copied to your hard drive just in case.

To see the master list of software components that you have and haven't yet installed, choose Start→Control Panel→Classic View→Programs and Features. Click the "Turn Windows features on or off" link at the left side of the window.

You've just launched the Windows Features Wizard—basically a list of all the optional Windows software chunks. Checkmarks appear next to some of them; these are the ones you already have. The checkboxes that aren't turned on are the options you still haven't installed. As you peruse the list, keep in mind the following:

► To learn what something is, point to it without clicking. A description appears in a tooltip balloon.

► Turn on the checkboxes for software bits you want to install. Clear the checkboxes of elements you already have, but that you'd like Windows to hide.

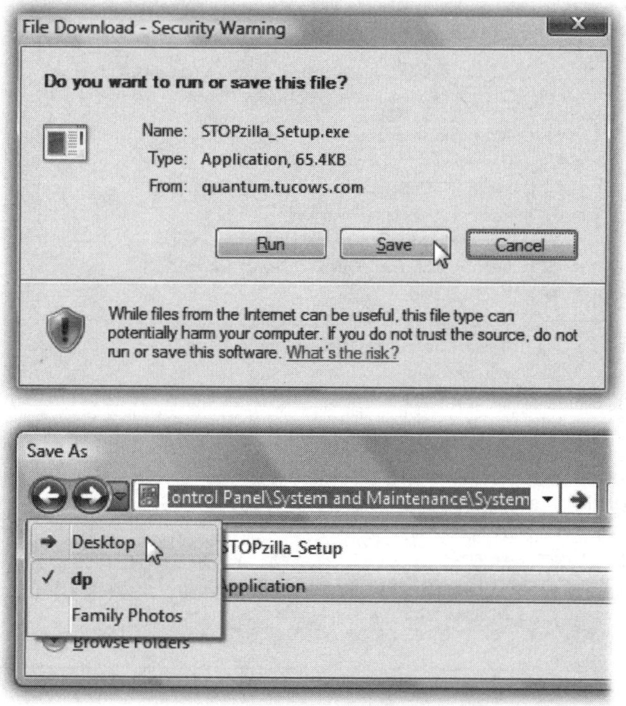

Figure 6-8: You can find thousands of Windows programs (demos, free programs, and shareware) at Web sites like *www.download.com, www. tucows.com,* or *www. versiontracker.com.*

Top: When you click a link to download something, this box appears. Click the Save button.

Bottom: To avoid losing the download in some deeply nested folder, click Desktop in the left-side pane. After the download is complete, quit your browser. Unzip the file, if necessary, and then run the downloaded installer.

___ **Note** _____

In Windows Vista, turning off an optional feature *doesn't* remove it from your hard drive, as it did in Windows XP. Turning off a feature simply hides it, and doesn't return any disk space to you. You can make a feature magically reappear just by turning the checkbox back on (without having to hunt down your Vista installation disc).

▶ Some of these checkboxes' titles are just titles for bigger groups of independent software chunks (see Figure 6-9).

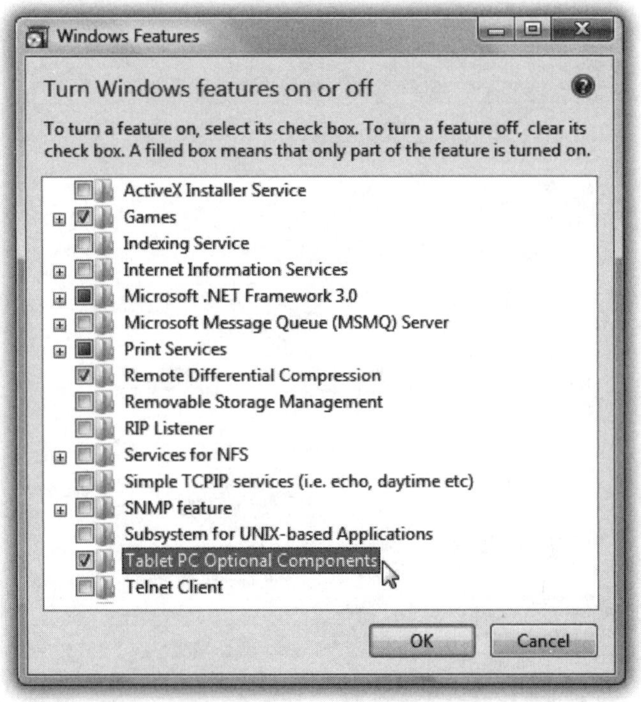

Figure 6-9: Most of the optional installations involve networking and administrative tools designed for corporate computer technicians. Still, you might want to turn off Games if you don't have that kind of time to kill, or Tablet PC Optional Components if your computer doesn't have a touch screen.

Uninstalling Software

When you've had enough of a certain program and want to reclaim the disk space it occupies, don't just delete its folder. The typical application installer tosses its software components like birdseed all over your hard drive; therefore, only some of the program is actually in the program's folder.

Instead, ditch software you no longer need using the "Programs and Features" control panel described above. Click the "Uninstall a program" link at the top left, and then proceed as shown in Figure 6-10.

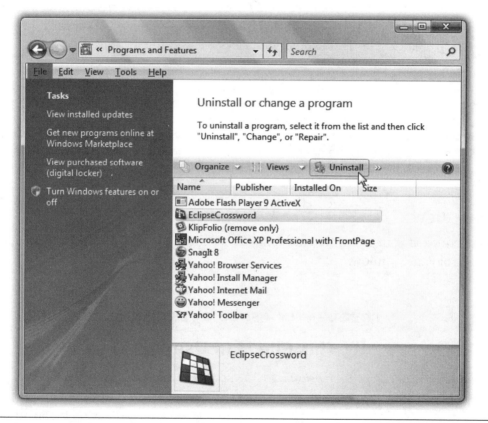

Figure 6-10: To vaporize a program, click its name to reveal the toolbar above it, as shown here, and then click the Uninstall button. Here's a tip—right-click the column headings to add or remove columns. If you choose More, you'll see some really useful ones, like Last Used On (shows you the last date you ran this program) and Used (how often you've run it—Frequently, Rarely, or whatever).

Even after you uninstall a program, the folder that contained it may still exist, especially if it contains configuration files, add-ons, or documents that you created while the program was still alive. If you're sure you won't need those documents, it's safe to remove the folder (discussed later in this section), along with the files inside it.

The Control Panel

Like the control panel in the cockpit of an airplane, the Control Panel is an extremely important feature of Windows Vista. It's teeming with miniature applications (or *applets*) that govern every conceivable setting for every conceivable component of your computer. Some are so important, you may use them (or their corresponding notification-area icons) every day. Others are so obscure you'll wonder what on earth inspired Microsoft to create them. This chapter describes a few of the most useful ones.

--- **Note** ---

> Here and there, within the Control Panel, you'll spot a little Windows security-shield icon. It tells you that you're about to make an important, major change to the operating system, something that will affect everyone who uses this PC—fiddling with its network settings, for example, or changing its clock. To prove your worthiness (and to prove that you're not an evil virus attempting to make a nasty change), you'll be asked to *authenticate* yourself; see the box on page 127 for details.

Home View

To have a look at your Control Panel collection, choose Start→Control Panel to open the Control Panel window.

FREQUENTLY ASKED QUESTION

This File Is in Use

Hey, I tried to uninstall a program using Programs and Features, like you said. But during the process, I got this scary message saying that one of the deleted program's files is also needed by other programs. It asked me if I was sure I wanted to delete it!

Heck, I wouldn't have the faintest idea. What should I do?

Don't delete the file. Leaving it behind does no harm, but deleting it might render one of your other applications nonfunctional.

You'll see that for the third straight Windows edition, Microsoft has rejiggered the layout in an attempt—not altogether successful—to make the thing easier to navigate.

The most important change is the pair of links at the left side of the window: *Control Panel Home* and *Classic View*.

The Control Panel Home view puts all of Vista's control panels into categories (Figure 6-11, top). From here, you're supposed to drill down.

For example, suppose you wanted to delete all your Web browser's cookies (stored Web-page preference files). You might first guess that this task's category would be Network and Internet, or maybe Security; you'd be right either way. (Microsoft put some tasks in

Figure 6-11: The Control Panel is available in two flavors: Home view (top), which requires your clicking one category link after another; and Classic View (bottom), which lists every control panel individually. To identify an icon, point without clicking; a tooltip pops up, telling you what's inside.

several different categories, just in case.) After you click that heading, you see individual tasks like "Delete browsing history and cookies." Clicking that link opens the dialog box that lets you do the deed.

Classic View

The category concept sounds OK in principle, but it'll drive veterans nuts. You don't want to guess what category Fax wound up in—you just want to open the old Print and Fax control panel, right now.

Fortunately, Classic View is still available. That's where the Control Panel displays all 50 icons in alphabetical order (Figure 6-11, bottom). Just double-click the icon of the applet you'd like to use.

Tip

The Icon view, unfortunately, chops off a lot of applets' names. For that reason—and to see more applets in less space—consider switching Classic View into Details view or List view. Do that by right-clicking a blank spot of the window; from the shortcut menu, choose View→Details or View→List.

The same shortcut menu lets you group, stack, and sort the icons to your heart's content.

Classic View is the perfect structure for a chapter that describes each Control Panel applet, since it's organized in alphabetical order. The rest of this chapter assumes that you're looking at the Control Panel in Classic View.

And now, a quick rundown of the most important control panel applets.

Date and Time

Your PC's conception of what time it is can be very important. Every file you create or save is stamped with this time, and every email you send or receive is marked with it. When you drag a document into a folder that contains a different draft of the same thing, Windows warns that you're about to replace an older version with a newer one (or vice versa)—but only if your clock is set correctly.

On the Date and Time tab, you can change the time, date, and time zone for the computer—if, that is, you'd rather not have the computer set its own clock.

Internet Options

A better name for this program would have been "Web Browser Options," since all of its settings apply to Web browsing—and, specifically, to Internet Explorer. As a matter of fact, this is the same dialog box that opens from the Tools→Internet Options menu command within Internet Explorer. Its tabs break down like this:

▶ **General, Security, Privacy, and Content.** These tabs control your home page, cache files, search field defaults, and history list. They also let you define certain Web pages as off-limits for your kids and manage RSS feeds (page 239), as well as block pop-up windows.

▶ **Connections.** Controls when your PC modem dials.

▶ **Programs.** Use this tab to manage browser add-ons, decide whether or not Internet Explorer should warn you whenever it is not the default browser (for your protec-

---

WORKAROUND WORKSHOP

Where'd I Put that Setting?

Ever try to configure a setting in the Control Panel, but forget which applet it's in? Happens all the time. In the pre-Vista days, there could be some guessing in your future, as you clicked through likely categories, or opened and closed a few applet icons. Now, however, you can use the handy-dandy Search field located in the upper-right corner of the window.

For example, let's say you can't remember exactly where to go to set up Sticky Keys for your keyboard. Is that a keyboard setting or an Ease of Access setting? Don't worry about it. In Control Panel Home view, type *sticky* into the search box. Presto: you get a list of all tasks that might involve *sticky*. From there, it's easy to go directly to the setting you're looking for.

Unfortunately, this trick doesn't work in Classic view. In Classic view, for some reason, Microsoft allows you to search only by icon name. Otherwise, it gives you a polite suggestion to change your view.

---

tion, of course), or choose the default programs that open, should you click a link to email someone, open a media file, or view the HTML source of a Web page (View menu→Source).

▶ **Advanced.** On this tab, you'll find dozens of checkboxes, most of which are useful only in rare circumstances and affect your Web experience only in minor ways. For example, "Enable personalized favorites menu" shortens your list of bookmarks over time, as Internet Explorer hides the names of Web sites you haven't visited in a while. (A click on the arrow at the bottom of the Favorites menu makes them reappear.)

Similarly, turning off the "Show Go button in Address bar" checkbox hides the Go button at the right of the Address bar. After you've typed a Web address (URL), you must press Enter to open the corresponding Web page instead of clicking a Go button on the screen. And so on.

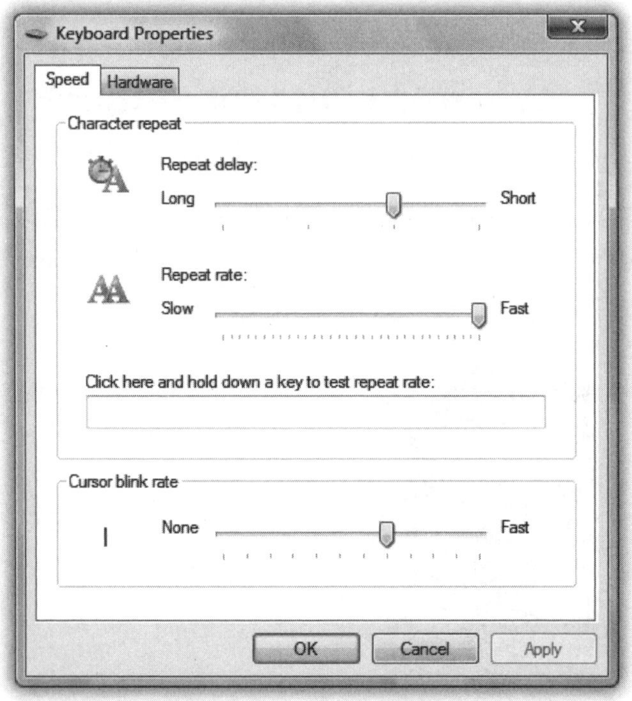

Figure 6-12: How fast do you want your keys to repeat? This dialog box also offers a Hardware tab, but you won't go there very often. You'll use it exclusively when you're trying to troubleshoot your keyboard or its driver.

Keyboard

You're probably too young to remember the antique known as a *typewriter*. On some electric versions of this machine, you could hold down the letter X key to type a series of XXXXXXXs—ideal for crossing something out in a contract, for example.

On a PC, *every* key behaves this way. Hold down any key long enough, and it starts spitting out repetitions, making it easy to type, "No WAAAAAY!" or "You go, grrrrrl!" for example. (The same rule applies when you hold down the arrow keys to scroll through the text document, hold down the = key to build a separator line between paragraphs, hold down Backspace to eliminate a word, and so on.) The Speed tab of this dialog box (Figure 6-12) governs the settings.

▶ **Repeat delay.** This slider determines how long you must hold down the key before it starts repeating (to prevent triggering repetitions accidentally).

▶ **Repeat rate.** The second slider governs how fast each key spits out letters once the spitting has begun.

   After making these adjustments, click the "Click here and hold down a key" test box to try out the new settings.

▶ **Cursor blink rate.** The "Cursor blink rate" slider actually has nothing to do with the *cursor,* the little arrow that you move around with the mouse. Instead, it governs the blinking rate of the *insertion point,* the blinking marker that indicates where typing will begin when you're word processing, for example. A blink rate that's too slow makes it more difficult to find your insertion point in a window filled with data. A blink rate that's too rapid can be distracting.

Mouse

All of the icons, buttons, and menus in Windows make the mouse a very important tool. And the Mouse dialog box is its configuration headquarters (Figure 6-13).

Buttons tab

This tab offers three useful controls: button configuration, double-click speed, and ClickLock.

▶ **Button configuration.** This checkbox is for lefties. Turning on this checkbox lets you switch the functions of the right and left mouse buttons, so that your index finger naturally rests on the primary button (the one that selects and drags).

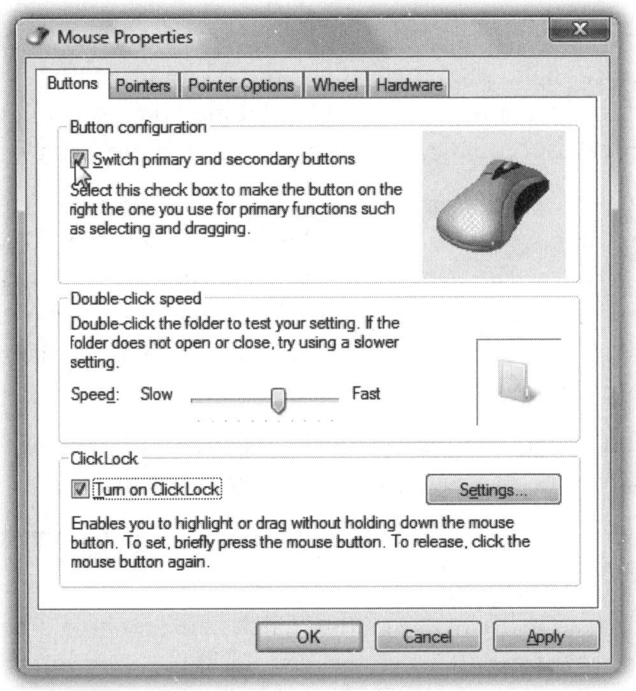

Figure 6-13: If you're a southpaw, you've probably realized that the advantages of being left-handed when you play tennis or baseball were lost on the folks who designed the computer mouse. It's no surprise, then, that most mice are shaped poorly for lefties—but at least you can correct the way the buttons work.

▶ **Double-click speed.** Double-clicking isn't a very natural maneuver. If you double-click too slowly, the icon you're trying to open remains stubbornly closed. Or worse, if you accidentally double-click an icon's name instead of its picture, Windows sees your double-click as two single clicks, which tells Windows that you're trying to rename the icon.

The difference in time between a double-click and two single clicks is usually well under a second. That's an extremely narrow window, so let Vista know what you consider to be a double-click by adjusting this slider. The left end of the slider bar represents 0.9 seconds, and the right end represents 0.1 seconds. If you need more time between clicks, move the slider to the left; by contrast, if your reflexes are highly tuned (or you drink a lot of coffee), try sliding the slider to the right.

Each time you adjust the slider, remember to test your adjustment by double-clicking the little folder to the right of the Speed slider. If the folder opens, you've successfully double-clicked. If not, adjust the slider again.

Not Your Father's Keyboard

Keyboards built especially for using Windows contain some extra keys on the bottom row:

On the left, between the Ctrl and Alt keys, you may find a key bearing the Windows logo (⊞). No, this isn't just a tiny Microsoft advertising moment; you can press this key to open the Start menu without having to use the mouse. (On desktop PCs, the Windows key is usually on the bottom row; on laptops, it's sometimes at the top of the keyboard.)

On the right, you may find a duplicate ⊞ key, as well as a key whose icon depicts a tiny menu, complete with a microscopic cursor pointing to a command. Press this key to simulate a right-click at the current location of your cursor.

Even better, the ⊞ key offers a number of useful functions when you press it in conjunction with other keys. For example:

⊞+**Space bar** opens the Sidebar.

⊞+**number key** opens the corresponding icon on the Quick Launch toolbar (⊞+1, ⊞+2, etc.).

⊞+**D** hides or shows all of your application windows (ideal for jumping to the desktop for a bit of housekeeping).

⊞+**E** opens an Explorer window (Chapter 3).

⊞+**F** opens the Search window (Chapter 4).

⊞+**G** cycles through your Sidebar gadgets.

⊞+**L** locks your screen. Everything you were working on is hidden by the login screen; your password is required to get past it.

⊞+**M** minimizes all open windows, revealing the desktop. (⊞+D is better, however, since the same keystroke also returns the windows.)

⊞+**Shift**+M restores all minimized windows.

⊞+**R** opens the Run command, where advanced Windowsveterans get their kicks by typing hyper-efficient text commands.

⊞+**T** cycles through the Taskbar buttons.

⊞+**U** opens the Ease of Access center (formerly the Universal Access center).

⊞+**X** opens the new Mobility Center, a central control panel filled with laptop-related controls (battery life, wireless networking, and so on).

⊞+**Tab** switches through all the application buttons on the taskbar.

⊞+**Break** opens the System Properties dialog box.

▶ **ClickLock.** ClickLock is for people blessed with large monitors or laptop trackpads who, when dragging icons onscreen, get tired of keeping the mouse button pressed continually. Instead, you can make Vista "hold down" the button automatically, avoiding years of unpleasant finger cramps and messy litigation.

When ClickLock is turned on, you can drag objects on the screen like this. First, point to the item you want to drag, such as an icon. Press the left mouse or trackpad button for the ClickLock interval. (You can specify this interval by clicking the Settings button in this dialog box.)

When you release the mouse button, it acts as though it's still pressed. Now you can drag the icon across the screen by moving the mouse (or stroking the trackpad) without holding any button down.

To release the button, hold it down again for your specified time interval.

Pointers tab

Here, you can change the shape of your cursor.

Pointers Options tab

This tab offers a few more random cursor-related functions.

▶ **Pointer speed.** It comes as a surprise to many people that the cursor doesn't move five inches when the mouse moves five inches on the desk. Instead, you can set things up so that moving the mouse one *millimeter* moves the pointer one full *inch*—or vice versa—using the Pointer speed slider.

It may come as an even greater surprise that the cursor moves farther when you move the mouse faster. How *much* farther depends on how you set the "Select a pointer speed" slider.

The Fast setting is nice if you have an enormous monitor, since it prevents you from needing an equally large mouse pad to get from one corner to another. The Slow setting, on the other hand, can be frustrating, since it forces you to constantly pick up and put down the mouse as you scoot across the screen. (You can also turn off the disproportionate-movement feature completely by turning off "Enhance pointer precision.")

▶ **Snap To.** A hefty percentage of the times when you reach for the mouse, it's to click a button in a dialog box. If you, like millions of people before you, usually click the *default* (outlined) button—such as OK, Next, or Yes—the Snap To feature can save you the effort of positioning the cursor before clicking.

When you turn on Snap To, every time a dialog box appears, your mouse pointer jumps automatically to the default button, so that all you need to do is click. (And to click a different button, such as Cancel, you have to move the mouse only slightly to reach it.)

▶ **Display pointer trails.** *Pointer trails* are ghost images of your mouse pointer that trail behind the pointer like ducklings following their mother. In general, this stuttering-cursor effect is irritating.

▶ **Hide pointer while typing.** Hiding the mouse pointer while you're typing is useful if you find that it sometimes gets in the way of the words on your screen. As soon as you use the keyboard, the pointer disappears; just move the mouse to make the pointer reappear.

▶ **Show location of pointer when I press the CTRL key.** If you've managed to lose the cursor on an LCD projector or a laptop with an inferior screen, this feature helps you gain your bearings. When you press and release the Ctrl key after turning on this checkbox, Windows displays an animated concentric ring each subsequent time you press the Ctrl key to pinpoint the cursor's location.

Wheel tab

The scroll wheel on the top of your mouse may be the greatest mouse enhancement since they got rid of the dust-collecting ball on the bottom. It lets you zoom through Web pages, email lists, and documents with a twitch of your index finger.

Use these controls to specify just how *much* each wheel notch scrolls. (You may not see this tab at all if your mouse doesn't have a wheel.)

Power Options

The Power Options program manages the power consumption of your computer. That's a big deal when you're running off a laptop's battery, of course, but it's also important if you'd like to save money (and the environment) by cutting down on the juice consumed by your *desktop* PC.

The options you see depend on your PC's particular features. Figure 6-14 displays the Power Options for a typical computer.

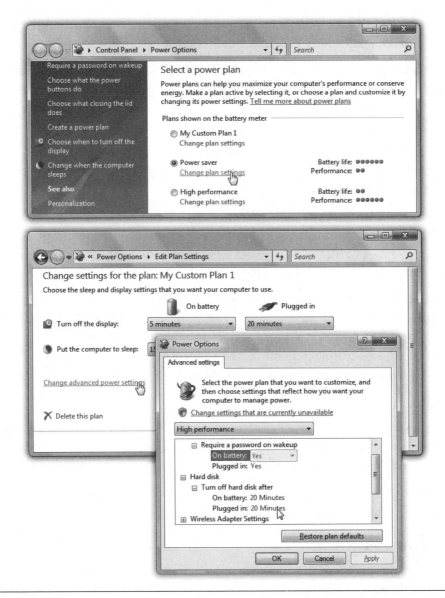

Figure 6-14: Top: The factory setting power plan, reasonably enough, is the Balanced plan. To take a look at the settings, click "Change plan settings." Middle: At first glance, it looks like you can change only a couple of settings, like when the computer sleeps and when the display turns off. Bottom: But if you click the "Change advanced power settings" link, you can see that the dialog box has more settings. Now you've got the full range of control over your screen, hard drive, wireless antenna, processor, installed PCI cards, and other power-related elements. Click the + sign to expand a topic, and then twiddle with the settings.

In Vista, Microsoft has tried to simplify the business of managing the electricity/speed tradeoff in two ways. First, it has abandoned the old name *power scheme* and adopted a new one: *power plan.* You can feel the clouds breaking up already.

(A power plan dictates things like how soon the computer goes to sleep, how bright the screen is, what speed the processor cranks at, and so on.)

Second, it presents you right up front with three premade power plans:

▶ Balanced, which is meant to strike a balance between energy savings and performance. When you're working hard, you'll get all the speed your PC can deliver; when you're thinking or resting, the processor slows down to save juice.

▶ Power Saver slows down your computer, but saves power—a handy one for laptop luggers who aren't doing anything more strenuous than word processing.

▶ High Performance sucks power like a black hole, but grants you the computer's highest speed possible.

___ Tip _____

You don't have to open the Control Panel to change among these canned plans. On a laptop, for example, you can just click the battery icon on your notification area (lower-right corner of the screen) and choose from the pop-up menu.

_____

Programs and Features

Programs and Features is about managing the software you have installed, managing updates, and buying software online. It replaces the old Add/Remove Programs program. ("Add" was dropped from the name because it was unnecessary; all programs these days come with their own installer. When was the last time you installed a program through Add/Remove Programs?)

This window is useful for fixing (which might simply mean reinstalling), changing, and uninstalling existing programs, and is the only place you can go to turn on (or off) Windows features like Fax and Scan, Games, Meeting Space, and more.

Regional and Language Options

Windows Vista can accommodate any conceivable arrangement of date, currency, and number formats; comes with fonts for dozens of Asian languages; lets you remap your keyboard to type non-English symbols of every ilk; and so on.

The Regional and Language Options allow you to install multiple input language kits on your computer and switch between them when the mood strikes. The key term here is *default input language*; the language for the operating system doesn't change. If you installed Vista in English, you'll still see the menus and dialog boxes in English.

But when you switch the input language, your keyboard can type the characters necessary for the selected language.

Sound

In Vista, the Sound dialog box contains only three tabs that control every aspect of your microphone and speakers: Playback, Record, and Sounds.

Playback and Recording tabs

These tabs simply contain the icons for each attached sound device (speakers, headset, and so on). To change a device's settings, select it, and then click Configure.

Sounds tab

Windows Vista comes with beeps, musical ripples, and chords that play when you turn on the PC, trigger an error message, empty the Recycle Bin, and so on. And if you like, you can hear them on many other occasions, such as when you open or exit a program, open a menu, restore a window, and so on. This tab lets you specify which sound effect plays for which situation (Figure 6-15).

See the Program list of system events? A speaker icon represents the occasions when a sound will play. If you click the name of some computer event (say, Low Battery Alert), you can:

▶ Remove a sound from the event by choosing (None) from the Sounds drop-down list.

▶ Change an assigned sound, or add a sound to an event that doesn't have one, by clicking the Browse button and choosing a new sound file from the list in the Open dialog box.

When you select a sound, its filename appears in the Sounds drop-down list. Click the triangular Play button to the right of the box to hear the sound.

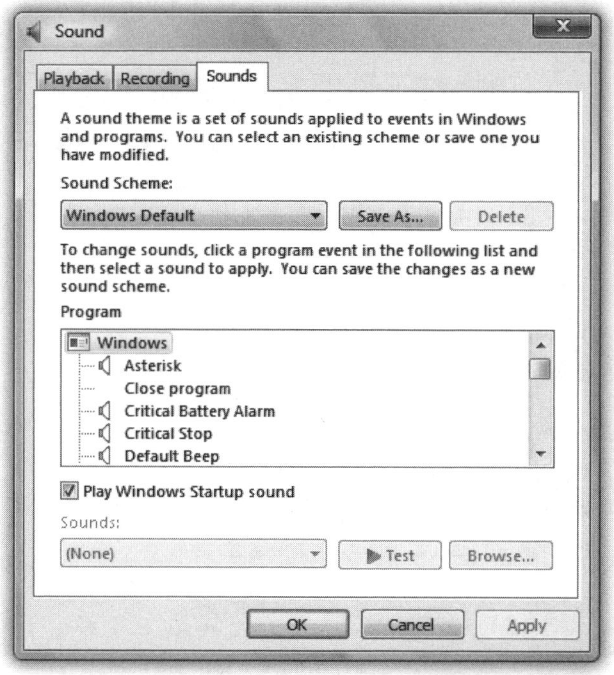

Figure 6-15: The Sounds tab lists every single bing, bong, and beep that your computer makes. If one annoys you, replace it with your own .wav file.

System

This advanced control panel contains the various settings that identify every shred of circuitry and equipment inside, or attached to, your PC.

When you open the System icon in Control Panel, you're taken to the System window (Figure 6-16).

Here you can find out what edition of Vista is installed on your computer (Home Basic, Business, or whatever); your PC's performance rating (page 23); the model name and speed of your PC's processor chip (such as Pentium 4, 2.6 GHz); how much memory your PC has; what network you're on; whether or not your operating system is activated (Microsoft's copy-protection method); what the Product ID key (serial number) is for your system; and so on.

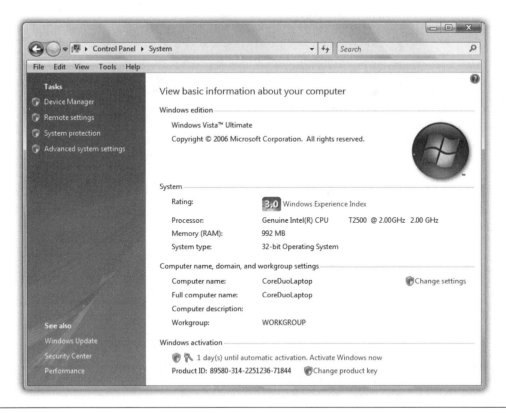

Figure 6-16: The System window is a one-stop shop for all things computer-related. From your hardware (and what Vista thinks of it) to your product ID key, System's got you covered.

PHOTOS, MUSIC, AND MOVIES

▶ Windows Photo Gallery
▶ Windows Media Player
▶ DVD Movies

Let's face it: the PC is no longer the center of the universe. Cellphones handle communications and the Internet. Palmtops can handle documents. The iPod has become the music hub. The PC just isn't the all-purpose, all-knowing central hub it once was.

On the other hand, the PC, for most people, is still the center of the electronics universe. Among other things, it's the place where all of those photos, movies, and songs come to rest. And in Windows Vista, Microsoft has addressed organizing/editing problem with a vengeance. Windows Photo Gallery and Windows Media Player are newly written (or newly beefed-up) programs that stand ready to manage your photos, music, and DVD movies.

Windows Photo Gallery

Your digital camera is brimming with photos. You've snapped the perfect graduation portrait, captured that jaw-dropping sunset over the Pacific, or compiled an unforgettable photo essay of your 2-year-old attempting to eat a bowl of spaghetti. It's time to use your PC to gather, organize, and tweak all these photos so you can share them with the rest of the world. And that's a job for Photo Gallery.

To open Photo Gallery, choose its name from the Start→Programs menu, or double-click a photo in your Pictures folder. You arrive at the program's main window, the basic elements of which are shown in Figure 7-1.

Getting Pictures into Photo Gallery

The very first time you open it, Photo Gallery displays all the digital photos it can find in your Pictures folder (Start→Pictures).

This is important: you're looking at the *actual files* on your hard drive. If you delete a picture from Photo Gallery, you've just deleted it from your PC. (Well, OK, you've actually moved it to your Recycle Bin. But still, that's a step closer to oblivion.)

Photos from a digital camera

Every modern camera comes with a USB cable that connects to your PC. That's handy, because it makes the photo-transfer process happen practically by itself.

▶ **If Photo Gallery is already running:** Choose File→Import from Camera or Scanner. In the dialog box that appears, click the name of your camera, and then click Import.

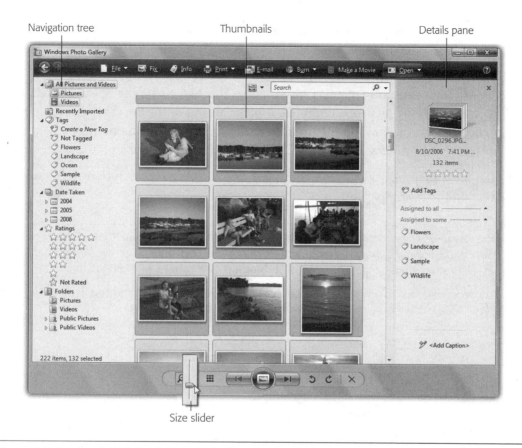

Navigation tree   Thumbnails   Details pane

Size slider

Figure 7-1: Here's what Photo Gallery looks like when you first open it. The large photo-viewing area is where thumbnails of your imported photos appear. The icons at the top of the window represent all the stuff you can do with your photos. To adjust the size of the photo thumbnails (miniatures), click the magnifying-glass icon. Don't release the mouse button yet. Instead, drag the vertical slider up or down. All the thumbnails expand or contract simultaneously. Cool!

▶ **If Photo Gallery isn't yet running:** Connect the camera to one of your PC's USB jacks. You see the box shown in Figure 7-2. Click "Import using Windows." (After the importing is finished, Photo Gallery opens automatically to show your newly acquired pix—unless you've turned off this feature in Photo Gallery's Options.)

Either way, unless you've turned off this option in Options, Photo Gallery now invites you to apply a *tag* to each of the incoming photos. Typing in a name for each new batch—*Disney, First Weekend* or *Baby Meets Lasagna*, for example—will help you organize and find your pictures later on.

In either case, Windows sets about sucking in all the photos from the camera and placing them into your Pictures folder.

Not all loose and squirming—that'd be a mess. Instead, it neatly creates subfolders, named for today's date and whatever tag you gave this batch (for example, "2007-2-15 Ski Trip"). Each photo gets auto-renamed, too, according to the tag (Ski Trip 001.jpg, Ski Trip 002.jpg, and so on), on the premise that you'll find *those* names more helpful than the names the *camera* gave them (DSC_IMG_0023.jpg, for example).

This "Tag these pictures" dialog box also offers a direct link to the Options box shown in the box on the facing page.

___ Note _____

Most cameras these days can also capture cute little digital movies. Photo Gallery can import and organize them, as long as they're in .wmv, .asf, .mpeg, or .avi format. (Unfortunately, that list doesn't include .mov, a common movie format of digital cameras.)

You don't have to do anything special to import movies; they get slurped in automatically. If you double-click one, it opens up and begins to play immediately.

Figure 7-2: When you connect a digital camera, Vista offers to import the photos from it. After the import, turn off the camera, and then unplug it from the USB cable.

The Post-Dump Slideshow

If you're like most people, the first thing you want to do after dumping the photos from your camera into your PC is to see them at full size, filling your screen. That's the beauty of Photo Gallery's slideshow feature.

To begin the slideshow, specify which pictures you want to see. For example:

▶ To see the pictures you most recently imported, click Recently Imported.

▶ Click a folder, tag, rating row, or another heading in the Navigation tree at the left side of the screen.

▶ If "All Pictures and Videos" (your whole library) is selected, click one of the photo-batch headings in the main window—for example, "2007—351 items."

Now click the unlabeled Play button at the bottom of the window (see Figure 7-3)—or just hit F11. Photo Gallery fades out of view, and a big, brilliant, full-screen slideshow of the new photos—and even self-playing videos—begins.

What's really useful is the slideshow control bar shown in Figure 7-3. You make it appear by wiggling your mouse as the show begins.

Click Exit, or press any key, to end the slideshow.

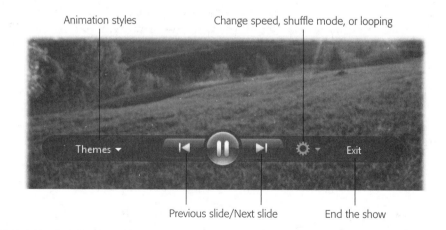

Figure 7-3: As the slideshow progresses, you can pause the show, go backward, rotate a photo, or change the transition effects, all courtesy of this control bar.

The Digital Shoebox

If you've imported your photos into Photo Gallery using any of the methods described above, you should now see a neatly arranged grid of thumbnails in Photo Gallery's main photo-viewing area. This is, presumably, your entire photo collection, including every last picture you've ever imported—the digital equivalent of that old shoebox you've had stuffed in the closet for the last 10 years.

Your journey out of chaos has begun. From here, you can sort your photos, give them titles, group them into smaller sub-collections (called *albums*), and tag them with keywords so you can find them quickly.

The Bigger Picture

If you point to a photo thumbnail without clicking, Photo Gallery is kind enough to display, at your cursor tip, a larger version of it. Think of it as a digital version of the magnifying loupe that art experts use to inspect gemstones and paintings.

> **Tip**
>
> If this feature gets on your nerves, choose File→Options, and then turn off "Show picture and video previews in tooltips."

You can also make *all* the thumbnails in Photo Gallery grow or shrink using the Size Control slider—click the blue magnifying-glass pop-up menu at the bottom of the Photo Gallery window. Drag the slider all the way down, and you get micro-thumbnails so small that you can fit 200 or more of them in the window. If you drag it all the way up, you end up with such large thumbnails that only a few fit the screen at a time.

For the biggest view of all, though, double-click a thumbnail. It opens all the way, filling the window. At this point, you can edit the picture, too, as described below.

The Navigation Tree

The *Navigation tree* at the left side of the window grows as you import more pictures and organize them—but right off the bat, you'll find icons like these:

▶ **All Pictures and Videos.** The first icon in the Navigation tree is a very reassuring little icon, because no matter how confused you may get in working with subsets of photos later in your Photo Gallery life, clicking this icon returns you to your entire picture collection. It makes *all* of your photos and videos appear in the viewing area.

Click the Pictures or Videos subhead to filter out the thumbnails so that *only* photos or *only* videos are visible.

▶ **Recently imported.** Most of the time, you'll probably work with the photos that you just downloaded from your camera. Conveniently, Photo Gallery always tracks your most recently added batch, so you can view its contents without much scrolling.

▶ **Tags.** As you work with your photos, you'll soon discover the convenience of adding *tags* (keywords) to them, like Family, Trips, or Baby Pix. Then, with one click on one of the tag labels in this list, you can see *only* the photos in your collection that match that keyword.

--- Tip ---

You can Ctrl-click several items in the Tags list at once. For example, if you want to see both Family photos *and* Vacation photos, click Family, then Ctrl-click Vacation.

This trick also works to select multiple months, years, star-rating categories, or folders (described below).

▶ **Date Taken.** Photo Gallery's navigation tree also offers miniature calendar icons named for the years (2005, 2006, 2007, and so on).

When you import photos, the program files each photo by the date you took it. You can click, say, the 2005 icon to see just the ones you took during that year.

By clicking the flippy triangle next to a year's name, furthermore, you expand the list to reveal the individual *months* in that year; click a month's flippy triangle to see the individual *dates* within that month. Photo Gallery shows *only* the months and dates in which you actually took pictures; that's why 2006, for example, may show only April, July, and October (Figure 7-4).

▶ **Ratings.** As you'll read in a moment, you can give your pictures star ratings: one star (or none) for the turkeys, five stars for the really great ones that are shoo-ins for your Web page or annual year-end calendar.

These little rows of stars make it easy to sort your entire collection by rating. Click the row of five stars, for example, to see *only* your five-starrers.

▶ **Folders.** At the bottom of the list, you'll see a collapsible list of the actual folders, sitting out there on your hard drive, that hold your photos and video clips. At the outset, you'll see only your Pictures and Videos folders (and maybe the Public versions of those, for use on a network).

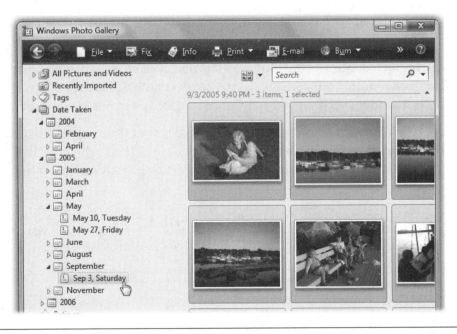

Figure 7-4: The year and month icons are very helpful when you're creating a slideshow or trying to pinpoint one certain photo. After all, you usually can remember what year you took a vacation or when someone's birthday was. These icons help you narrow down your search without requiring that you scroll through your entire library.

Working with Your Photos

All right: Enough touring Photo Gallery's main window. Now it's time to start *using* it.

Browsing, selecting, and opening photos is straightforward. Here's everything you need to know:

▶ Use the vertical scroll bar, or your mouse's scroll wheel, to navigate through your thumbnails.

▶ To create the most expansive photo-viewing area possible, you can temporarily hide the details pane at the right side of the window. To do so, click the tiny X button at its top—just *under* the ? button. (The red X *above* the Help button closes Photo Gallery.) Bring the Info pane back by clicking Info in the toolbar.

Selecting Photos

To highlight a single picture in preparation for printing, opening, duplicating, or deleting, click the thumbnail once with the mouse. That much may seem obvious. But first-time PC users may not know how to manipulate *more* than one icon at a time—an essential survival skill.

To highlight multiple photos in preparation for deleting, moving, duplicating, printing, and so on, use one of these techniques:

▶ **To select all the photos.** Select all the pictures in the set you're viewing by pressing Ctrl+A (the equivalent of the Edit→Select All command).

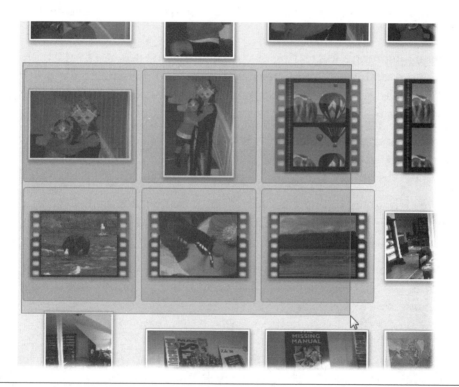

Figure 7-5: You can highlight several photos simultaneously by dragging a box around them. To do so, start from somewhere outside of the target photos and drag diagonally across them, creating a whitish enclosure rectangle as you go. Any photos touched by this rectangle are selected when you release the mouse.

▶ **To select several photos by dragging.** You can drag diagonally to highlight a group of nearby photos, as shown in Figure 7-5. You don't even have to enclose the thumbnails completely; your cursor can touch any part of any icon to highlight it. In fact, if you keep dragging past the edge of the window, the window scrolls automatically.

▶ **To select consecutive photos.** Click the first thumbnail you want to highlight, and then Shift-click the last one. All the files in between are automatically selected, along with the two photos you clicked. This trick mirrors the way Shift-clicking works in a word processor, the Finder, and many other kinds of programs.

▶ **To select random photos.** If you only want to highlight, for example, the first, third, and seventh photos in a window, start by clicking photo icon No. 1. Then Ctrl-click each of the others. Each thumbnail sprouts colored shading to indicate that you've selected it.

If you're highlighting a long string of photos and then click one by mistake, you don't have to start over. Instead, just Ctrl-click it again, and the dark highlighting disappears. (If you do want to start over from the beginning, however, just deselect all selected photos by clicking any empty part of the window.)

The Ctrl-key trick is especially handy if you want to select *almost* all the photos in a window. Press Ctrl+A to select everything in the folder, then Ctrl-click any unwanted photos to deselect them. You'll save a lot of time and clicking.

Once you've highlighted multiple photos, you can manipulate them all at once. For example, you can drag them en masse out of the window and onto your desktop—a quick way to export them.

In addition, when multiple photos are selected, the commands in the shortcut menu (right-click any *one* of them) apply to all of them simultaneously—like Rotate, Copy, Delete, Rename, or Properties.

Deleting Photos

As every photographer knows—make that every *good* photographer—not every photo is a keeper. You can relegate items to the Recycle Bin by selecting one or more thumbnails, and then pressing the Delete key on your keyboard.

If you suddenly decide you don't really want to get rid of any of these trashed photos, it's easy to resurrect them. Switch to the desktop, open the Recycle Bin, and then drag the thumbnails out of the window and back into your Pictures folder.

The Info Panel—and photo names

Behind the scenes, Photo Gallery stores a wealth of information about each individual photo in your collection. To take a peek, highlight a thumbnail, and then click the Info button on the toolbar. A new pane appears at the right side of the window (Figure 7-6), or It reveals that picture's name, rating, creation time and date, dimensions (in pixels), file size, and any comments you've typed into the Captions area.

Figure 7-6: The Info pane isn't just a place to look at the details of your pictures. You can also edit a lot of it. You can even change the date a photo was taken—a good tip to remember if you're a defense attorney.

Here, you can rename a photo easily enough. Just click its existing name in the Info panel, and then retype.

The best thing about adding comments is that they're searchable. After you've entered all this free-form data, you can use it to quickly locate a photo using Photo Gallery's search command.

Tags and Ratings

Tags are descriptive keywords—like *family*, *vacation*, or *kids*—that you can use to label and categorize your photos and videos. Ratings are, of course, star ratings from 0 to 5, meaning that you can categorize your pictures by how great they are.

The beauty of tags and ratings is that they're searchable. Want to comb through all the photos in your library to find every closeup taken of your children during summer vacation? Instead of browsing through dozens of folders, just click the tags *kids, vacation, closeup,* and *summer in the Navigation tree*. You'll have the results in seconds.

Or want to gather only the cream of the crop into a slideshow or DVD? Let Photo Gallery produce a display of only your five-star photos.

Microsoft offers you a few sample entries in the Tags list to get you rolling: Landscape, Travel, and so on. But these are intended only as starting points. You can add as many new tag labels as you want to create a meaningful, customized list.

To build your list, click "Create a New Tag" in the Navigation tree (Figure 7-7). Type the tag label and click OK.

Figure 7-7: You can drag thumbnails onto tags one at a time, or you can select the whole batch first, using any of the selection techniques described on page 175.

To edit or delete a tag, right-click it, and then, from the shortcut menu, choose Delete or Rename.

Applying Tags and Ratings

The best way to apply tags to photos is, paradoxically, to apply the *photos* to the *tags*. That is, drag relevant photos directly onto the tags in the Navigation tree, as shown in Figure 7-7.

To give a photo a new star rating, drag its thumbnail onto the appropriate row in the Navigation tree.

___ Tip ___

You can apply as many tags to an individual photo as you like. A picture of your cousin Rachel at a hot dog–eating contest in London might bear all these keywords: Relatives, Travel, Food, Humor, and Medical Crises. Later, you'll be able to find that photo no matter which of these categories you're hunting for.

Using Tags and Ratings

The big payoff for your diligence arrives when you need to get your hands on a specific set of photos, because Photo Gallery lets you *isolate* them with one quick click.

To round up all the photos with, say, the Kids tag, just click Kids in the Navigation tree at the left side of the window. Photo Gallery immediately rounds up all photos labeled with that tag, displays them in the photo-viewing area, and hides all others. Or, to find all your five-star photos, click the row of five stars in the Navigation tree.

More tips:

Editing Your Shots

Straight from the camera, digital snapshots often need a little bit of help. A photo may be too dark or too light. The colors may be too bluish or too yellowish. The focus may be a little blurry, the camera may have been tilted slightly, or the composition may be somewhat off.

Fortunately, Photo Gallery lets you fine-tune digital images in ways that, in the world of traditional photography, would require a fully equipped darkroom, several bottles of smelly chemicals, and an X-Acto knife.

All Photo Gallery editing is performed in a special editing mode, in which the photo appears at nearly full-screen size, and tool icons appear at the top (Figure 7-8). You enter Edit mode by double-clicking a photo's thumbnail, either in Photo Gallery or in an Explorer window, and then clicking the Fix button on the toolbar.

You exit Edit mode by clicking "Back To Gallery" (top left of the window).

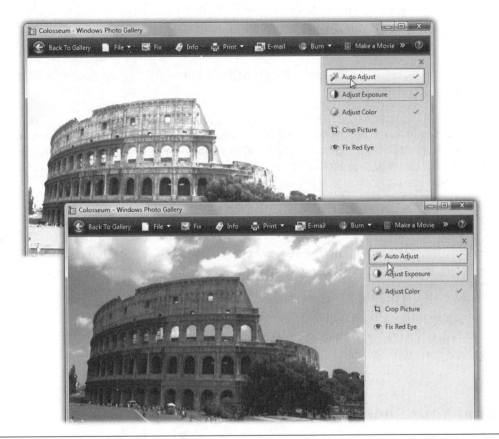

Figure 7-8: Photo Gallery's editing tools appear in a special toolbar. There's no Save command. Any changes you make to a photo are automatically saved. But don't worry; Photo Gallery always keeps the untouched, unedited original behind the scenes.

Ten Levels of Undo

As long as you remain in Edit mode, you can back out of your last 10 changes. To change your mind about the *last* change you made, just click the Undo button at the *bottom* of the Fix pane.

To retrace even more of your steps, click the ▾ button next to the Undo button. The resulting pop-up menu lists your last 10 editing steps. Choose how far you want to "rewind," or click Undo All to back out of everything you've done since opening the photo.

Auto Adjust

The Auto Adjust button provides a simple way to improve the appearance of less-than-perfect digital photos. One click makes colors brighter, skin tones warmer, and details sharper. (If you've used Photoshop, the Enhance button is a lot like the Auto Levels command.)

Cropping

Think of Photo Gallery's cropping tool as a digital paper cutter. It neatly shaves off unnecessary portions of a photo, leaving behind only the part of the picture you really want.

You'd be surprised at how many photographs can benefit from selective cropping. You can eliminate parts of a photo you just don't want, improve a photo's composition (filling the frame with your subject often has greater impact), or fit a photo to specific proportions (an important step if you're going to turn your photos into standard-size prints).

Here are the steps for cropping a photo:

1. **Open the photo for editing.**

   For example, double-click it, and then click Fix on the toolbar.

2. **In the Fix pane, click Crop.**

   The Crop controls appear.

3. **Make a selection from the Proportion pop-up menu, if you like** (Figure 7-9).

   The **Proportion** pop-up menu controls the behavior of the cropping tool. When the menu is set to Original, you can draw a cropping rectangle of any size and proportion, in essence going freehand.

   When you choose one of the other options in the pop-up menu, however, Photo Gallery constrains the rectangle you draw to preset proportions, like 4 x 6, 5 x 7, and so on. Limiting your cropping to one of these preset sizes guarantees that your cropped photos will fit perfectly into Kodak (or Shutterfly) prints. (If you don't constrain your cropping this way, Kodak—not you—will decide how to crop them to fit.)

Often, you'll want to give the cropping job the benefit of your years of training and artistic sensibility by *redrawing* the cropping area. Here's how:

Choose a standard print size

Figure 7-9: When you crop a picture, you draw a rectangle in any direction using the crosshair pointer to define the part of the photo you want to keep. (To deselect this area—when you want to start over, for example—click anywhere in the dimmed area.) Once you've drawn the rectangle and clicked Crop, the excess falls to the digital cutting room floor, thus enlarging your subject.

4. **Drag the tiny white control handles to reshape the cropping rectangle.**

   Drag inside the rectangle to move it relative to the photo itself.

5. **When the cropping rectangle is just the way you want, click Apply.**

   Photo Gallery throws away all the pixels outside the rectangle. Of course, the Undo and Revert commands are always there if you change your mind.

Red-Eye

Red-eye is light reflected back from your subject's eyes. The bright light of your flash passes through the pupil of each eye, illuminating and bouncing off of the blood-red retinal tissue at the back of the eye. Red-eye problems worsen when you shoot pictures in a dim room, because your subject's pupils are dilated wider, allowing even more light from the flash to shine on the retina.

The best course of action is to avoid red-eye to begin with—by using an external flash, for example. But if it's too late for that, and people's eyes are already glowing demonically, there's always Photo Gallery's Red-Eye tool.

To fix red-eye, zoom in and scroll so that you have a closeup view of the eye with the red-eye problem. Click the Red-Eye button, and then drag a box around each affected eye.

With each click, Photo Gallery neutralizes the red pixels, painting the pupils solid black. Of course, this means that everybody winds up looking like they have black eyes instead of red ones—but at least they look a little less like the walking undead..

Rotate

Unless your digital camera has a built-in orientation sensor, Photo Gallery imports all photos in landscape orientation (wider than they are tall). The program has no way of knowing if you turned the camera 90 degrees when you took your pictures.

To turn them right-side up, click one of the blue Rotate buttons at the bottom of the main Photo Gallery window.

Exposure and Color Adjustments

Plenty of photos need no help at all. They look fantastic right out of the camera. And plenty of others are ready for prime time after only a single click on the Auto Adjust button, as described earlier.

If you click Exposure or Adjust Color on the Fix pane, though, you can make *grada-tions* of the changes that the Auto Adjust button makes. For example, if a photo looks too dark and murky, you can bring details out of the shadows without blowing out the highlights. If the snow in a skiing shot looks too bluish, you can de-blue it. If the colors don't pop quite enough in the prize-winning-soccer-goal shot, you can boost their saturation levels.

In short, there are fixes the Adjust panels can make that no one-click magic button can touch.

Reverting to the Original

Photo Gallery includes built-in protection against overzealous editing—a feature that can save you much grief. If you end up cropping a photo too much, or cranking up the brightness of a picture until it seems washed out, or accidentally turning someone's lips black with the Red-Eye tool, you can undo all your edits at once with the Revert command. Revert strips away *every change you've ever made* since the picture arrived from the camera. It leaves you with your original, unedited photo—even if it's been months or years since you made the changes.

The secret of the Revert command: whenever you use any editing tools, Photo Gallery—without prompting and without informing you—instantly makes a duplicate of your original file. With an original version safely tucked away, Photo Gallery lets you go wild on the copy. Consequently, you can remain secure in the knowledge that in a pinch, Photo Gallery can always restore an image to the state it was in when you first imported it.

No longer must you make copies of your photos just so you'll have a safety copy if your edits don't work out, or dream up some elaborate naming and folder-filing scheme to accommodate them.

To restore an original photo, undoing all cropping, rotation, brightness adjustments, and so on, double-click the thumbnail of an edited photo. Click Fix on the toolbar, and then click Revert (at the bottom of the Fix pane). Photo Gallery asks you to confirm the change—after all, you're about to throw away all the editing you've done to this photo, which could represent a lot of time and effort—and then, if you click OK, swaps in the original version of the photo. You're back where you started.

Finding Your Audience

The last stop on your digital photos' cycle of greatness is, of course, a showing for other people. Photo Gallery offers several ways to make that happen.

Make Prints

If you highlight some photo thumbnails, and then click Print (in the Photo Gallery toolbar), the pop-up menu offers you two choices:

▶ **Print.** The dialog box appears. Here, you can specify what printer, paper, and quality options you want in order to print your own pictures at home—on an inkjet printer, for example.

▶ **Order Prints.** Even if you don't have a high-quality color printer, traditional prints of your digital photos are only a few clicks away—if you're willing to spend a little money, that is.

Slideshows

See "The Post-Dump Slideshow" on page 171.

Email

The most important thing to know about emailing photos is this: *full-size photos are usually too big to email.*

Suppose, for example, that you want to send three photos along to some friends—terrific shots you captured with your 8-megapixel camera.

Sending along just three shots would make at least a 9-megabyte package. It will take you a long time to send, and it will take your recipient a long time to download.

Worse, the average high-resolution shot is much too big for the screen. It does you no good to email somebody an 8-megapixel photo (3264 x 2448 pixels) when his monitor's maximum resolution is only 1900 x 1200. If you're lucky, his graphics software will intelligently shrink the image to fit his screen; otherwise, he'll see only a gigantic nose filling his screen.

Besides, the typical Internet account has a limited mailbox size. If the mail collection exceeds 5 MB or so, that mailbox is automatically shut down until it's emptied. Your massive photo package will push your hapless recipient's mailbox over its limit. She'll miss out on important messages that get bounced as a result.

Photo Gallery solves these problems neatly, as shown in Figure 7-10.

Here's how the process works:

1. **Select the thumbnails of the photo(s) you want to email.**

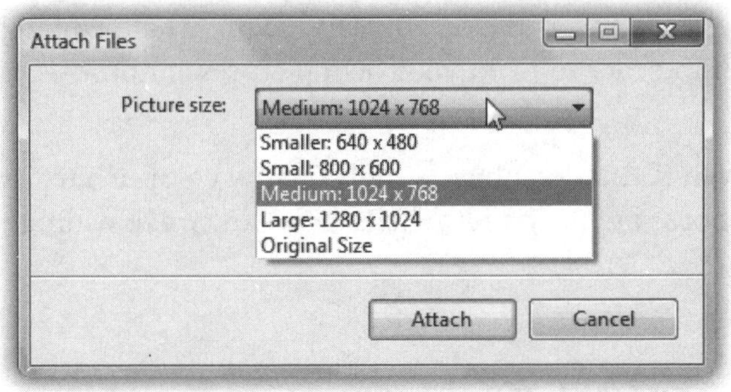

Figure 7-10: Instead of unquestioningly attaching a multimegabyte graphic to an email message, it offers you the opportunity to send a scaled-down, reasonably sized version of your photo instead. If you take advantage of this feature, your friends will savor the thrill of seeing your digital shots without enduring the agony of a half-hour email download.

You can use any of the picture-selecting techniques described on page 175.

2. **Click the Email icon on the toolbar.**

The dialog box shown in Figure 7-11 appears.

3. **Choose a size for your photo(s).**

This is the critical moment. The "Picture size" pop-up menu in the Attach Files dialog box offers four choices. **Small** and **Smaller** yield a file that will fill a nice chunk of your recipient's screen, with plenty of detail. It's even enough data to produce a small print. Even so, the file size (and download time) remains reasonable.

Use **Medium** and **Large** options sparingly. Save them for friends who have a cable modem or DSL. Even then, these big files may still overflow their email boxes.

No matter which you choose, keep an eye on the "Total estimated size" readout in the dialog box. Most email systems can't accept attachments greater than 5 MB.

4. **Click Attach.**

At this point, Photo Gallery processes your photos—converting them to JPEG format and, if you requested it, resizing them. It then launches your email program, creates a new message, and attaches your photos to it.

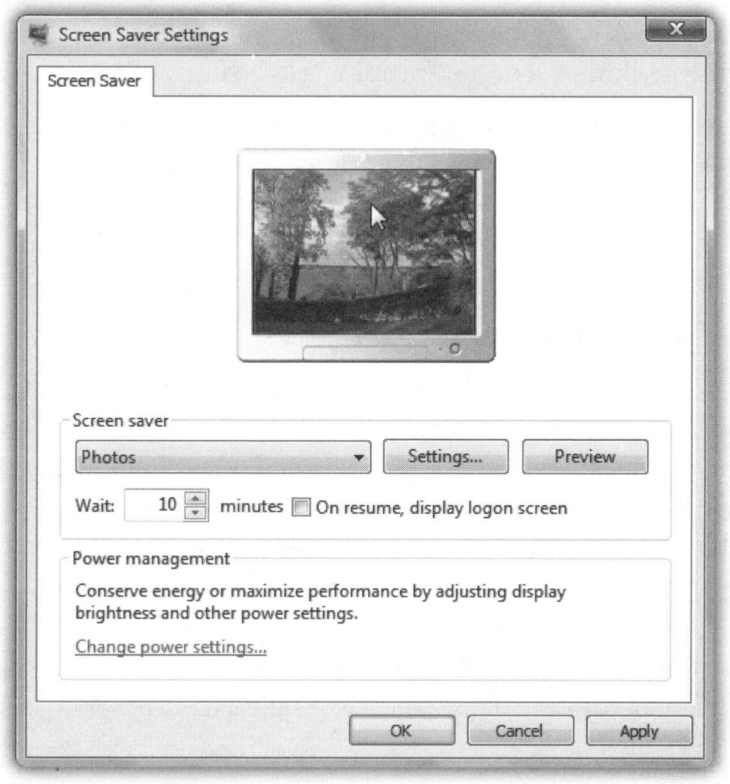

Figure 7-11: Below the horizontal line, you'll find three options that govern screen saver special effects, speed, and randomness. Click Save when it all looks good.

5. **Type your recipient's email address into the "To:" box, and then click Send.**

   Your photos are on their merry way.

Make a Slideshow Movie

If you highlight some photo thumbnails and then click Make a Movie in the toolbar, Vista automatically hands them off to Movie Maker, Vista's basic video-editing program, and lays them out in the timeline as a slideshow, all ready to go.

All you have left to do is rearrange them, add music and credits, and save as a digital movie file for distribution to your hip friends or publishing online.

When you've finished setting up the slideshow—that is, screen saver—click Save. When you return to the Screen Saver Settings dialog box, you can either click Preview to manually trigger the screen saver for your inspection, or click OK and wait 20 minutes for the screen saver to kick in by itself.

Windows Media Player

In the beginning, Windows Media Player was the headquarters for music and video on your PC. It was the Grand Central Terminal for things like music CDs (you could play 'em, copy songs off 'em, and burn 'em); MP3 files and other digital songs (you could sort 'em, buy 'em online, and file 'em into playlists); pocket music players of the non-iPod variety (fill 'em up, manage their playlists); Internet radio stations; DVD movies (watch 'em); and so on.

Media Player still does all that, and more. But it's no longer clear that this is the program you'll use for these activities. Gradually, the Media Player audience is splintering. Nowadays, a certain percentage of people is using alternative programs like:

▶ **iTunes.** If you have an iPod, you use Apple's iTunes software to do your music and video organizing.

▶ **Zune software.** If you have a Zune music player, you have to use yet *another* jukebox program—the software that came with it—for loading up and organizing your player.

▶ **Media Center.** Many of Media Player's functions are now duplicated in Windows Media *Center,* a specialized program (included only with the higher-priced versions of Windows Vista) that's designed to be operated with a remote control while your PC is hooked up to your television.

Still, most of the Windows world continues to use Windows Media Player as their music-file database. It's worth getting to know.

The Lay of the Land

Down the left side of the window is a Navigation tree, just as in Photo Gallery: a list of the music, videos, and playlists in your collection. The flippy triangles next to the major headings make it easy to collapse sections of the list. Under the Library headings, you can click Artist, Album, Songs, Genre, or whatever, to see your entire music library sorted by that criterion (Figure 7-12). (The Navigation tree isn't visible in some views—more on this in a moment.)

Figure 7-12: When you click a label at left, the main portion of the window changes to show you your music collection, using the actual album-cover artwork as their icons. It's very visual, but not especially stingy with screen space. Fortunately, you also have a more compact list view available—choose Details from the View Options pop-up menu identified here.

Media Player's top edge, as you may have noticed, offers several primary tabs, which cover the essential functions of Media Player. Here's a quick overview:

▶ **Now Playing.** Click this tab while music or video is playing from any source. This is where you can see a list of songs on the CD, a graphic equalizer, and a wild, psychedelic screen saver that pulses in time to the music. Here, too, is where you change the volume and other audio settings.

--- Tip ---
> To start playing a song, album, playlist, or whatever, just double-click its name. You can use the Space bar to pause or resume playback.

► **Library.** This screen lists every piece of music or video your copy of Media Player "knows about" on your hard drive; use the Navigation tree to sort and group the lists. This is also where you can sort your songs into subsets called *playlists*.

► **Rip.** Use this screen to copy songs from one of your music CDs onto your hard drive, as described later in this chapter.

► **Burn.** After transferring some songs to your hard drive—from the Internet or your own music CD collection—you can then burn your own CDs. This screen is the loading dock.

► **Sync.** Here's where you line up music or video that you'd like transferred to a portable music or video player, if you have one that Media Player understands.

► **Urge.** This page is a rabbit hole into Alice in Marketingland. It's the gateway to online music stores—MTV's Urge store is, obviously, the featured one—where you can buy songs for $1 each, or download all you want for $15 a month, with the understanding that you're just renting them; when you stop paying, you lose them all.

Playing Music CDs

For its first trick, Media Player can simulate a $25 CD player. To fire it up, just insert an audio CD into your computer's CD or DVD drive.

If this is the first time you've ever taken this dramatic action, you see the dialog box shown in Figure 7-13. It asks how you want Windows to handle inserted CDs. Do you want it to *play* them? Or *rip* them (start copying their songs to your hard drive)? And if you said "play," do you want to use Media Player or Media *Center*, if you have it?

For now, click "Play audio CD using Windows Media Player."

Media Player opens and the CD begins to play automatically. The screen even fills with a shimmering, laser-light show (called a *visualization*) that pulses along with the music.

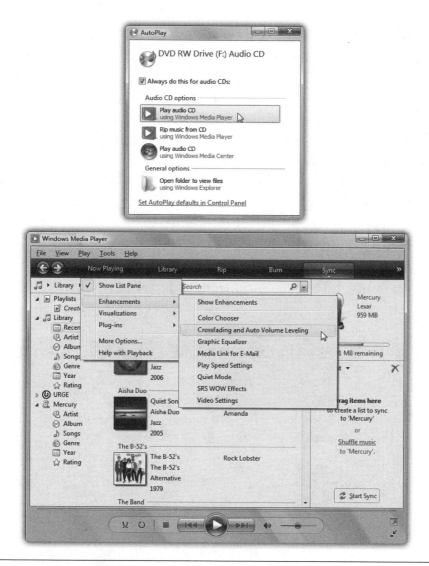

Figure 7-13: Top: Windows may ask what you want it to do with a music CD. If you accept the *"Play Audio CD using Windows Media Player"* option by clicking OK or pressing Enter, Media Player opens automatically and begins to play the songs on your CD.

Bottom: Most of the menu commands you'll need are hiding under the names of the main tabs (Now Playing, Library, and so on); click the tiny ▾ buttons to open the menus. There is, however, a proper menu bar—it's just hidden. Tap the Alt key to make it appear. Or, if you ache for the comfort of the traditional menu bar, press Ctrl+M.

Ripping CDs to Your Hard Drive

You can copy an album, or selected tracks, to your hard drive in the form of standalone music files that play when double-clicked. The process is called *ripping,* much to the consternation of sleepless record executives who think that it's short for *ripping off.*

Having CD songs on your hard drive is handy because you can listen to your songs without having to hunt for the CDs they came from. You can also build your own *playlists* (sets of favorite songs) consisting of tracks from different albums. And you can transfer the songs to a portable player or burn them onto a homemade CD.

If you're sold on the idea, open the Rip tab's pop-up menu. Inspect your settings. For example, unless you intervene by clicking the Change button near the top, Windows copies your song files into your Personal→Music folder.

Note, too, that Microsoft has designed Windows Media Player to generate files in the company's own format, called Windows Media Audio (.wma) format. But many people

Figure 7-14: Using this submenu, tell Windows how much to compress the song files (and sacrifice sound quality). If you don't need MP3 compatibility, Windows Media Audio (Variable Bit Rate) maximizes quality and minimizes file size by continuously adjusting the data rate along the song's length.

prefer, and even require, MP3 files. For example, most recent CD players and portable music players (including the iPod) can play back MP3 files—but won't know what to do with WMA files.

If you'd prefer the more universally compatible MP3 files, Rip→Format→MP3 (Figure 7-14).

Tip

If you have a stack of CDs to rip, don't miss the two commands in the Rip menu: "Rip CD Automatically When Inserted→Always" and "Eject CD After Ripping." Together, they turn your PC into an automated ripping machine, leaving nothing for you to do but feed it CDs and watch TV.

Finally, the Rip→Bit Rate submenu controls the tradeoff, in the resulting sound files, between audio quality and file size. For MP3 files, most people find the 192 Kbps setting (on the "Audio quality" slider) to produce great-sounding, relatively compact files. Let your ears (and the capacity of your portable music player) be your guide.

Here's how you rip:

1. **Insert the music CD. Click the Rip tab in Media Player.**

   The list of songs on the CD appears.

2. **Turn on the checkboxes of the tracks you want to copy.**

   You've waited all your life for this: at last, you have the power to eliminate any annoying songs and keep only the good ones.

3. **Click Start Rip.**

   You'll find this button at the lower-right corner of the window.

   Windows begins to copy the songs onto your hard drive. The Start Rip button changes to Stop Rip, which you can click to interrupt the process.

Organizing Your Music Library

Every CD transferred to your hard drive winds up with an entry on the Library tab. You can sort your collection by performer, album, year released, or whatever, just by clicking the corresponding icons in the Navigation tree. Whenever you want to play back some music, just double-click its name in this list—there's no need to hunt around in your shoeboxes for the original CD the songs came from.

But that's just the beginning of Media Player's organizational tools; see Figure 7-15.

Figure 7-15: To create a playlist, just start dragging tracks or whole albums to the Playlist pane. Switch views, or use the Search box, as necessary to find the tracks you want. Drag songs up and down in the Playlist pane to reorder them. Use the pop-up menu (where it now says Untitled Playlist) to scramble, sort, rename, or save the playlist.

Playlists

Microsoft recognizes that you may not want to listen to *all* your songs every time you need some tunes. That's why Media Player lets you create *playlists*—folders in the Navigation list that contain only certain songs. In effect, you can devise your own albums, mixing and matching songs from different albums for different purposes: one called Downer Tunes, another called Makeout Music, and so on.

To create a new playlist, start on the Library tab. The Playlist pane, at the right side of your screen, is empty. It says, "Drag items here to create a playlist." Well, hey—it's worth a try. See Figure 7-15.

Once you've created a playlist, click Save Playlist at the bottom of the pane. Type a name for your playlist, and thrill to the appearance of a new icon in My Playlists "category" of the Navigation tree.

Burning Your Own CDs

The beauty of a CD burner is that it frees you from the stifling restrictions put on your musical tastes by the record companies. You can create your own "best of" CDs that play in any CD player—and that contain only your favorite songs in your favorite order. The procedure goes like this:

1. **Click the Burn tab. Insert a blank CD.**

    On the right side of the screen, the Burn pane appears. If your PC has more than one disc burner, click Next Drive until Media Player identifies the correct one.

___ **Note** _____

If you've inserted a rewriteable disc like a CD-RW, and you've burned it before, right-click its icon in the Navigation tree, and then, from the shortcut menu, choose "Erase disc" before you proceed.

2. **Specify which songs you want to burn by dragging them into the Burn List (where it says "Drag items here" in the Burn pane).**

    You can add music to your CD-to-be in just about any kind of chunk: individual songs, whole albums, playlists, random audio files on your hard drive, and so on; see Figure 7-16.

    As you go, keep an eye on the "time remaining" readout at the top of the Burn List. It lets you know how much more your CD can hold. If you go over the limit, Media Player will burn additional CDs as necessary.

___ **Tip** _____

Media Player adds two seconds of silence between each song, which might explain why you may not be able to fit that one last song onto the disc even though it seems like it should fit.

3. **Click Start Burn.**

    It takes a while to burn a CD. To wind up with the fewest "coasters" (mis-burned CDs that you have to throw away), allow your PC's full attention to focus on the task. Don't play music, for example.

Figure 7-16: Use the Navigation tree to pull up the display you want. For example, to see a complete list of your songs or albums, click Songs or Albums, and then drag individual songs or albums directly into the Burn list. To add a playlist to the Burn List, drag the name of the playlist right across the screen from the Navigation tree. To add a file that's not already in Media Player, drag it out of its Explorer window directly into the Burn List.

Copying Music or Videos to a Portable Player

If you have a pocket gizmo that's capable of playing music (like a SanDisk Sansa or a Pocket PC) or even videos (like a Portable Media Center), the process for loading your favorite material onto it is very similar to burning your own CD. The only difference in the procedure is that you do your work on the Sync tab instead of the Burn tab.

Just connecting the player to Media Player brings it up-to-date with whatever songs you've added or deleted on your PC. As your library grows, shrinks, or gets edited, you can sleep soundly, knowing that your portable gadget's contents will be updated automatically the next time you hook it up to your PC's USB port.

Online Music Stores

Right from within Media Player, you can search or browse for millions of pop songs, classical pieces, and even comedy excerpts—and then buy them or rent them. (You can pay $1 per song to own it, or about $15 per month to download as many songs as you want, with the understanding that they'll all go *poof!* if you ever stop paying the fee.)

At first, the Online Store tab features Urge, which is MTV's music store. But with a little effort, you can also access Napster, eMusic, XM Satellite Radio, and other music and movie stores.

___ **Note** _____

Two stores you *can't* get to from here are iTunes and Zune Marketplace. You have to get to those using the software that came with your iPod or Zune, as noted earlier in this chapter.

_____

To look over your options, open the Urge menu and then choose Browse All Online Stores. Now Media Player window ducks into a phone booth and becomes a Web browser, filled with company logos. Anything you buy gets gulped right into your Library, ready for burning to a CD or syncing with an audio player, if the store's copy-protection scheme allows it.

Songs from most online stores are copy-protected—gently. For example, the $1-a-song sites generally permit you to play the songs on up to five computers at once, and to burn a playlist containing the songs 10 times.

The $15-a-month rental (subscription) plans generally don't let you burn CDs at all.

Internet Radio

The 21st century's twist on listening to the radio as you work is listening *without* a radio. Media Player itself can tune in to hundreds of Internet-based radio stations all over the world, which may turn out to be the most convenient music source of all. They're free, they play 24 hours a day, and their music collections make yours look like a drop in the bucket.

Figure 7-17: Top: In the list at the right side of Media Guide, click Internet Radio. Bottom: Click through the music genres to find what you're up for. Click a station that looks interesting, and then click the little Play button beneath its listing. (The higher the number in the Speed column, the better the sound quality. Note, though, that 128 Kbps is generally too rich for dial-up modems, and may sputter.) Wait for your PC to connect to the Internet site, and then let the music begin!

For radio, use the rightmost tab (the Online Stores tab). Click the ▼ button; from the menu, choose Media Guide.

Media Guide is a window onto *www.windowsmedia.com*. It's a promotional/news site that plugs new movies, songs, movies, videos, and so on.

Oh—and it lists radio stations. See Figure 7-17 for details.

___ **Note** _____

Unfortunately, there's no easy way to capture Internet broadcasts or save them onto your hard drive.

_____

DVD Movies

If your PC has a drive that's capable of playing DVDs—and if you're running Windows Vista, it probably does—you're in for a treat. Media Player can play rented or purchased Hollywood movies on DVD as though it was born for the job.

Figure 7-18: Once the DVD is playing, you control the playback using the standard Media Player controls (bottom edge of the window). To switch to a different "chapter," click the ▶▶ button. To change language or parental-control options, right-click the screen; from the shortcut menu, choose Audio and Language Tracks. When you're playing the movie full-screen, the playback controls reappear when you move the mouse a bit.

Watching movies on your screen couldn't be simpler. Just insert the DVD. Windows automatically detects that it's a video DVD—as opposed to, say, one that's just filled with files.

The dialog box shown in Figure 7-18 appears, or at least it does the very first time you insert a DVD. Click "Play DVD movie using Windows Media Player"— if, indeed, that's the program you want to play the DVD. You may have other programs that can play DVDs, with their own buttons in this dialog box.

Now Media Player opens, and your movie begins playing, full-screen. Most of the time, there's nothing for you to do now but watch. But if you're the interactive sort, you can also take action like this:

▶ **Switch between full-screen mode and window mode** by pressing Alt+Enter. In window mode, the movie plays within the Media Player window, surrounded by the usual controls. The pane at the right side of the window lists the DVD chapters (scenes), which is handy if you want to jump around in the DVD.

▶ **Pause, skip, adjust the volume** by wiggling your mouse. Playback controls appear for a few seconds at the bottom of the screen, permitting you to pause, adjust the volume, or skip backward or forward, and then fade away so as not to obscure Arnold Schwarzenegger's face.

Alternatively, you can right-click anywhere on the "movie screen" itself to reveal a menu of disc-navigation features.

— Tip —————————————————————————————
    For real fun, turn on *English* subtitles but switch the *soundtrack* to a foreign language. No matter how trashy the movie, you'll gain respect from your friends when you say you're watching a foreign film.
————————————————————————————————————

PART THREE: VISTA ONLINE

GETTING ONLINE—SECURELY

▶ Broadband Connections
  (Cable Modems and DSL)

▶ Wireless Networks

▶ Dial-Up Connections

▶ Connection Management

▶ Internet Security

▶ Hot Spot Security

▶ Parental Controls

Plenty of people buy a PC to crunch numbers, scan photos, or cultivate their kids' hand-eye coordination. But for millions of people, Reason One for using a PC is to get on the Internet. Few computer features have the potential to change your life as profoundly as the World Wide Web and email.

If you upgraded to Windows Vista from an earlier version of Windows, then you can already get online, as the Vista installer is thoughtful enough to preserve your old Internet settings. (So is Windows Easy Transfer, described in Appendix A.)

Broadband Connections (Cable Modems and DSL)

A growing fraction of the world's Internet citizens get online over *broadband* connections—that is, high-speed connections like cable modems and DSL boxes. These contraptions offer gigantic advantages over dial-up modems. For example:

▶ **Speed.** These modems operate at 5 to 50 times the speed of a traditional dial-up modem. For example, you might wait 5 minutes to download a 2 MB file with a standard modem—a job that would take about 10 *seconds* with a cable modem.

▶ **No dialing.** You're hooked up permanently, full time, so you don't waste time connecting or disconnecting—ever. You're *always* online.

▶ **No weekends lost to setup.** A representative from the phone company (DSL) or cable TV company (cable modems) generally comes to your home or office to install the cable modem or DSL box and configure Windows to use it.

▶ **Possible savings**. At this writing, cable modems and DSL services cost $30 to $45 a month. That includes the Internet account for which you'd ordinarily pay $20 if you signed up for a traditional ISP. And since you're connecting to the Internet via cable TV wires or unused signal capacity on your telephone lines, you may save even more money by canceling the second phone line you were using for dialup.

Virtually all cable TV companies offer cable modem service, and most phone companies offer DSL (depending on how far you live from the central office).

So how do you get online once you've got one of these services? You don't—you're *already* online, always and forever (except when the service goes out). Just open up your Web browser, email program, chat program, or whatever—and it just works.

Wireless Networks

A broadband connection like a cable modem or DSL is heaven, but it's not the penthouse floor of heaven. These days, the ultimate bliss is connecting without wires, from anywhere in your house or building—or, if you're a laptop warrior, someone *else's* house or building, like Starbucks, McDonald's, airport lounges, hotel lobbies, and anywhere else that a WiFi Internet "hot spot" has been set up.

Those are places where somebody has set up an *WiFi access point* (or base station), which is a glorified antenna for their cable modem or DSL box. Any computer that's been equipped with a corresponding wireless networking card (as most new laptops are these days) can hop online at high speed with only a couple of clicks.

— Tip _____

> Whenever you try to get online, Windows Vista automatically hunts for a working connection—wired or wireless. That's a blessing for laptops. When you're at the office plugged into an Ethernet cable, you get the security and speed of a wired network. When you're in some hotel-lobby hot spot, and your laptop can't find the Ethernet cable, it automatically hops onto the wireless network, if possible.
>
> (And how does the dial-up modem enter into all this? That's up to you. Open Internet Options in your Control Panel, click the Connections tab, and turn on, for example, "Dial whenever a network connection is not present" or "Never dial a connection." Keep the "Never dial" option in mind if the Connect dialup dialog box starts popping up every time your WiFi signal hiccups.)

For details on connecting to a wireless network (using a laptop in a hotel lobby, for example), see Figure 8-1.

— Tip _____

> In the delightful event that more than one hot spot is available at once, you can tell Windows which ones you want to connect to first. Choose Start→Network; in the toolbar, click "Network and Sharing Center." From the links at left, click "Manage wireless networks" to see the list of all your WiFi networks' names. Drag the networks' names up or down in the list to change their preferred connection order.

Dial-Up Connections

High-speed Internet is where it's at, baby! But there are plenty of reasons why you may be among the 50 percent of the Internet population that connects via dial-up modem,

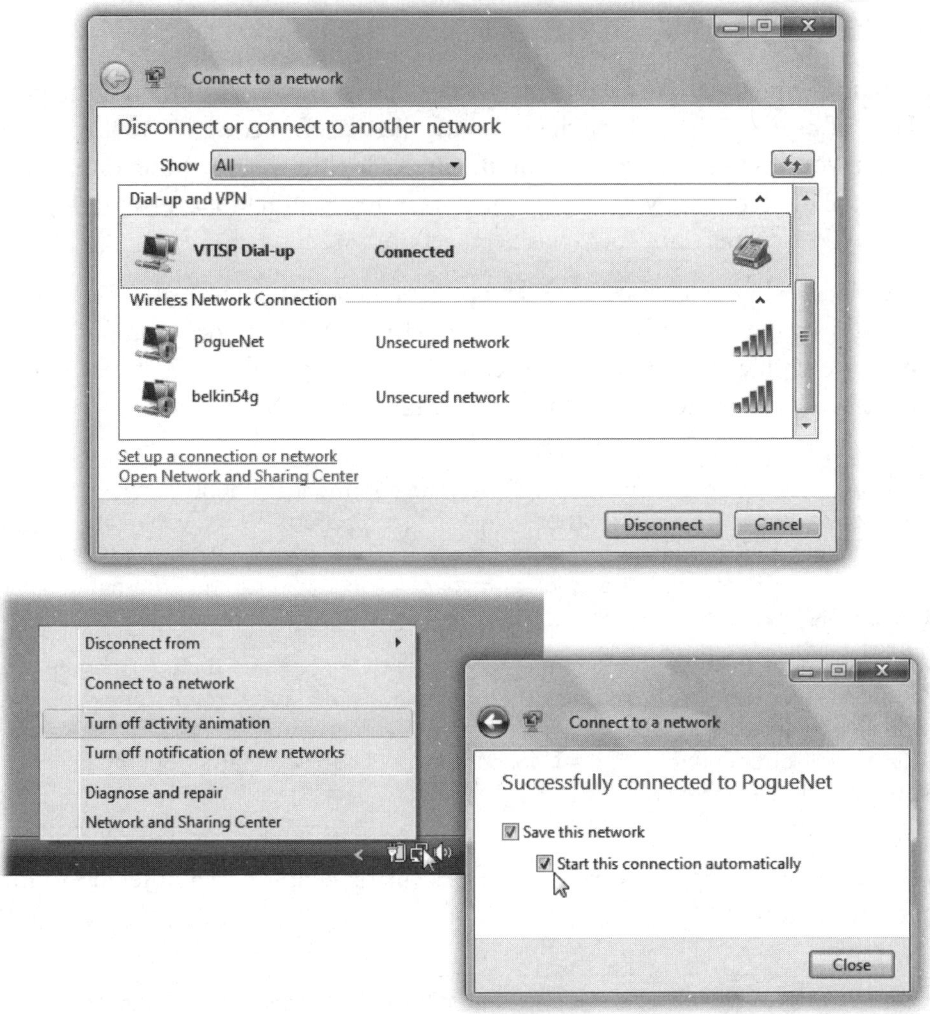

Figure 8-1: Top: Windows Vista no longer notifies you when you've entered a WiFi hot spot. You just sort of have to know, or you can check for hot spots by choosing Start→Connect To, which produces the dialog box shown here.

Middle: You can also get here by choosing "Connect to a network" from the taskbar icon shown here.

Bottom: When you double-click one of the networks, you're asked to type in the password, if one is required. Then you see this: You're asked if you want Vista to memorize this network and even auto-connect to it the next time you're in range—no muss, no dialog boxes.

slow though it is. Dial-up is a heck of a lot less expensive than broadband. And its availability is incredible—you can find a phone jack in almost any room in the civilized world, in places where the closest Ethernet or WiFi network is miles away.

To get online by dial-up, you need a dial-up *account.* You sign up with a company called an Internet service provider (or *ISP,* as insiders and magazines inevitably call them).

National ISPs like EarthLink, AT&T, and AOL (which still offers $10-a-month dialup access) have local telephone numbers in every U.S. state and many other countries. If you don't travel much, you may not need such broad coverage. Instead, you may be able to save money by signing up for a local or regional ISP. In fact, you can find ISPs that are absolutely free (if you're willing to look at ads), or that cost as little as $4 per month (if you'll promise not to call for tech support). Google can be your friend here.

Even if you have a cable modem or DSL, you can generally add dial-up access to the same account for another few bucks a month. You'll be happy to have that feature if you travel a lot (unless your cable modem comes with a *really* long cord).

In any case, dialing the Internet is a local call for most people.

___ Tip _____

The Internet is filled with Web sites that list, describe, and recommend ISPs. To find such directories, visit Google and search for *ISP listings.* One of the best Web-based listings, for example, can be found at
www.boardwatch.com. (Of course, until you've actually got your Internet account working, you'll have to conduct this research on a PC that *is* online, like the free terminals available at most public libraries.)

Vista expects that you've contacted an ISP on your own. It assumes that you're equipped with either (a) a setup CD from that company, or (b) a user name, password, and dial-up phone number from that ISP, which is pretty much all you need to get online.

Your only remaining task is to plug that information into Windows. (And, of course, to plug your computer into the phone jack on the wall.)

Here's how you do it.

1. **Choose Start→Network.**

    The Network window opens.

2. **On the toolbar, click Network and Sharing Center. In the task list at left, click "Set up a connection or network."**

It's one of the links at the left side of the window. In any case, the "Choose a connection option" dialog box opens.

3. **Click "Set up a dial-up connection"** (Figure 8-2, top), **and then click Next.**

If your modem isn't hooked up to a phone line, you get a "could not detect a dial-up modem" dialog box. Either fix the problem, or click "Set up a connection anyway." Windows will save your settings, and you can connect later, once you've solved your hardware problems.

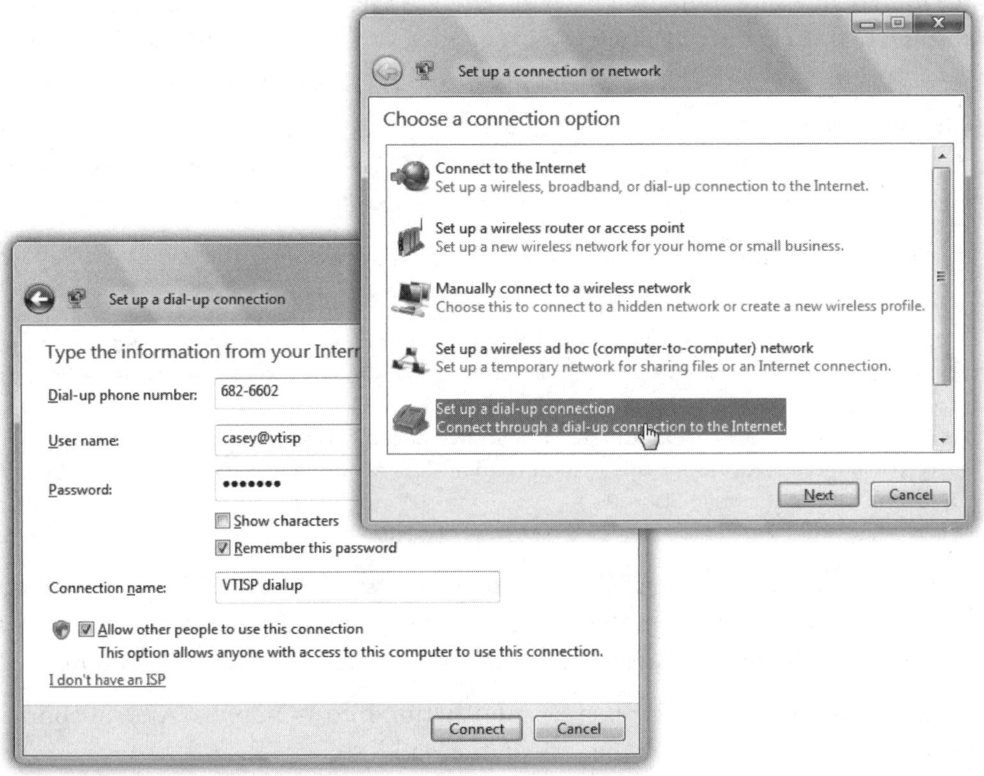

Figure 8-2: Top: You can use this same New Connection Wizard to set up a small office network, a corporate network, and so on, but for now, you want the Connect to the Internet option. To sign up for a standard Internet account, click "Set up a dial-up connections."

Bottom: If the gods are smiling, you'll never have to see this dialog box again. It's where you put in your dial-up account information.

4. **Fill in the phone number, user name, and password your ISP provided** (Figure 8-2, bottom).

   You can call your ISP for this information, or consult the literature delivered by postal mail when you signed up for an ISP account.

   If you were given a setup CD instead, click "I don't have an ISP," and then click "Use the CD I received from an ISP." Insert the disc when you're asked.

   Otherwise, complete the final step.

5. **Click Connect.**

   Assuming a phone line is plugged in, your PC dials and makes its connection with the mother ship.

6. **Make a decision: is this network Public or Private?**

   When the "Choose a location" dialog box appears, click Home, Work, or Public after you've read what the heck that means; see the box on the the next page. (Hint—"Public" is the most secure option for dial-up.)

GEM IN THE ROUGH

Cellular Wireless

WiFi hot spots are fast and usually cheap—but they're hot *spots*. Beyond 150 feet away, you're offline.

No wonder laptop luggers across America are getting into *cellular* Internet services. All of the big cellphone companies offer PC cards or ExpressCards that let your laptop get online at high speed *anywhere* in major cities. No hunting for a coffee shop; with a cellular Internet service, you can check your email while zooming down the road in a taxi. (Outside of the metropolitan areas, you can still get online wire-lessly, though much more slowly.)

Verizon and Sprint offer the fastest such networks, using a technology called EV-DO. Cingular and T-Mobile's offerings are much slower.

So why isn't the world beating a path to this delicious technology's door? Because it's expensive—$30 to $60 a month on top of your phone bill.

You may also be able to get your laptop online by connecting it to your cellphone with a cable—a lower-priced, slower option. Ask your cellphone carrier.

The First Time:
Home, Work, or Public Location

This gets a little technical, so hold onto your hat.

The first time you connect to a new network—the first time you use a wireless hot spot, first time you connect to a dial-up ISP, first time you plug into an office network—you see this dialog box.

It's asking you to categorize the network you've just joined. Is this a *public* network, like a coffee-shop hot spot? Is it a Work network—a corporate network that's likely to be staffed by security-conscious network geeks? Or is it your own home network, where you don't have to worry so much about hackers?

The choice you make here has absolutely nothing to do with the physical *location,* no matter what the dialog box says. Instead, it tells Windows how much *security* to apply to the network you've just joined.

If you choose Public, for example, Windows makes your computer invisible to other computers nearby. (Technically, it turns off the Vista feature called *network discovery.*) That's not ideal for file sharing, printer sharing, and so on—but it means

that hackers have a harder time "sniffing" the airwaves to detect your presence.

If you say a network is Public, you may be visited quite a bit by the "Unblock?" messages from the Windows firewall. That's Windows just being insecure, asking for permission every time any program (like a chat program) tries to get through the firewall.

If those messages are driving you crazy, maybe you should change the location to the Home or Work settings, which are less paranoid. In these "location" settings, network discovery is turned on, so you and your PCs can see each other on the network and share files, music, printers, and so on.

To change a connection from one location (that is, security scenario) to another, connect to the network in question. Choose Start→Network. On the toolbar, click Network and Sharing Center. Click Customize, and then click either Public or Private (meaning home and office networks). Authenticate yourself (page 127). Click Next, and then Close.

Connection Management

No matter what crazy combination of Internet connections you've accumulated on your computer, Windows represents each one as a *connection icon.* You can view them, rename them, change their settings, or just admire them by opening the window shown at top in Figure 8-3.

To get there, choose Start→Network. On the toolbar, click Network and Sharing Center. Click "Manage network connections" (in the left-side task pane).

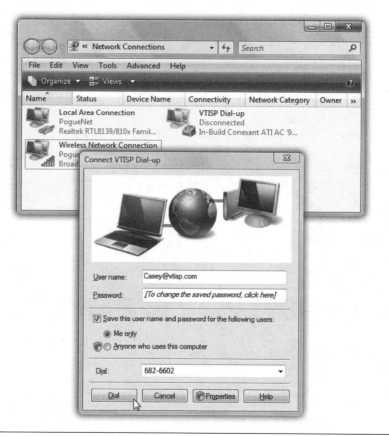

Figure 8-3: Top: This lucky individual has three different ways to get to the Internet: a dial-up account (listed first), a wireless network, and (courtesy of an Ethernet cable) a wired network. One of the many ways to go online is to double-click the connection you want to use. Bottom: Double-clicking the dial-up account name produces this dialog box, where you can click Dial to go online. (Turning on "Save this user name and password" eliminates the need to type your password each time—in general, a great idea.)

Tip _____

> If you travel frequently between the same couple of cities, consider making a differ-
> ent dial-up connection icon for each city—with the local access phone number already
> stored in each. To do that, right-click the first dial-up icon (Figure 8-3); from the shortcut
> menu, choose Create Copy. Authenticate yourself (page 127), then double-click the newly
> hatched icon to change its built-in phone number.

These icons are handy because their Properties dialog boxes are crammed with useful
information. A dial-up connection icon stores your name, password, phone number,
and so on; a broadband icon stores various technical Internet connection details.

In such situations, you need a way to make manual changes to your connections. To do
so, right-click a connection icon; from the shortcut menu, choose Properties.

The Notification Area Icon

The Network icon in the notification area (Figure 8-4) is a handy status meter, no matter how you're getting online.

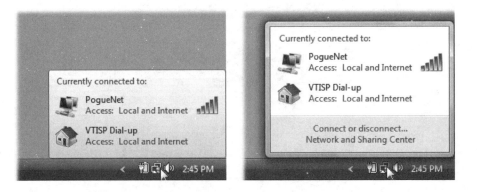

Figure 8-4: Top: If you point to this icon without clicking, you'll see a tooltip showing your WiFi signal
strength and, if you're dialing up, whether or not you're connected.

Bottom: If you click it, you get additional links to key control centers. And if you right-click it, you
get a shortcut menu that lets you disconnect, troubleshoot, or display "activity animation"—blinky
screens on the two tiny computers, illustrating the transfer of data. (Figure 8-1 shows that one.)

If it bears a red X, for example, it means that your PC isn't connected to any network at
all.

Internet Security

If it weren't for that darned Internet, personal computing would be a lot of fun. After all, it's the Internet that lets all those socially stunted hackers enter our machines, unleashing their viruses, setting up remote hacking tools, feeding us spyware, trying to trick us out of our credit-card numbers, and otherwise making our lives an endless troubleshooting session. It sure would be nice if they'd cultivate some other hobbies.

In the meantime, these low-lifes are doing astronomical damage to businesses and individuals around the world—along the lines of $100 billion a year (the cost to fight viruses, spyware, and spam).

A big part of the problem was the design of Windows itself. In the quaint old-fashioned days of 2000, when Windows XP was designed, these sorts of Internet attacks were far less common. Microsoft left open a number of back doors that were intended for convenience (for example, to let system administrators communicate with your PC from across the network) but wound up being exploited by hackers.

Microsoft wrote Windows Vista for a lot of reasons: to give Windows a cosmetic makeover, to give it up-to-date music and video features, to overhaul its networking plumbing—and, of course, to make money. But Job Number One was making Windows more secure. Evil strangers will still make every attempt to make your life miserable, but one thing is for sure: They'll have a much, much harder time of it.

Lots of Vista's security improvements are invisible to you. They're deep in the plumbing, with no buttons or controls to show you.

If you're scoring at home, they include features called Application Isolation, Service Hardening, Protected Mode, Address Space Layout Randomization, PatchGuard, Code Integrity, and so on.

The rest of this chapter describes features that *aren't* invisible and automatic—the ones that you can control.

Note, however, that built-in security tools can't do the whole job of keeping your PC safe; you play a role, too. So keep in mind these tips before you or your family go online:

▶ **Don't trust a pretty face.** It doesn't take much expertise to build a snazzy-looking Web site. Just because a Web site looks trustworthy doesn't mean that you can trust it. If you're visiting a little-known Web site, be careful what you do there.

▶ **Don't download from sites you don't know.** The Web is full of free software offers. But that free software may, in fact, be spyware or other malware. (Malware is a general term for viruses, spyware, and other Bad Software.) So be very careful when downloading anything online.

▶ **Don't click pop-up ads.** Pop-up ads are more than mere annoyances; some of them, when clicked, download spyware to your PC. As you'll see later in this chapter, Internet Explorer includes a pop-up blocker, but it doesn't block all pop-ups. So to be safe, don't click.

Security Center

If you're looking for at-a-glance information about the current state of your Internet security, head to the Security Center, by choosing Control Panel→Security→Security Center, shown in Figure 8-5.

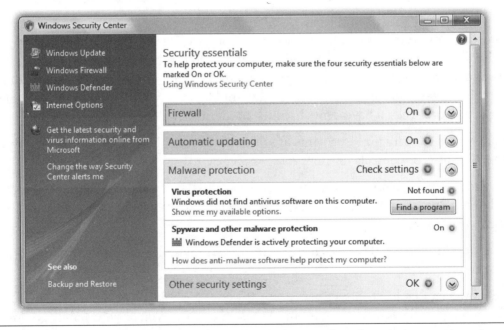

Figure 8-5: The Security Center shows you at a glance where you're safe and where you're not. Click the buttons or arrows on the right side of the screen to get more details about your security in any category. But if you want to change those settings, use the links on the left side of the screen instead.

Its status readouts cover several important Windows security features, described on the following pages. Green means you're protected; yellow means you're partially protected; red means that you're open to attack.

In the malware protection area, for example, you'll see green if you're running both Windows Defender (Vista's anti-spyware feature) and antivirus software; yellow if you're running only one of them; and red if neither one is turned on. For details, expand the panel by clicking the colored button or down arrow.

The Security Center isn't just a status display. It also alerts you (using a color-coded icon in the notification area [page 68], plus a pop-up balloon) whenever any of your security settings drops to yellow or red. Double-click the icon to open the Security Center and find out what it's worried about.

The Security Center is also a central control panel whose links let you change the most important Internet-related security settings: Windows Firewall, Windows Update, Windows Defender, and general Internet options. Read on.

Windows Firewall

If you have a broadband, always-on connection, you're connected to the Internet 24 hours a day. It's theoretically possible for some cretin to use automated hacking software to flood you with files or take control of your machine. Fortunately, Vista's *firewall* feature puts up a barrier to such mischief.

The firewall acts as a gatekeeper between you and the Internet. It examines all Internet traffic, and lets through only communications that it knows are safe; all other traffic is turned away at the door. (Vista's firewall is a big improvement over the Windows XP firewall, because it protects both inbound *and* outbound traffic. The Windows XP firewall handled only inbound traffic.)

You don't need to do anything to turn on the Windows Firewall. When you turn on Windows Vista, it's already at work.

Now, the firewall isn't always your friend. It can occasionally block a perfectly harmless program from communicating with the outside world—a chat program, for example.

Fortunately, whenever that happens, Windows lets you know with a message like the one in Figure 8-6. Most of the time, you'll know exactly what program it's talking about, because it's a program you just opened *yourself.* In other words, it's not some rogue spyware trying to talk to the mother ship. Click Unblock and get on with your life.

Security Center and Antivirus

The Security Center alerts you when it discovers that you don't have antivirus software on your PC. Since Vista doesn't actually come with any antivirus software, you'll almost certainly see these software nags until you download and install one. (Yes, even with all of Vista's fortifications, you still need antivirus software.)

Some PCs come with a trial version of some antivirus program; you have to pay an annual fee to keep it up-to-date. If your PC didn't come with any antivirus software at all, or if you've upgraded your PC from an earlier version of Windows, getting some antivirus software should be at the top of your To Do list.

Important: Vista requires antivirus software written especially for Vista. Antivirus software from the Windows XP days won't work.

Tip

Installing antivirus software doesn't necessarily mean paying for it. Several very good antivirus programs are free for personal use, like Avast (*www.avast.com*).

Figure 8-6: From time to time, your life with Vista will be interrupted by this message. It's your firewall speaking. It's trying to tell you that a program is trying to get online, as though you didn't know. Most of the time, you can just hit Unblock and get on with your life.

Windows Defender

Spyware is software that you don't know you have. You usually get it in one of two ways. First, a Web site may try to trick you into downloading it. You'll see what looks like an innocent button in what's actually a phony Windows dialog box, or maybe you'll get an empty dialog box—and clicking the Close box actually triggers the installation.

Second, you may get spyware by downloading a program that you *do* want—"cracked" software (commercial programs whose copy protection has been removed) is a classic example—without realizing that a secret program is piggybacking on the download.

Once installed, the spyware may make changes to important system files, install ads on your desktop (even when you're not online) or send information about your surfing habits to a Web site that blitzes your PC with pop-up ads related in some way to your online behavior.

Spyware can do a lot of damage beyond tracking what you do on the Internet. It can, for example, hijack your home page or search page, so every time you open your browser, you wind up at a Web page that incapacitates your PC with a blizzard of pop-ups. *Keylogger* spyware can record all of your keystrokes, passwords and all, and send them to a snooper.

Fortunately, Microsoft has provided, in Windows Vista, its first-ever anti-spyware program. It's called Windows Defender (Control Panel→Security→Windows Defender).

FREQUENTLY ASKED QUESTION

Laptop's Lament:
Away from the Cable Modem

When I'm home, I connect my laptop to my cable modem. But when I'm on the road, of course, I have to use my dial-up ISP. Is there any way to automate the switching between these two connection methods?

If there weren't, do you think your question would have even appeared in this chapter?

The feature you're looking for is in the

Control Panel. In Classic view, double-click Internet Options, click the Connections tab, and then turn on "Dial whenever a network connection is not present."

From now on, your laptop will use its dial-up modem only when it realizes that it isn't connected to your cable modem.

Windows Defender protects you against spyware in two ways. First, it's a kind of silent sentinel that sits in the background, watching your system. When it detects a piece of spyware trying to install itself, Defender zaps it. Second, it scans your hard drive for infections every day, and removes what it finds.

You don't need to do anything to turn Windows Defender on. It runs every time you start Windows. And every night at 2 a.m., if your PC is turned on, Defender scans your system, killing any spyware it finds.

Hot Spot Security

One of the greatest computing conveniences of the new millennium is the almighty public wireless hot spot, where and your WiFi laptop can connect to the Internet at high speed, often for free. There are thousands of them at cafés, hotels, airports, and other public locations (see *www.jiwire.com* for a national directory).

But unless you're careful, you'll get more than a skinny latte from your local café if you connect to their hot spot—you may get eavesdropped as well. It's theoretically possible for someone sitting nearby, using free and easy-to-find shareware programs, to "sniff" the transmissions from your laptop. He can intercept email messages you send, names and passwords, and even the images from the Web pages you're visiting.

Now, there's no cause for alarm; you don't have to sell your laptop and move to the Amish country over this. There are, however, a few simple steps that will go a long way toward keeping yourself safe:

▶ **Tell Windows it's a public network.** When you first connect to a wireless network, Windows Vista asks whether it's a public or private one. Choosing Public gives you extra built-in protection. Technically speaking, Vista turns off *network discovery,* the feature that makes your PC announce its presence to others on the network. (Unfortunately, lurking criminals using special scanning software can still find you if they're determined.)

▶ **Turn off file sharing.** You certainly don't want any of your over-caffeinated neighbors to get access to your files. Turn off file sharing by going to Control Panel Control→"Set up file sharing." Turn off file sharing and Public folder sharing.

▶ **Watch for the padlock.** You generally don't have to worry about online stores and banks. Whenever you see the little padlock icon in Internet Explorer (or whenever the URL in the Address bar begins with https instead of http), you're visiting a secure

Web site. Your transmissions are encrypted in both directions, and can't be snooped.

▶ **Look over your shoulder.** Hacking isn't always high-tech stuff; it can be as simple as "shoulder surfing," in which someone looks over your shoulder to see the password you're typing. Make sure no one can look at what you're typing.

▶ **Don't leave your laptop alone.** Coffee has a way of moving through your system fast, but if you have to leave for the rest room, don't leave your laptop unattended. Pack it up into its case and take it with you, or bring along a lock that you can use to lock your laptop to a table.

▶ **Use a Virtual Private Network (VPN).** Even if somebody intercepts your "hi, Mom" email, it may not be the end of the world. If you're doing serious corporate work, though, and you want maximum safety, you can pay for wireless virtual private network (VPN) software that encrypts all of the data that you're sending and receiving. Nobody will be able to grab it out of the air using snooping software at a hot spot.

For example, HotSpotVPN (*www.hotspotvpn.com*) costs $3.88 per day or $8.88 per month. You get a password, user name, and the Internet address of a VPN server.

Go to Control Panel→Network and Internet→Network and Sharing Center→"Set up a connection or network." Select "Connect to workplace" and follow the prompts for creating a new VPN connection with the information provided to you by Hot-SpotVPN.

Parental Controls

Many parents reasonably worry that it's far too easy for kids to find upsetting material on the Internet, accidentally or not: violence, pornography, hate speech, illegal drug sites, and so on.

A new Vista feature gives you a fighting chance at keeping this stuff off your PC: parental controls. They're easy to use and fairly complete.

Go to Control Panel→"Set up Parental Controls for any users" (in the User Accounts and Family Safety category). Authenticate yourself (page 127).

The dialog box shown in Figure 8-7 appears, listing all the user *accounts* on the PC (Chapter 15). One of the key advantages of the accounts system is that you can set up separate "worlds" for each person in your family—and now comes the payoff.

Click your kid's account to open up its parental controls screen. (If you haven't yet created accounts for your kids, you can create them here first.)

Under the Parental Controls setting, click "On, enforce current settings"—the master switch. You can now set up these limits for your offspring's PC use:

▶ **Windows Vista Web Filter** blocks access to objectionable Web sites—and prevents any Web downloads.

When you click the link, you're sent to a configuration screen that lets you select how restrictive you want the controls to be. You'll have the chance to turn on *automatic*

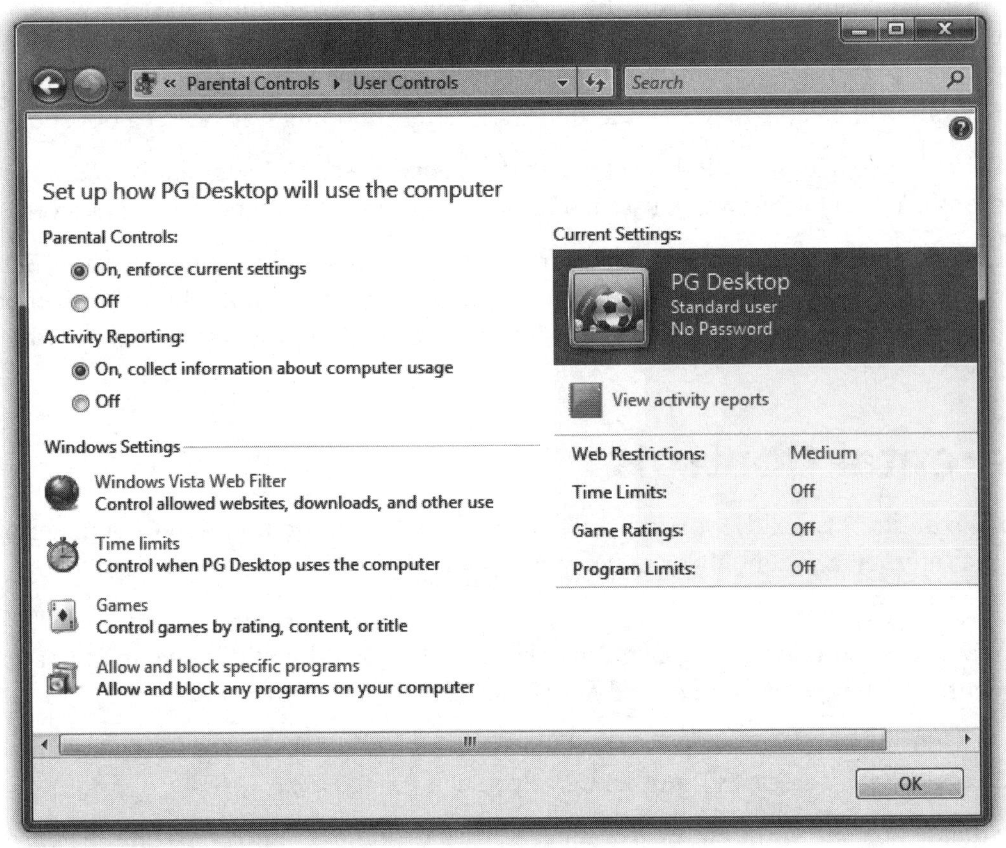

Figure 8-7: Parental Controls lets you control how your children use the PC and the Internet. Most parents will be most interested in the Windows Vista Web Filter, which lets you filter out objectionable Web sites, and lets you stop children from downloading software.

blocking based on what's on each site, using canned settings like High, Medium, None, or Custom (Figure 8-8).

— Tip —

The High setting permits Internet Explorer to open *only* Web sites that are specifically designed for children.

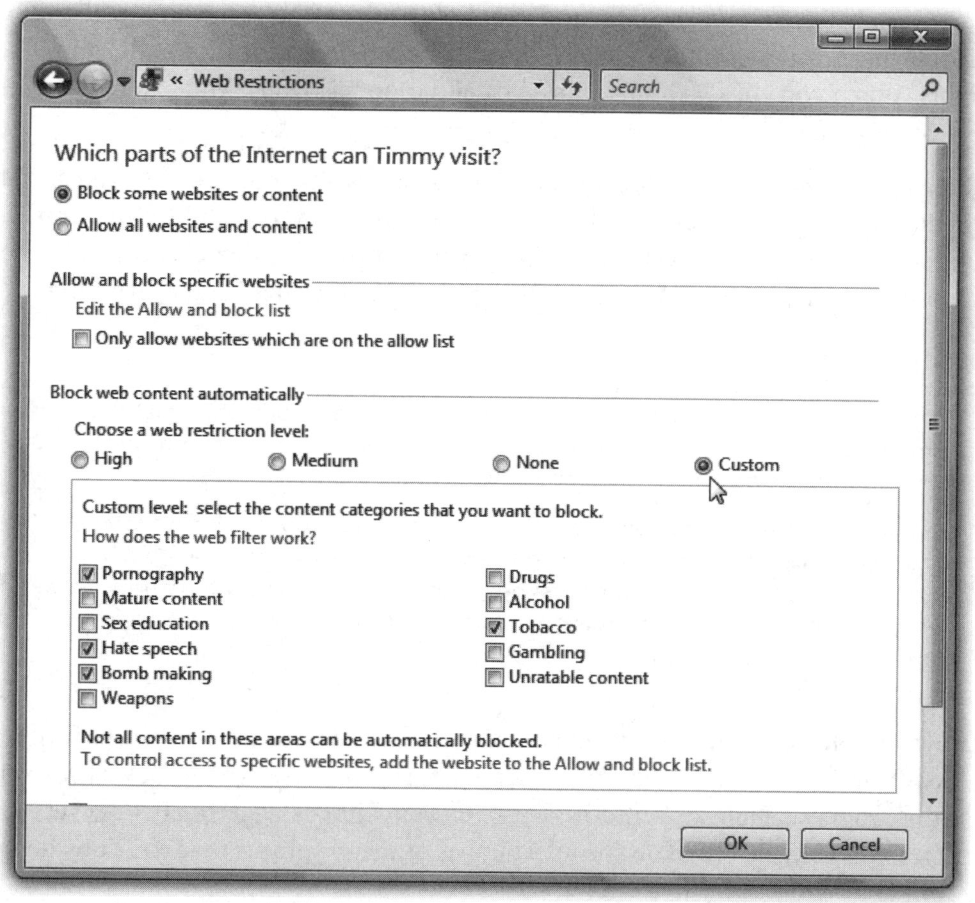

Figure 8-8: The Custom option lets you specify exactly what you consider objectionable. After all, you might find Weapons OK for your 12-year-old, but not Pornography or Bomb making. Don't let the 12-year-old actually see this list, however; it may serve as an inspiration rather than a deterrent.

Alternatively, you can type in the addresses of *individual* Web sites that you want to declare off-limits by turning on "Only allow websites which are on the allow list," and then clicking "Edit the Allow and Block list."

Finally, don't miss the "Block file downloads" checkbox. If you really want a safe PC, turn this one on. Your kid won't be able to download anything from the Web at all: no songs, games, videos—and no viruses, spyware, or worms.

▶ **Time Limits** lets you set the days and times of the week that your little tyke can use the Internet. You might, for example, decide to keep your kids off the PC on school nights. When you click "Time limits," a calendar opens, where you can block times by selecting them.

▶ **Games** prevents your youngsters from playing games altogether, or lets you specify which kinds of games they can play: Early Childhood, say, or Adults Only. You can even customize any level, by blocking specific upsetting depictions within the games—everything from "Animated Blood" to "Use of Drugs" and everything in between.

--- Note ---

To make this feature work, Vista consults a tiny GDF (game definition file) that software companies can put into their game. Game companies usually use ratings bestowed by a ratings board like the Entertainment Software Ratings Board (ESRB).

If a publisher uses information from a different ratings board, or doesn't have a rating file (GDF) at all, Vista consults Microsoft's own 2,000-game database. And if even *that* source draws a blank, Vista considers the game unrated. You may have noticed that the Games screen in Parental Controls offers a "Block games with no rating" option, which is designed just for such situations.

▶ **Allow and block specific programs** lets you declare individual programs on your PC to be off-limits. On the configuration screen, turn on "Casey [or whoever] can only use the programs I allow." Windows presents you with a staggering list of every single program on your PC; turn on the checkboxes of the programs that you consider appropriate for your kid. Click OK.

▶ **View activity reports.** Parental Controls reports are exceptionally detailed; they let you see pretty much everything that your kids have been doing on the PC. For example, it shows the 10 most popular Web sites they've each visited, the most recent Web sites blocked, files downloaded, and file downloads blocked. You also see how when your kid logged onto the PC, and the amount of time spent during each session. And that's just the beginning.

The final step is explaining the new limits to the young account holder. (Windows Vista has no new features to help you with that one.)

INTERNET EXPLORER 7

9

- ▶ IE7: The Grand Tour
- ▶ Tabbed Browsing
- ▶ Favorites (Bookmarks)
- ▶ History List
- ▶ RSS: The Missing Manual
- ▶ Tips for Better Surfing
- ▶ The Phishing Filter
- ▶ Privacy and Cookies
- ▶ The Pop-up Blocker

Microsoft has gone to great lengths to integrate the Internet into every cranny of Windows. Links and buttons that take you online are everywhere: on the Help screens, in the Windows freebie programs, and even in the "Send error report to Microsoft?" dialog boxes that appear after a program crashes. Once you've got your Internet connection working (Chapter 8), you may find that it's easier to go online than it is *not* to.

Internet Explorer (or IE, as it's often abbreviated) is the most famous Web browser on earth. The greatly revamped version 7 offers boatloads of new features. A *huge* number of them are related to security, since most bugs and viruses enter your PC from the Internet: the new phishing filter, pop-up blocker, download blocker, Windows Defender, cookies manager, ActiveX blocking, Protected Mode, parental controls, and so on.

There are lots of great new productivity features, too, though: an RSS reader, tabbed browsing, a new Search bar, a new interface design, and so on. This chapter is all about using Internet Explorer to surf the Web.

(Hey, it could happen.)

IE7: The Grand Tour

You can open Internet Explorer in a number of ways— for example, you can choose its name from the Start menu or click its shortcut on the Quick Launch toolbar.

As you can see in Figure 9-1, the Internet Explorer window is filled with tools that are designed to facilitate a smooth trip around the World Wide Web.

A *link* (or hyperlink) is a bit of text, or a little graphic, that's been programmed to serve as a button. When you click a link, you're transported from one Web page to another. One may be the home page of General Motors; another might have baby pictures posted by a parent in Omaha. About a billion pages await your visit.

Tip _____

Text links aren't always blue and underlined. In fact, modern Web designers sometimes make it very difficult to tell which text is clickable, and which is just text. When in doubt, move your cursor over some text. If the arrow changes to a pointing-finger cursor, you've found yourself a link.

Actually, you can choose to hide *all* underlines, a trick that makes Web pages look cleaner and more attractive. Underlines appear only when you point to a link (and wait a moment). If that arrangement appeals to you, open Internet Explorer. Choose Tools→Internet Options, click the Advanced tab, scroll down to "Underline links," select the Hover option, then click OK.

Menus and Gizmos

Internet Explorer 7 doesn't have a traditional menu bar (although you can make the old one come back if you press Alt or F10). Instead, it offers five tiny menu *icons* at the upper-right corner. Each little ▼ is, in fact, a menu.

Here's a look at the other basic controls—the doodads that surround your browser window.

Figure 9-1: The Internet Explorer window offers tools and features that let you navigate the Web almost effortlessly; these various toolbars and status indicators are described in this chapter. Chief among them: the Address bar, which displays the address (URL) of the Web page you're currently seeing, and the standard buttons, which let you control the Web-page loading process.

The Address Bar

When you type a new Web page address (URL) into this strip and press Enter, the corresponding Web site appears. (If only an error message results, then you may have mistyped the address, or the Web page may have been moved or dismantled—a relatively frequent occurrence.)

Because typing out Internet addresses is so central to the Internet experience and such a typo-prone hassle, the Address bar is rich with features that minimize keystrokes. For example:

▶ You don't have to click in the Address bar before typing; just press Alt+D.

▶ You don't have to type out the whole Internet address. You can omit the *http://www* and *.com* portions if you press Ctrl+Enter after typing the name; Internet Explorer fills in those standard address bits for you.

To visit Amazon.com, for example, a speed freak might press Alt+D to highlight the Address bar, type *amazon,* and then press Ctrl+Enter.

GEM IN THE ROUGH

Let AutoFill Do the Typing

Internet Explorer can remember the user names and passwords you type into those "please sign in" Web sites.

You can't miss this feature; each time you type a password into a Web page, this dialog box appears.

It's a great time- and brain-saver, even though it doesn't work on all Web sites. (Of course, use it with caution if you share an account on your PC with other people.)

When you want IE to "forget" your passwords—for security reasons, for example—choose Tools→Options. Click the Content tab, click Settings, and click OK.

Here in this dialog box, you'll also find checkboxes that control *what* Internet Explorer memorizes: Web addresses (autocomplete in the Address bar), forms (your name, address, and so on), and user names and passwords.

▶ Even without the Ctrl+Enter trick, you can still omit the *http://* from any Web address. (Most of the time, you can omit the *www.*, too.) To jump to today's Dilbert cartoon, type *dilbert.com* and then press Enter.

▶ When you begin to type into the Address bar, the AutoComplete feature compares what you're typing against a list of Web sites you've recently visited. IE displays a drop-down list of Web addresses that seem to match what you're typing. To spare yourself the tedium of typing out the whole thing, just click the correct complete address with your mouse, or use the down arrow key to reach the desired listing and then press Enter. The complete address you selected then pops into the Address bar.

(To make AutoComplete *forget* the Web sites you've visited recently—so that nobody will see what you've been up to—you have to delete your History list; see page 238.)

Topside Doodads

Around the Address bar, you'll find several important buttons. Some of them lack text labels, but all offer tooltip labels:

▶ **Back button, Forward button.** Click the Back button to revisit the page you were just on. (*Keyboard shortcut:* Backspace and Shift+Backspace, or Alt+left arrow and Alt+right arrow.)

— Tip —

Pressing Shift as you turn your mouse's scroll wheel up or down also navigates forward and back. Cool.

Once you've clicked Back, you can then click the Forward button (or press Alt+right arrow) to return to the page you were on *before* you clicked the Back button. Click the ▾ button for a list of all the Web pages you've visited during this online session (that is, within this browser window, as opposed to your long-term History list).

▶ **Refresh button.** Click this double-arrow button (just to the right of the Address bar) if a page doesn't look or work quite right, or if you want to see the updated version of a Web page (such as a stock ticker) that changes constantly. This button forces Internet Explorer to redownload the Web page and reinterpret its text and graphics.

▶ **Stop (X) button.** Click this button, at the far right end of the Address bar, to interrupt the downloading of a page you requested (-by mistake, for example). (*Keyboard shortcut:* Esc.)

▶ **Search bar.** There's no tidy card catalog of every Web page. Because Web pages appear and disappear hourly by the hundreds of thousands, such an exercise would be futile.

The best you can do is to use a search engine, a Web site that searches *other* Web sites. You might have heard of the little engine called Google, for example.

But why waste your time plugging in *www.google.com?* Here's one of Internet Explorer's most profoundly useful features—a Search box that accesses Google automatically—or any other search page you like. Type something you're looking for into this box—*electric drapes*, say—and then press Enter. You go straight to the Google results page.

Actually, the factory setting is Microsoft's own search page, Live.com, not Google. It takes a moment to reprogram the Search box so that it uses Google or another search service, but it's worth the effort. From the ▾ button to the right of the magnifying glass icon, choose Find More Providers. See Figure 9-2 for the next steps.

Tip

Truth is, it's often faster to type your search phrase into the *Address bar itself,* if for no other reason than you have a keyboard shortcut to get your cursor in there (Alt+D). When you press Enter, IE does a Web search for that term, using the same search service you've set up for the Search box.

Window Controls

These last items wrap up your grand tour of Internet Explorer's window gizmos:

▶ **Scroll bars.** Use the scroll bar, or the scroll wheel on your mouse, to move up and down the page—or to save mousing, press the Space bar each time you want to see more. Press Shift+Space bar to scroll *up.* (The Space bar has its traditional, space-making function only when the insertion point is blinking in a text box or the Address bar.)

You can also press your up and down arrow keys to scroll. Page Up and Page Down scroll in full-screen increments, while Home and End whisk you to the top or bottom of the current Web page.

▶ **Home button.** Click to bring up the Web page you've designated as your home page—your starter page.

And which page is that? Whichever one you designate. Open a good startup page (Google, NYTimes.com, Dilbert.com, whatever), and then choose Add or Change Home Page from this icon's pop-up menu.

Figure 9-2: Top: To add search services to this pop-up menu, start by choosing Find More Providers. Middle: This page lists lots of popular search services, including Google, Yahoo, Ask.com, and more specialized pages: Amazon for books, ESPN for sports, and so on. You can even add new ones using the Create Your Own section. Bottom: When you click a search service's name, you're asked to confirm—and you're given the chance to make it your default search, the one that IE always uses. Click Add Provider.

▶ **Status bar.** The status bar at the bottom of the window tells you what Internet Explorer is doing (such as "Opening page…" or "Done"). When you point to a link without clicking, the status bar also tells you which URL will open if you click it.

And when you're opening a new page, a graph appears here, showing that your PC is still downloading (receiving) the information and graphics on the Web page. In other words, you're not seeing everything yet.

Tabbed Browsing

Beloved by hard-core surfers the world over, *tabbed browsing* is a way to keep a bunch of Web pages open simultaneously—in a single, neat window, without cluttering up your taskbar with a million buttons.

Figure 9-3 illustrates.

Shortcut-O-Rama

Turning on tabbed browsing unlocks a whole raft of Internet Explorer shortcuts and tricks, which are just the sort of thing power surfers gulp down like Gatorade:

▶ **To open a new, empty tab** in front of all others, press Ctrl+T (for *tab*), or click the New Tab stub identified in Figure 9-3, or double-click anywhere in the empty area of the tab row. From the empty tab that appears, you can navigate to any site you want.

▶ **To open a link into a new tab,** Ctrl-click it. Or click it with your mouse wheel.

Or, if you're especially slow, right-click it and, from the shortcut menu, choose Open in New Tab.

--- **Note** ---

Ctrl-clicking a link opens that page in a tab *behind* the one you're reading. That's a fantastic trick when you're reading a Web page and see a reference you want to set aside for reading next, but you don't want to interrupt whatever you're reading.

But if you want the new tab to appear in *front,* add the Shift key.

▶ **To close a tab,** either click the X on it, press Ctrl+W, press Alt+F4, or click the tab with your mouse wheel or middle mouse button, if you have one.

If you press Ctrl+Alt+4, you close all tabs *except* the one that's in front.

▶ **Switch from one tab to the next** by pressing Ctrl+Tab. Add the Shift key to move backwards through them.

One more note to tab fans: When you close Internet Explorer, a dialog box appears asking if you really want to close *all* the tabs. If you click Show Options at this point, you're offered an opportunity to "Open these the next time I use Internet Explorer." Turn that on and click Close Tabs; the next time you go a-browsing, you'll pick up right from the tabs where you left off.

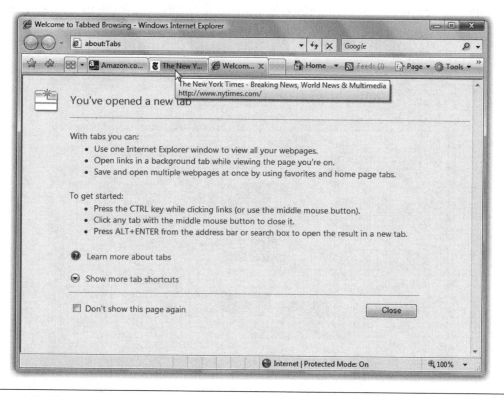

Figure 9-3: When you Ctrl+Shift-click a link, or type an address and press Alt+Enter or ⌘-Enter, you open a new *tab,* not a new window as you ordinarily would. You can now pop from one open page to another by clicking the tabs above the window, or close one by clicking its X button (or pressing Ctrl+W).

___ Note _____

If you find all this tabby business confusing and unnecessary, you can turn off the whole feature. In Internet Explorer, choose Tools→Internet Options. Click the General tab; under Tabs, click Settings. Turn off Enable Tabbed Browsing, and then click OK twice.

Quick Tabs (Thumbnails)

Once you've got a bunch of tabs open, you may face a horizontal screen-space crunch. How much, exactly, of the text "Welcome to Bass World—The Internet's Global Resource for Bass Fisherfolk" can you see on a half-inch tab?

Not much. But how, then, are you supposed to tell your tabs apart?

By using another new Internet Explorer feature called Quick Tabs. Figure 9-4 shows all.

Quick Tabs tab

Figure 9-4: Quick Tabs shows you thumbnails of all the Web pages you've opened into tabs, making it simple to tell them apart. One click on a thumbnail returns it to full size, with that tab in front of the others. All you have to learn is the Quick Tabs keystroke, which is Ctrl+Q—or the location of the Quick Tabs button, shown here. (Repeat the trigger to exit the Quick Tabs view without changing anything.)

— Tip —

> You can *close* a tab directly from the Quick Tabs screen, too—just click the X button in the upper-right corner of the thumbnail.

Favorites (Bookmarks)

When you find a Web page you might like to visit again, press Ctrl+D. That's the Add to Favorites command. (The long way is to click the Add to Favorites button identified in Figure 9-5.) Type a shorter or more memorable name, if you like, and click Add.

Figure 9-5: Top: When you want to flag a Web page for visiting later, using this menu is one way to do it. Bottom: Internet Explorer offers to add this Web page's name (or a shorter name that you specify for it) either to the Favorites menu itself, or to a "folder" (category) *within* that menu. The next time you want to visit that page, just select its name from the star-shaped menu at the top left of the window.

The Web page's name appears instantly in the "Favorites center," which is the menu indicated by the yellow star (Figure 9-5). The next time you want to visit that page, open this menu—or press Alt+C—and click the Web site's name in the list.

___ Tip ___
You can send your list of Favorites to or from other browsers or other PCs, which can save you a lot of time.

To do that, open the Add to Favorites menu (Figure 9-5); choose Import and Export. The Import/Export wizard appears to guide you through the process. Consider saving them onto, for example, a flash drive, for ease in transporting to another location or computer.

You can rearrange the commands in your Favorites menu easily enough. Open the Favorites center (Figure 9-6), and then drag the bookmarks up and down in the list.

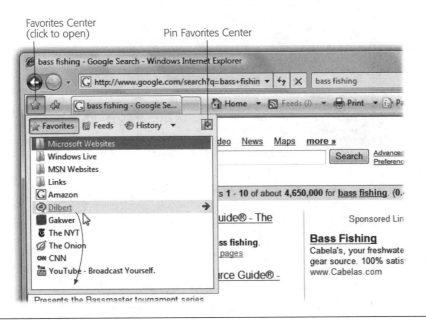

Figure 9-6: When the Favorites menu opens, you can drag names up or down to rearrange the list, as shown. Or right-click one to access the commands that rename, delete, or file a favorite into a folder. (Unfortunately, the Favorites menu covers up part of the Web page you're reading. It hides itself soon enough, but you might also want to freeze the Favorites Center open so that it *doesn't* cover the page. To do that, click the Pin the Favorites Center button shown here.)

Or, for more elaborate organizing tasks—creating and deleting folders, renaming sites, and so on—click the Add to Favorites button (Figure 9-5) and, from the shortcut menu, choose Organize Favorites. You get a little dialog box that makes all of those tasks easy.

History List

This *history* is a list of the Web sites you've visited. It's the heart of three IE features: AutoComplete, described at the beginning of this chapter; the drop-down list at the right side of the Address bar; and the History list itself.

That's the pane that appears when you click the Favorites (star) button and then click History—or just press Ctrl+H. Figure 9-7 presents the world's shortest History class.

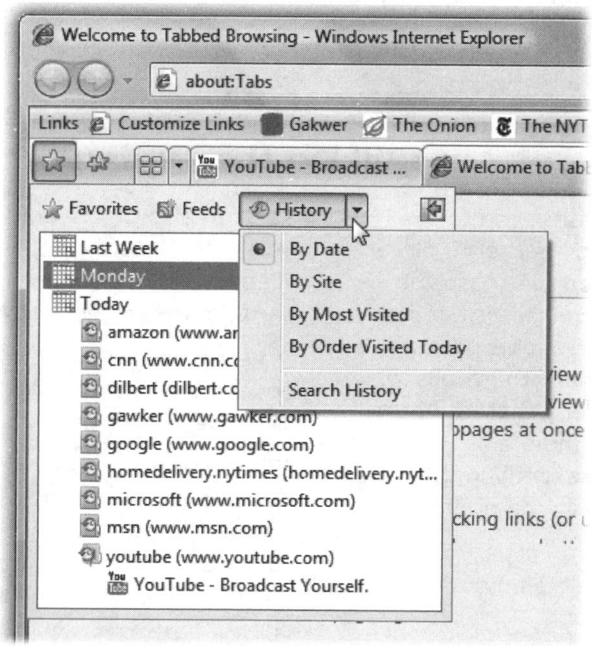

Figure 9-7: If you click the little ▾ button next to the word History, you'll see that you can view the list sorted by Web site, date, frequency of visits—or you can see only the sites you've visited *today*, in order. The same little pop-up menu offers a command called Search History, so that you can search for text in the History list—not the actual text *on* those pages, but text within the page addresses and descriptions.

The History pane lists the Web sites you've visited in the last week or so, neatly organized into subfolders like "Today" and "Last Week." These are great features if you can't recall the URL for a Web site that you remember having visited recently.

Click one of the time-period icons to see the Web sites you visited during that era. Click the name of a Web site to view a list of each visited page *within* that site—and click an actual URL to reopen that Web page in the main window.

You can configure the number of days for which you want your Web visits tracked. To do so, choose Tools→Internet Options→General; where it says "Browsing history," click Settings. At the bottom of the dialog box, you'll see the "Days to keep pages in history" control.

To *erase* your History list for security purposes, choose Tools→Delete Browsing History. In the resulting dialog box, click "Delete history."

Let AutoFill Do the Typing

You'd be surprised and shocked to see the kinds of information Internet Explorer stores about you. Behind the scenes, it logs every Web site you ever visit. It stashes your cookies, of course, plus passwords and information you type into Web Now, some people find it creepy that Internet Explorer maintains a complete list of every Web site they've seen recently, right there in plain view of any family member or co-worker who wanders by.

Fortunately, you can delete any or all of these tracks easily enough.

To delete just one particularly incriminating History listing, right-click it in the History list. From the shortcut menu, choose Delete. You've just rewritten History.

You can also delete any other organizer icon in the History list: one of the little Web-site folders, or even one of the calendar folders like "Three Weeks Ago."

To erase the entire History menu, choose Tools→Delete Browsing History, and then click "Delete history."

The same dialog box offers individual buttons for deleting the other kinds of tracks—the passwords, cache files, and so on. Or, if you really want a clean slate, you can click Delete All to purge all of it at once.

This is good information to know; after all, you might be nominated to the Supreme Court some day.

The more days IE tracks, the easier it is for you to refer to those addresses quickly. On the other hand, the more days you keep, the longer the list becomes, which may make it harder to use the list easily and efficiently.

Oh, and if you set "Days to keep pages in history" to 0, Internet Explorer won't track your movements at all. (You know who you are.)

RSS: The Missing Manual

In the beginning, the Internet was an informational Garden of Eden. There were no banner ads, pop-ups, flashy animations, or spam messages. People loved the Internet.

Those days, unfortunately, are long gone. Web browsing now entails a constant battle against intrusive advertising and annoying animations. And with the proliferation of Web sites and blogs, just reading your favorite sites can become a full-time job.

Enter RSS, a technology that lets you subscribe to *feeds*—summary blurbs provided by thousands of sources around the world, from Reuters to Microsoft to your nerdy next-door neighbor. News and blog sites usually publish RSS feeds, but RSS can also bring you podcasts (recorded audio broadcasts), photos, and even videos.

You used to need a special RSS *reader* program to tune into them—but no longer. Internet Explorer 7 can "subscribe" to updates from such feeds, so you can read any new articles or postings at your leisure.

The result? You spare yourself the tedium of checking for updates manually, plus you get to read short summaries of new articles without ads and blinking animations. And if you want to read a full article, you can click its link in the RSS feed to jump straight to the main Web site.

___ Note ___

RSS either stands for Rich Site Summary or Really Simple Syndication. Each abbreviation explains one aspect of RSS—either its summarizing talent or its simplicity.

Viewing an RSS Feed

So how do you sign up for these free, automatic RSS "broadcasts"? Watch your tab bar as you're surfing the Web. When Internet Explorer's Feeds button (Figure 9-8) turns orange, IE is telling you, "This site has an RSS feed available."

(Sometimes, in fact, the site has *multiple* feeds available—for example, in different formats—in which case you can choose among them using the ▾ menu next to the RSS icon.)

___ Tip _____
To find more RSS feeds, visit a site like *www.feedster.com*.

To see what the fuss is all about, click that button. Internet Explorer switches into RSS-viewing mode, as shown in Figure 9-8.

At this point, you have three choices:

▶ **Subscribe.** Click the Add to Favorites button, and then click Subscribe to This Feed. From now on, you'll be able to see whether the RSS feed has had any new articles posted—without actually having to visit the site. Figure 9-8 has the details.

▶ **Massage the feed.** Once you're looking at the feed, you can sort the headline items by date, title, and author, or use the Search box to find text among all the articles.

▶ **Close the RSS feed altogether.** To do so, just click the Feeds button again. You're left back where you started, at whatever Web page you were visiting.

___ Tip _____
Once you've subscribed to some feeds, you don't actually have to fire up Internet Explorer just to see what's new in your world. Remember the Sidebar? The Gadgets described in Chapter 6?

One of them, you may recall, is called Feed Headlines. Yes, right there on your desktop, you'll see headlines from your subscribed Web sites, updating themselves as the news breaks. Click a headline to open a minipreview window; double-click to open Internet Explorer and view the actual Web page.

Tips for Better Surfing

IE is filled with shortcuts for better speed and more pleasant surfing. For example:

Picking a Home Page

The first Web site you encounter when IE connects to the Internet is a Microsoft Web site—or Dell, or EarthLink; the point is, *you* didn't choose it. This site is your factory-set *home page*.

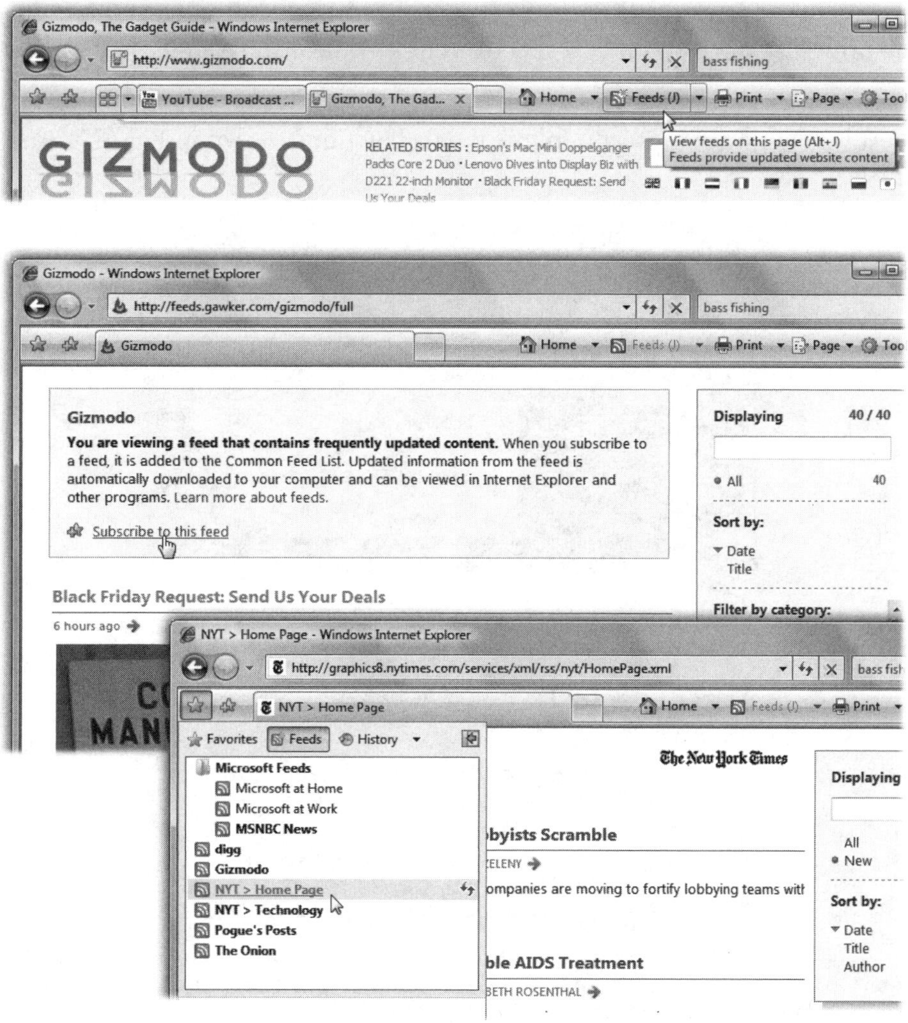

Figure 9-8: Top: When the Feeds button changes color, you've got yourself a live one: a Web site that publishes a feed. Click the Feeds button.

Middle: Now you get a sneak peek at what the feed looks like. If you like, subscribe, as shown here.

Bottom: To read your feed, click the Favorites button (the star) and, at the top of the pane, click Feeds. Click the one you want to read.

Unless you actually work for Microsoft, Dell, or EarthLink, however, you'll probably find Web browsing more fun if you specify your *own* favorite Web page as your startup page.

The easiest way to go about it is to follow the instructions shown in Figure 9-9.

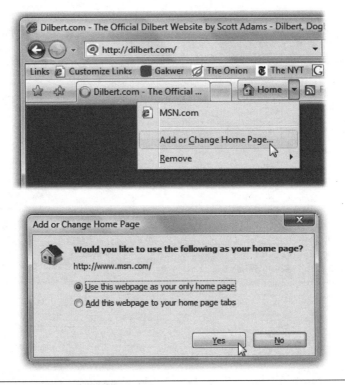

Figure 9-9: Top: Start by visiting the page you want to designate as your home page. Then, from the Home menu identified here, choose Add or Change Home Page.

Bottom: In this dialog box, choose "Use this webpage as your only home page," and click Yes.

Google makes a nice home page; so does a news site. But here are a couple of possibilities that might not have occurred to you:

▶ **A blank page.** If you can't decide on a home page, or your mood changes from day to day, set up a blank—empty—home page. This setup makes IE load very quickly when you first launch it. Once this window opens, *then* you can tell the browser where you want to go today.

To set this up, open the Home menu (Figure 9-9) and choose Remove→Remove All; in the confirmation box, click Yes.

▶ **Multiple home page tabs.** This is a cool one. Now that Internet Explorer can display tabs, you can designate a bunch of them to open all at once each time you fire up Internet Explorer. It's a great way to avoid wasting time by calling up one site after another, because they'll all be loading in the background as you read the first one.

The quickest way to set up a Home tab set: Open all the Web sites into their own tabs, just the way you'll want IE to do automatically in the future. Then, from the Home menu, choose Add or Change Home Page. Next, in the dialog box (Figure 9-9, bottom), select "Use the current tab set as your home page," and click Yes.

Thereafter, you can always add additional tabs to this starter set by choosing "Add this webpage to your home page tabs," the bottom option shown in Figure 9-9.

Bigger Text, Smaller Text

When your eyes are tired, you might like to make the text bigger. When you visit a site designed for Macintosh computers (whose text tends to look too large on PC screens), you might want a smaller size. You can adjust the point size of a Web page's text using the Page→Text Size commands.

Zooming In and Out

So much for magnifying the *text;* what about the whole Web page?

There are plenty of ways to zoom in or out of the whole affair:

▶ If you have a scroll-wheel mouse, press the Ctrl key as you turn the mouse's wheel. (This works in Microsoft Office programs, too.)

▶ Press Ctlr+plus or Ctrl+minus on your keyboard.

▶ Use the pop-up menu in the lower-right corner of the window (where it probably says "100%" at the moment). Just clicking the digits repeatedly cycles the page among 100, 125, and 150 percent of actual size. Alternatively, you can use its ≥ menu to choose any degree of zoom from 50 to 400 percent—or choose Custom to type anything in between.

Saving Pages

You can make Internet Explorer *store* a certain Web page on your hard drive so that you can peruse it later—on your laptop during your commute, for example.

The short way is to choose Page→Save As. For greatest simplicity, choose "Web Archive, single file (*.mht)" from the "Save as type" drop-down list. (The other options here save the Web page as multiple files on your hard drive—a handy feature if you intend to edit them, but less convenient if you just want to read them later.) Name the file and click the Save button. You've just preserved the Web page as a file on your hard drive, which you can open later by double-clicking it.

Printing Pages

The decade of chopped-off printouts is over. Now, when you choose Print (the little printer icon) *all* of the Web page's text is auto-shrunk to fit within the page.

Tip

You can print only *part* of a page, too. Drag through the portion you want, press Ctrl+P, click Selection, and then click Print.

Faster Browsing Without Graphics

Sure, sure, graphics are part of what makes the Web so compelling. But they're also responsible for making Web pages take so long to arrive on the screen. Without them, Web pages appear almost instantaneously. You still get fully laid-out Web pages; you still see all the text and headlines. But wherever a picture would normally be, you see an empty rectangle containing a generic "graphic goes here" logo, usually with a caption explaining what that graphic would have been.

To turn off graphics, choose Tools→ Internet Options, which opens the Internet Options dialog box. Click the Advanced tab, scroll down halfway into the list of checkboxes, and turn off "Show pictures" (in the Multimedia category of checkboxes).

Now try visiting a few Web pages. You'll feel a substantial speed boost, especially if you're connected by dial-up modem.

And if you wind up on a Web page that's nothing without its pictures, you can choose to summon an individual picture. Just right-click its box and choose Show Picture from the shortcut menu.

Better yet, if you choose Print→Print Preview, you get a handsome preview of the end

Turn Off Animations

If blinking ads make it tough to concentrate as you read a Web-based article, choose Tools→Internet Options→Advanced tab, and then scroll down to the Multimedia heading. Turn off "Play animations in web pages" to stifle most animated ads. Alas, it doesn't stop *all* animations; the jerks of the ad-design world have grown too clever for this option.

Take a moment, too, to look over the other annoying Web page elements that you can turn off, including sounds.

Internet Options

Internet Explorer's Options dialog box offers roughly 68,000 tabs, buttons, and nested dialog boxes. Most of the useful options have been described, in this chapter, with their appropriate topics (like Tabbed Browsing). Still, by spending a few minutes adjusting Internet Explorer's settings, you can make it more fun (or less annoying) to use.

To open this cornucopia of options, choose Tools→Internet Options.

The Phishing Filter

The criminal mind knows no bounds. How else do you explain the clever nefariousness of *phishing* attacks?

In a phishing attack, you're sent what appears to be legitimate email from a bank, eBay, PayPal, or some other financial Web site. The message tells you that the site needs to confirm account information, or warns that your account has been hacked, and needs you to help keep it safe.

If you, responsible citizen that you are, click the provided link to clear up the supposed problem, you wind up on what looks like the bank/eBay/PayPal Web site. But it's a fake, carefully designed to look like the real thing; it's run by a scammer. If you type in your password and login information, as requested, the next thing you know, you're getting credit-card bills for $10,000 charges at high-rolling Las Vegas hotels.

The fake sites look so much like the real ones that it can be extremely difficult to tell them apart. (That's *can* be; on some of the phishing sites, spelling mistakes a fourth grader wouldn't make are a clear giveaway.) To make the site seem more realistic, the scam artist often includes legitimate links alongside phony ones. But if you click the login link, you're in trouble.

Internet Explorer 7's new phishing filter protects you from these scams. You don't need to do anything to turn it on; it's always running.

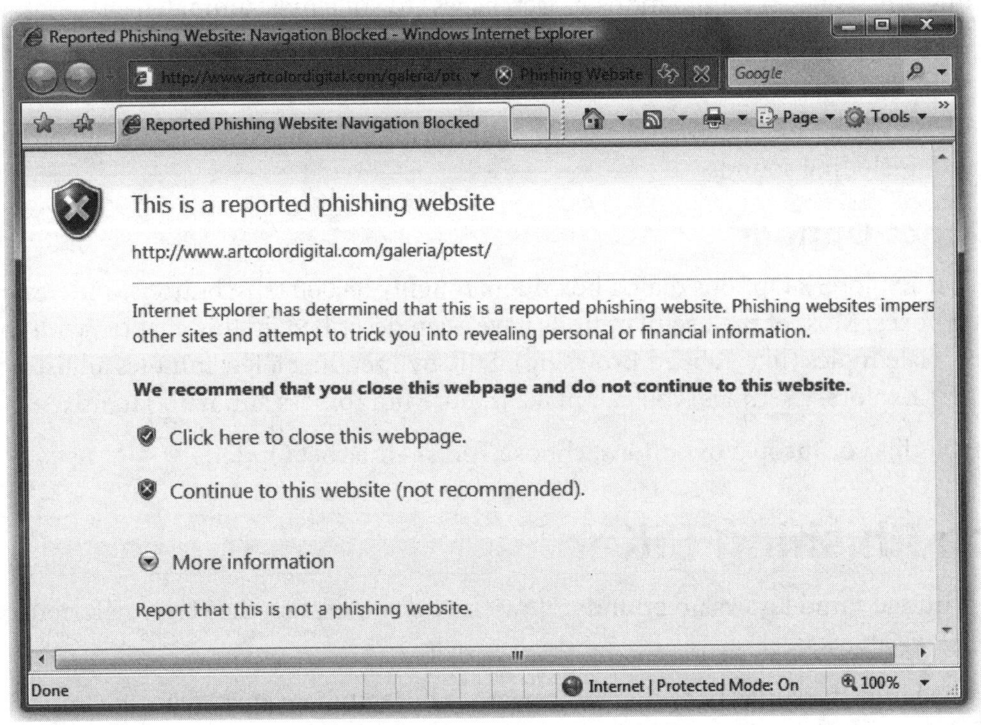

Figure 9-10: Don't go there: Internet Explorer blocks you from visiting known phishing sites. It uses a variety of methods for determining what's a legitimate site and what's a phishing site, including getting updated lists of known phishing sites.

One day, though, when you least expect it, you'll be on your way to visit some Web site—and Internet Explorer will stop you in your tracks with a pop-up warning that you're about to open to a "reported phishing website" (Figure 9-10).

In that situation, click the *green checkmark button* to close the page. Do not click the red X button; it will send you through to the phony site.

If Internet Explorer isn't quite sure about a certain site's phishiness, but it has a funny feeling in its bones, a yellow button appears next to the Address bar that says, "Suspicious Website." Unless you absolutely know the site is legitimate, it's a good idea to head somewhere else.

Privacy and Cookies

Cookies are something like Web page preference files. Certain Web sites—particularly commercial ones like Amazon.com—deposit them on your hard drive like little bookmarks, so that they'll remember you the next time you visit. On Amazon, in fact, a greeting says "Hello, Casey" (or whatever your name is), thanks to the cookie it uses to recognize you.

Most cookies are perfectly innocuous—and, in fact, are extremely helpful. They can let your PC log into a site automatically, or let you customize what the site looks like and how you use it.

But fear is on the march, and the media fan the flames with tales of sinister cookies that track your movement on the Web. Some Web sites rely on cookies to record which pages you visit on a site, how long you spend on a site, what kind of information you like to find out, and so on.

If you're worried about invasions of privacy—and you're willing to trade away some of the conveniences of cookies—Internet Explorer is ready to protect you.

Choose Tools→Internet Options→Privacy to get to the Privacy tab. The slider on the left side lets you pick your compromise on the convenience/privacy scale, ranging from Accept All Cookies to Block All Cookies (Figure 9-11).

— **Note** ───

> Some sites don't function well (or at all) if you choose to reject all cookies. So if you choose High Privacy, and you run into trouble browsing your favorite sites, return here and change the setting to Medium High. (Internet Explorer's factory setting is Medium.)

───

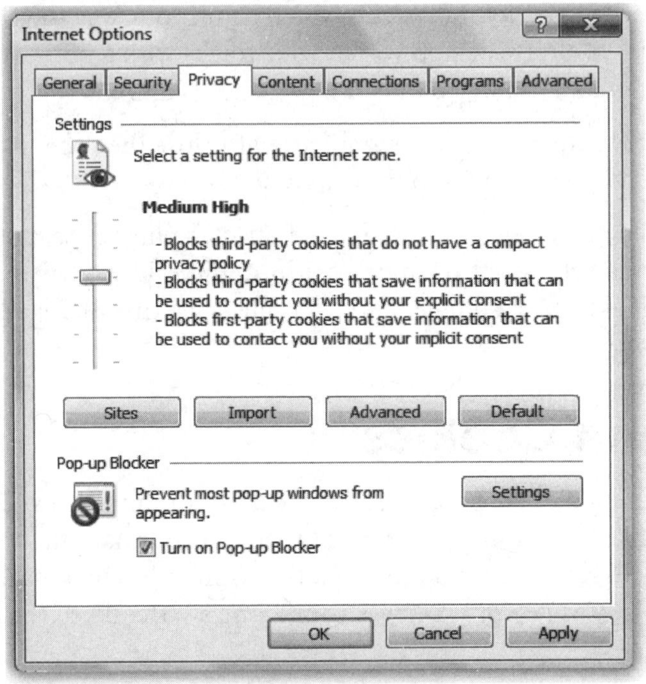

Figure 9-11: This box helps you keep your private information private—it lets you control how your PC works with cookies, which are bits of data put on your hard disk by Web sites. Medium High is a good setting that balances your privacy with Web sites' needs to use cookies for purposes like automated logins.

The Pop-up Blocker

The ad banners at the top of every Web page are annoying enough—but nowadays, they're just the beginning. The world's smarmiest advertisers have begun inundating us with *pop-up* and *pop-under* ads: nasty little windows that appear in front of the browser window, or, worse, behind it, waiting to jump out the moment you close your browser. They're often deceptive, masquerading as error messages or dialog boxes… and they'll do absolutely anything to get you to click inside them (Figure 9-12).

Pop-ups are more than just annoying; they're also potentially dangerous. They're a favorite trick that hackers use to deposit spyware on your PC. Clicking a pop-up can begin the silent downloading process. That's true even if the pop-up seems to serve a legitimate purpose—asking you to participate in a survey, for example.

Internet Explorer, fortunately, has a pop-up *blocker*. It comes automatically turned on; you don't have to do anything. You'll be browsing along, and then one day you'll see the "Pop-up blocked" message in the yellow Information bar (Figure 9-12, top).

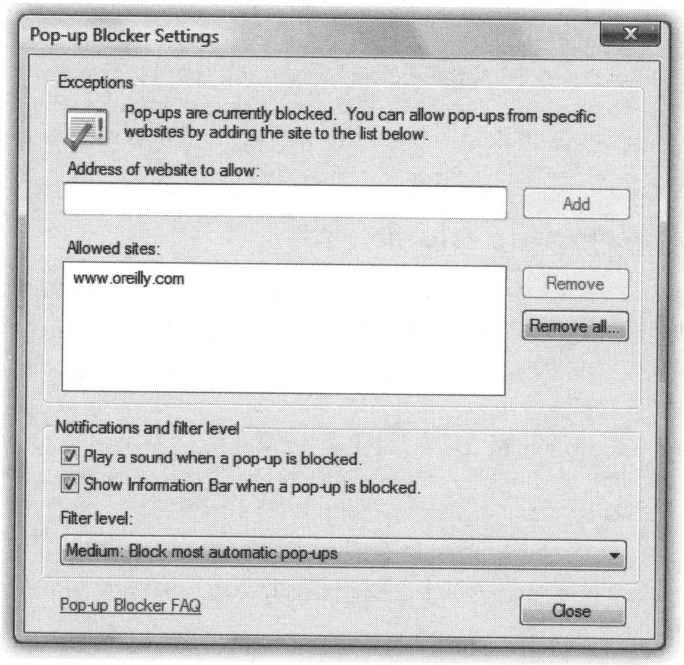

Figure 9-12: Top: If you click the "pop-up blocked" message, you can choose Temporarily Allow Pop-ups, which lets you see what IE is blocking—or just press Ctrl+Alt. Or if pop-ups are important on a certain page (like the confirmation screen on a travel-booking site), choose Always Allow Pop-ups from This Site.

Bottom: Later, you can always manage the list of "pop-ups permitted" sites by choosing Tools→Pop-up Blocker→Pop-up Blocker Settings. This dialog box appears, listing all pop-up–approved Web sites (and offering a Remove button if you're having second thoughts). Here, too, you can turn off the "blocked pop-up" sound, eliminate the Information bar, or adjust the level of the pop-up filter (High, Medium, or Low).

Note that IE blocks only pop-ups that are spawned *automatically,* not those that appear when you click something (like a seating diagram on a concert-tickets site). And it doesn't block pop-ups from your local network, or from Web sites you've designated as Trusted (choose Tools→Internet Options→Security, click "Trusted sites," and then click Sites).

Overriding the Pop-up Block

Sometimes, though, you *want* to see the pop-up. Some sites, for example, use pop-up windows as a way to deliver information—a seating chart when you're buying plane or concert tickets, for example.

In those situations, click the Information Bar. A dialog box appears that lets you manage pop-ups from this particular Web site.

Your options:

▶ **Temporarily Allow Pop-ups** lets this Web site's pop-ups through just for this browsing session. Next time, pop-ups will be blocked again.

▶ **Always Allow Pop-ups from This Site** does what it says.

▶ **Settings** lets you configure the Pop-up Blocker. From the menu that appears, select Turn Off Pop-up Blocker to turn the blocker off. Turn off Show Information Bar for Pop-ups if you don't even want the yellow Information bar to appear when a pop-up is blocked. Select More Settings, and a screen appears that lets you always allow or block pop-ups from specific sites (Figure 9-13).

This dialog box also lets you control how you're notified in the event of a pop-up: with a sound, with a note in the Information bar, or neither. You can also use the Filter Level pop-up menu to tone down Internet Explorer's aggressiveness in blocking pop-ups. The High level, for example, blocks *all* pop-ups, even ones that Internet Explorer determines to be necessary for the site to run properly.

Tip ──

If you've installed some other company's pop-up blocker, you can turn off IE's version by choosing Tools→Pop-up Blocker→Turn Off Pop-up Blocker.

Figure 9-13: This alert can get annoying after a while, so consider turning it off by clicking "Don't show this message again" and then clicking OK.

Windows Vista for Starters: The Missing Manual

WINDOWS MAIL

10

▶ Setting Up Windows Mail

▶ Sending Email

▶ Reading Email

▶ Junk Email

Email is a fast, cheap, convenient communication medium; these days, it's almost embarrassing to admit that you don't have an email address. To spare you that humiliation, Windows Vista includes Windows Mail (which, in previous versions of Windows, was called Outlook Express).

If you do have an email address, or several, Mail can help you manage your email accounts, messages, and contacts better than ever (Figure 10-1).

To use Mail, you need several technical pieces of information: an email address, an email server address, and an Internet address for sending email. Your Internet service provider or your network administrator is supposed to provide all of these ingredients.

Setting Up Windows Mail

The first time you use Mail (Start→All Programs→Windows Mail), you're prompted to plug in the Internet addresses and codes that tell the program where to find your email.

Figure 10-1: Meet Windows Mail—and the very first message you'll see here. It's a canned message from Microsoft containing information about Mail, its features, and how to use it.

__ Note _____

> If you used the Vista program called Easy Transfer Wizard to bring over your files and
> settings from an older PC, Windows Mail is probably already set up quite nicely. If that's
> the case, skip to the next section.

Click Next to step through the wizard's interview process, during which you'll provide the following information:

▶ **Display Name.** The name that should appear in the "From:" field of the email you send.

▶ **Email Address.** The email address you chose when you signed up for Internet services, such as *billg@microsoft.com.*

▶ **Mail Servers.** Enter the information your ISP provided about its mail servers: the type of server, the name of the incoming mail server, and the name of the outgoing mail server. Most of the time, the incoming server is a *POP3 server* and its name is connected to the name of your ISP. It might be *popmail.mindspring.com, for example, or mail.comcast.net.*

The outgoing mail server (the *SMTP server*) usually looks something like *mail.mindspring.com or smpt.comcast.net.*

▶ **Logon Name and Password.** Enter the name and password provided by your ISP. This is generally your full email address and the password you already created.

If you wish, turn on "Remember password," so that you won't have to enter it each time you want to collect mail. (Turn on Secure Password Authentication [SPA] only if instructed by your ISP or network administrator.)

Click Finish to close the wizard and open Windows Mail.

Sending Email

When you finally arrive at the main Mail screen, you've already got mail. The Inbox contains a welcome from Microsoft, but it wasn't actually transmitted over the Internet; it's a starter message just to tease you. Fortunately, all your future mail will come via the Internet.

To receive and send new mail, click the Send/Receive button on the toolbar.

___ Tip _____

> You can set up Mail to check your email accounts automatically according to a schedule. Just choose Tools→Options. On the General tab, you'll see the "Check for new messages every ___ minutes" checkbox, which you can change to your liking.

Now Mail retrieves new messages and sends any outgoing messages.

In the list on the right side of your screen, the names of new messages show up in bold type; folders containing new messages show up in bold type, too (in the Folders list at the left side of the screen). The bold number in parentheses after the word "Inbox" represents how many messages you haven't read yet. Figure 10-2 shows Mail after a few weeks of use.

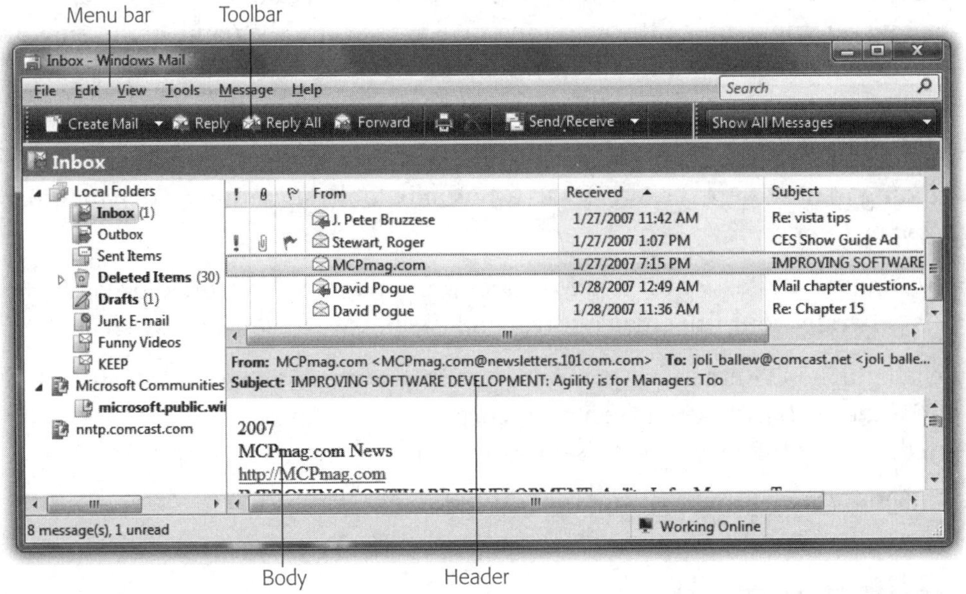

Figure 10-2: A message has two sections: the *header*, which holds information about the message, and the *body*, which contains the message itself. The menu bar and a toolbar harbor other useful features for composing and sending messages.

Mail folders in Windows Mail

At the left side of the screen, Windows Mail organizes your email into *folders*. To see what's in a folder, click it once:

▶ **Inbox** holds mail you've received.

▶ **Outbox** holds mail you've written but haven't sent yet.

▶ **Sent Items** holds copies of messages you've sent.

▶ **Deleted Items** holds mail you've deleted. It works a lot like the Recycle Bin, in that messages placed there don't actually disappear. Instead, they remain in the Deleted Items folder, awaiting rescue if you opt to retrieve them. To empty this folder, right-click it and then choose "Empty 'Deleted Items' Folder" from the shortcut menu (or simply choose Edit→Empty 'Deleted Items' Folder).

> **Tip**
>
> To make the folder empty itself every time you exit Mail, choose Tools→Options, click the Advanced tab, and then click the Maintenance button. From the Maintenance dialog box, turn on "Empty messages from the 'Deleted Items' folder on exit."

▶ **Drafts** holds messages you haven't finished—and don't want to send just yet.

▶ **Junk E-Mail** holds messages deemed as junk (spam) by Mail's Junk E-Mail Protection. (More about that later.)

You can also add to this list, creating folders for your own organizational pleasure— Family Mail, Work Mail, or whatever. See page 267.

Composing and sending messages

To send a message, click Create Mail on the toolbar. The New Message form opens (Figure 10-3).

> **Tip**
>
> You can also start writing a message by clicking Contacts in the toolbar. In the Contacts window that results, click the person's name, and then click E-Mail on the toolbar. A blank, outgoing piece of mail appears, already addressed to the person whose name you clicked.
>
> Come to think of it, it's faster to hit Ctrl+N.

Composing the message requires several steps:

1. **Type the email address of the recipient into the "To:" field.**

   If you want to send a message to more than one person, separate their addresses using semicolons, like this: *bob@snow.net; billg@microsoft.com; steve@apple.com.*

There's no need to type out all those complicated email addresses, either. As you begin typing the person's plain-English name, the program attempts to guess who you mean (if it's somebody in your Contacts list)—and fills in the email address automatically.

If it guesses the correct name, great; press Tab to move on to the next text box. If it guesses wrong, just keep typing. The program quickly retracts its suggestion and watches what you type next.

Tip

You can also click the tiny envelope icon next to the "To:" box to open your Contacts list; double-click a name to address your message.

As in most Windows dialog boxes, you can jump from blank to blank in this window (from the "To:" field to the "CC:" field, for example) by pressing the Tab key.

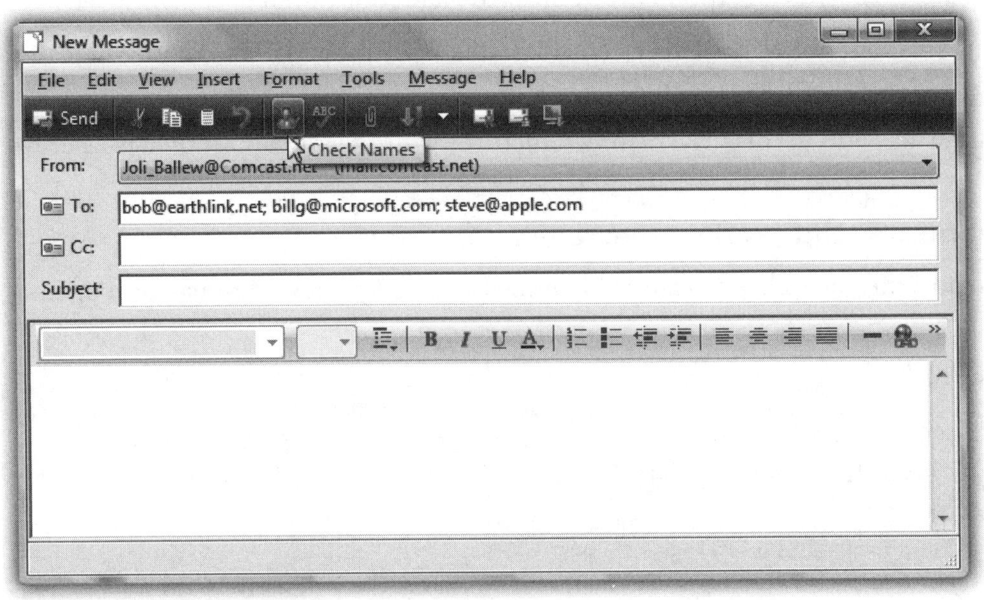

Figure 10-3: In the New Message window, type the name of the recipients, separated by semicolons, in the "To:" field. If Windows Mail doesn't automatically complete the name for you (by consulting your address book and recent recipients list), click Check Names.

2. **To send a copy of the message to other recipients, enter the additional email address(es) in the "CC:" field.**

CC stands for *carbon copy*. There's very little difference between putting all your addressees on the "To:" line (separated by semicolons) and putting them on the "CC:" line. The only difference is that using the "CC:" line implies, "I sent you a copy because I thought you'd want to know about this correspondence, but I'm not expecting you to reply."

Press Tab when you're finished.

3. **Type the topic of the message in the "Subject:" field.**

Some people get bombarded with email. That's why it's courteous to put some thought into the Subject line. (For example, use "Change in plans for next week" instead of "Hi.")

Press the Tab key to move your cursor into the message area.

4. **Choose a format (HTML or plain text), if you like.**

When it comes to formatting a message's body text, you have two choices: *plain text* or *HTML* (Hypertext Markup Language).

Plain text means that you can't format your text with bold type, color, specified font sizes, and so on. HTML, on the other hand, is the language used to create Web pages, and it lets you use formatting commands (such as font sizes, colors, and bold or italic text).

But there's a catch: HTML mail is much larger, and therefore slower to download, than plain-text messages, and some older e-mail programs don't display the formatting anyway. Plain text tends to feel more professional, never irritates anybody— and you're guaranteed that the recipient will see exactly what was sent.

To specify which format Windows Mail *proposes* for all new messages (plain text or HTML), choose Tools→Options. Click the Send tab. Next, in the section labeled Mail Sending Format, choose either the HTML or Plain Text button, and then click OK.

No matter which setting you specify there, however, you can always switch a *particular* message to the opposite format. Just choose Format→Rich Text (HTML), or Format→Plain Text, in the New Message window.

If you choose the HTML option, clicking in the message area activates the HTML toolbar, shown in Figure 10-4.

Just remember: less is more. If you go hog-wild formatting your email, the message may be difficult to read, especially if you apply stationery (a background).

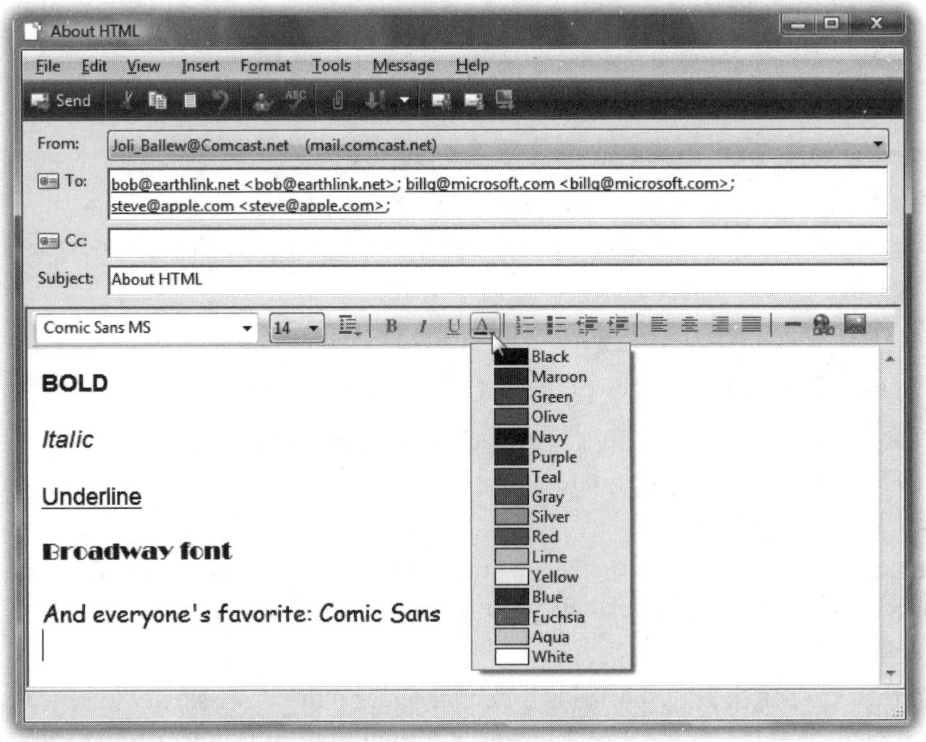

Figure 10-4: When you're composing an email using the HTML format, the New Message window gives you options for choosing fonts, formatting options like Bold, Italic, and Underline, and colors (from a handy color palette).

5. **Enter the message in the message box (the bottom half of the message window).**

    You can use all standard editing techniques, including Cut, Copy, and Paste, to rearrange the text as you write it.

6. Add a signature, if you wish.

Signatures are bits of text that get stamped at the bottom of outgoing email messages. They typically contain a name, a mailing address, or a Star Trek quote.

POWER USERS' CLINIC

The Mighty Morphing Interface

You don't have to be content with the factory-installed design of the Windows Mail screen; you can control which panes are visible, how big they are, and which columns show up in list views.

To change the size of a pane, drag its border to make it larger or smaller, as shown here. You can also hide or show the toolbar, folder list, status bar, search bar, or preview pane using the View→Layout command; in the dialog box, turn off the checkboxes for the window elements you could do without.

The View→Layout command also lets you control where the preview pane appears: under the message list, as usual, or to its right—a great arrangement if you have a very wide screen.

Mail lets you decide what columns are

displayed in the list pane. For example, if you don't particularly care about seeing the Flag column, you can hide it, leaving more space for the Subject and Received columns. To switch columns on or off, choose from the list in the View→Columns dialog box.

You can also *rearrange* the columns, which can be handy if you'd rather see the Subject column first instead of the sender, for example. Just drag the column's name *header* horizontally; release when the vertical dotted line is where you want the column to wind up. To make a column wider or narrower, drag the short black divider line between column names horizontally, much the way you'd resize a folder window list-view column.

To create a signature, choose Tools→Options, click the Signatures tab, and then click the New button. The easiest way to compose your signature is to type it into the Edit Signatures text box at the bottom of the window. (If you poke around long enough in this box, you'll realize that you can actually create multiple signatures—and even assign each one to a different outgoing email account.)

Once you've created a signature (or several), you can tack it onto your outgoing mail for all messages (by turning on "Add signatures to all outgoing messages" at the top of this box) or on a message-by-message basis (by choosing Insert→Signature in the New Message window).

7. **Click the Send button.**

Alternatively, press Alt+S, or choose File→Send Message. Your PC connects to the Internet and sends the message.

The Contacts list

Accumulating names in a Contacts list eliminates the need to enter complete email ad-

---

dresses whenever you want to send a message. Click the Contacts button on the toolbar; then, to begin adding names and email addresses, click New Contact.

Attaching files to messages

Sending little text messages is fine, but it's not much help when you want to send somebody a photograph, a sound recording, a Word or Excel document, and so on. Fortunately, attaching such files to email messages is one of the world's most popular email features.

To attach a file to a message, use either of two methods:

▶ **The long way.** Click the Attach button (the paper-clip icon) on the New Message dialog box toolbar. Alternatively, you could select Insert→File Attachment. When the Open dialog box appears, locate the file and select it. (In the resulting navigation window, Ctrl-click multiple files to attach them all at once.)

Now the name of the attached file appears in the message, in the Attach text box. When you send the message, the file tags along.

▶ **The short way.** If you can see the icon of the file you want to attach—in its folder window behind the Mail window, on the Desktop, or wherever—then attach it by *dragging* its icon directly into the message window. That's a handy technique when you're attaching many different files.

Reading Email

Just seeing a list of the *names* of new messages in Mail is like getting wrapped presents—the best part's yet to come. There are two ways to read a message: using the preview pane, and opening the message into its own window.

To preview a message, click its name in the list pane; the body of the message appears in the preview pane below. Don't forget that you can adjust the relative sizes of the list and preview panes by dragging the gray border between them up or down.

To open a message into a window of its own, double-click its name in the list pane. An open message has its own toolbar, along with Previous and Next message buttons (which look like upward- and downward-pointing arrows).

Once you've read a message, you can view the next one in the list either by pressing Ctrl +U (for the next *unread* message), or by clicking its name in the list pane. (If you're using preview mode, and haven't opened a message into its own window, you can also press the up or down arrow key to move from one message to the next.)

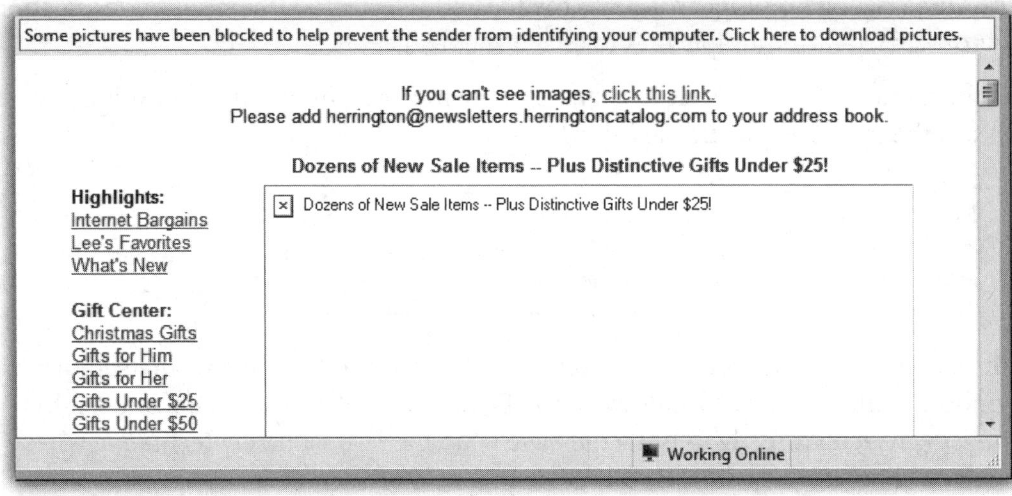

Figure 10-5: To view blocked images in a message, click the warning itself (top). Or, to make Mail quit blocking pictures altogether, choose Tools→Options→Security; next, turn off "Block images and other external content in HTML messages."

When Pictures are Part of the Message

Sending pictures in email is a globally popular activity—but Mail doesn't want you to see them.

Mail comes set up to block images, because these images sometimes serve as "bugs" that silently report back to the sender whether you received and opened the message. At that point, the spammers know that they've found a live, working email address—and, better yet, a sucker who opens mail from strangers. And presto, you're on their "safe senders" list, and the spam flood *really* begins.

You'll know if pictures were meant to appear in the body of a message; see the strip that appears at the top in Figure 10-5.

How to Process a Message

Once you've read a message and savored the feeling of awe brought on by the miracle of instantaneous electronic communication, you can handle the message in several ways.

Deleting messages

Sometimes it's junk mail, sometimes you're just done with it; either way, it's a snap to delete a message. Click the Delete button on the toolbar, press the Delete key. (You can also delete a batch of selected messages simultaneously.)

The messages don't actually disappear. Instead, they move to the Deleted Items folder. If you like, click this folder to view a list of the messages you've deleted. You can even rescue some simply by dragging them into another folder (even right back into the Inbox).

Mail doesn't truly vaporize messages in the Deleted Items folder until you "empty the trash." You can empty it in any of several ways:

▶ Right-click the Deleted Items folder. Choose "Empty 'Deleted Items' Folder" from the shortcut menu.

▶ Click a message, or a folder, within the Deleted Items Folder list and then click the Delete button on the toolbar (or press the Delete key). You're asked to confirm its permanent deletion.

▶ Set up Mail to delete messages automatically when you quit the program. To do so, choose Tools→Options→Advanced. Click the Maintenance button, and then turn on "Empty messages from the 'Deleted Items' folder on exit." Click OK.

Replying to Messages

To reply to a message, click the Reply button in the toolbar, or press Ctrl+R. Mail creates a new, outgoing email message, preaddressed to the sender's return address. (If the message was sent to you *and* a few other people, and you'd like to reply to all of them at once, click Reply All in the toolbar.)

To save additional time, Mail pastes the entire original message at the bottom of your reply (either indented, if it's HTML mail, or marked with the > brackets that serve as Internet quoting marks); that's to help your correspondent figure out what you're talking about.

Mail even tacks *Re:* ("regarding") onto the front of the subject line.

Your insertion point appears at the top of the message box. Now, begin typing your reply. You can also add recipients, remove recipients, edit the subject line or the message, and so on.

— **Tip** —————————————————————————————————
Use the Enter key to create blank lines within the bracketed original message in order to place your own text within it. Using this method, you can splice your own comments into the paragraphs of the original message, replying point by point. The brackets preceding each line of the original message help your correspondent keep straight what's yours and what's hers. Also, if you're using HTML formatting for the message, you can format what you've written in bold, italic, underlined, or even in another color for easier reading.

———————————————————————————————————————

Forwarding Messages

Instead of replying to the person who sent you a message, you may sometimes want to *forward* the message—pass it on—to a third person.

To do so, click Forward in the toolbar, choose Message→Forward, or press Ctrl+F. A new message opens, looking a lot like the one that appears when you reply. Once again, before forwarding the message, you have the option of editing the subject or the message. (For example, you may wish to precede the original message with a comment of your own, along the lines of: "Frank: I thought you'd be interested in this joke about Congress.")

All that remains is for you to specify who receives the forwarded message. Just address it as you would any outgoing piece of mail.

Printing Messages

Sometimes there's no substitute for a printout of an email message—an area where Mail shines. Click Print in the toolbar, choose File→Print, or press Ctrl+P. The standard Print dialog box pops up, so that you can specify how many copies you want, what range of pages, and so on. Make your selections, and then click Print.

Filing Messages

Mail lets you create new folders in the Folders list; by dragging messages from your Inbox onto one of these folder icons, you can file away your messages into appropriate cubbies. You might create one folder for important messages, another for order confirmations from shopping on the Web, still another for friends and family, and so on. In fact, you can even create folders *inside* these folders, a feature beloved by the hopelessly organized.

To create a new folder, see Figure 10-6.

___ Tip _____

To rename an existing folder, right-click it and choose Rename from the shortcut menu.
_____

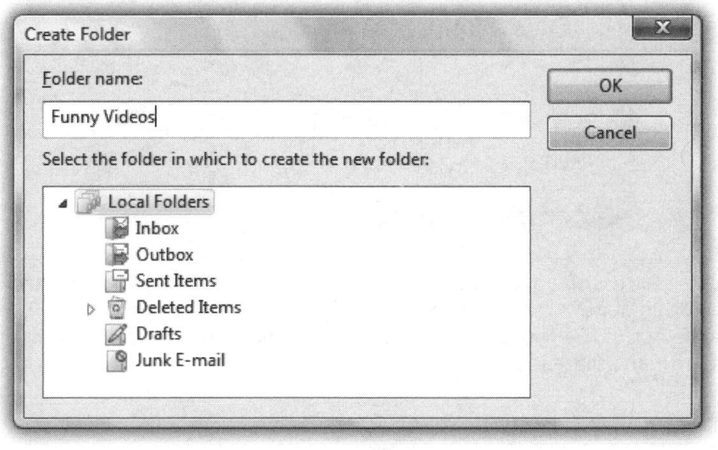

Figure 10-6: To create a new folder, choose File→Folder→New, or right-click the Local Folders icon (in the folder list), and choose New Folder from the shortcut menu. Either way, this window appears. Name the folder and then, by clicking, indicate which folder you want this one to appear in. Usually, you'll want to click Local Folders (that is, not inside any other folder).

To move a message into a folder, drag it out of the list pane and onto the folder icon. You can use any part of a message's "row" in the list as a handle. You can also drag messages en masse onto a folder after selecting them.

Opening Attachments

Just as you can attach files to a message, people can send files to you. You know when a message has an attachment because a paper-clip icon appears next to its name in the Inbox.

To free an attached file from its message, releasing it to the wilds of your hard drive, use one of the following methods:

▶ Click the attachment icon, select Save Attachments from the shortcut menu, and then specify the folder in which you want the file saved (Figure 10-7).

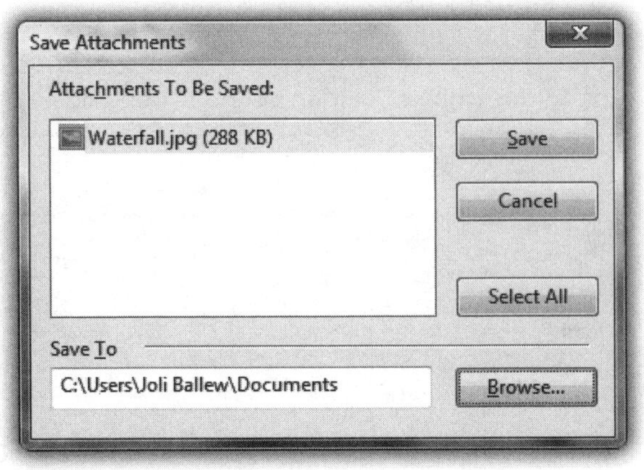

Figure 10-7: One way to rescue an attachment from an email message is to click the paper-clip icon and choose Save Attachments. You can also drag an attachment's icon onto your desktop. Either way, you take the file out of the Mail world and into your standard Windows world, where you can file it, trash it, open it, or manipulate it as you would any file.

▶ Click the attachment icon, and select the attachment to open. Choose the name of the attachment in order to open the file directly (in Word, Excel, or whatever).

▶ If you've double-clicked the message so it appears in its own window, drag the attachment icon out of the message window and onto any portion of your desktop.

▶ Again, if you've opened the message into its own window, you can double-click the attachment's icon in the message. Once again, you're asked whether you want to open the file or save it to the disk.

Junk Email

Windows Mail now offers Junk E-Mail Options, which automatically channel what it believes to be spam into the Junk E-Mail folder in the folder list. Its factory setting is Low, meaning that only the most obvious spam gets sent to the Junk E-Mail folder. You'll probably still get a ton of spam, but at least almost no legitimate mail will get mistakenly classified as spam.

You can configure the level of security you want in the Junk E-Mail Options window, shown in Figure 10-8.

Junk E-Mail Options

Junk E-Mail options offers five tabs. The Options tab is shown in Figure 10-8. The other tabs are:

Windows Mail doesn't always get it right, however. It labels some good messages as junk, and some spam messages as OK.

Selecting Messages

In order to process a group of messages simultaneously—to delete, move, or forward them, for example—you must first master the art of multiple message selection.

To select two or more messages that appear consecutively in your message list, click the first message, then Shift-click the last. Known as a *contiguous selection*, this trick selects every message between the two that you clicked.

To select two or more messages that *aren't* adjacent in the list (that is, skipping a few messages between selected ones), Ctrl-click the messages you want. Only the messages you click get selected—no filling in of messages in between, this time.

After using either technique, you can also *deselect* messages you've managed to highlight—just Ctrl-click them again.

Over time, though, it's supposed to get better—*if* you patiently help it along. Every time you see a good piece of email in the Junk E-Mail folder, click it, and then click Not Junk on the Toolbar.

Better yet, use the Message→Junk E-Mail submenu to choose one of these two options:

▶ **Add Sender to Safe Senders List.** No future mail from this person will be misfiled.

▶ **Add Sender's Domain to Safe Senders List.** No future mail from this person's entire company or ISP will be marked as spam.

The news isn't so good if you find a piece of spam in your Inbox; there's no This is Junk button on the toolbar, or even a similar command in the Message menu.

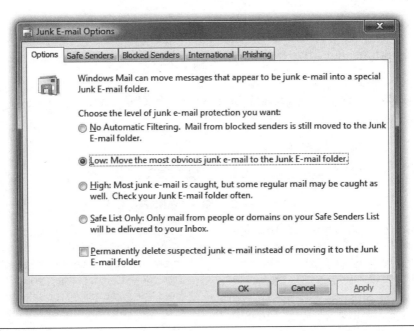

Figure 10-8: To visit this dialog box, choose Tools→Junk E-Mail Options. Choose No Automatic Filtering, Low, High, or Safe List Only. You can also opt to permanently delete suspected spam instead of moving it to the Junk E-Mail folder. No matter what setting you choose, though, always go through the Junk E-Mail folder every few days to make sure you haven't missed any important messages that were flagged as spam incorrectly.

You can use the Message→Junk E-Mail→Add Sender (or Sender's Domain) to Blocked Senders List, of course. But since spammers rarely use the same address or domain twice, it's probably faster just to hit the Delete key.

Canning Spam

Help! I'm awash in junk email! How do I get out of this mess?

Spam is a much-hated form of advertising that involves sending unsolicited emails to thousands of people. While there's no instant cure for spam, you can take certain steps to protect yourself from it.

1. Use one email account for online shopping, Web site and software registration, and newsgroup posting; use a second one for person-to-person email.

   Spammers have automated software robots that scour every public Internet message and Web page, automatically locating and recording email addresses they find. These are the primary sources of spam, so at least you're now restricting the junk mail to one secondary mail account.

2. Whenever you receive a piece of junk mail, choose Message→Junk E-Mail→Add Sender to Blocked Senders List. Windows Mail no longer accepts email from that sender.

3. When filling out forms or registering products online, look for checkboxes requesting permission for the company to send you email or share your email address with its "partners." Just say no.

4. When posting messages in any public area of the Web, insert the letters NOSPAM, SPAMISBAD, or something similar somewhere into your email address. Anyone replying to you via email must manually remove it from your email address, which, while a hassle, keeps your email address away from the spammer's robots. (They're getting smarter every day, though; a trickier insert may be required, along the lines of REMOVETOEMAIL or SPAMMERSARESCUM.)

5. Create *message rules* to filter out messages containing typical advertising words such as *casino, Rolex, herbal,* and so forth. (You'll find instructions in this chapter.)

6. Buy an antispam program like SpamAssassin.

Windows Vista for Starters: The Missing Manual

PART FOUR: BEYOND THE BASICS

PRINTING AND FAXING

Technologists got pretty excited about "the paperless office" in the 1980s, but the PC explosion had exactly the opposite effect. Thanks to the proliferation of inexpensive, high-quality PC printers, the world generates far more printouts than ever. Fortunately, there's not much to printing from Windows Vista.

Installing a Printer

A printer is a peripheral device—something outside of the PC—and as such, it won't work without a piece of *driver software* explaining the new hardware to Windows. In general, getting this driver installed is a simple process. It's described in more detail in Chapter 12; here are a few notes on the process to get you started.

USB Printers

If the technology gods are smiling, then installing the driver for a typical inkjet USB printer works just as described in Chapter 12: you connect the printer, turn it on, and marvel as Vista autodetects it and autoinstalls the driver, thanks to its secret cache of hundreds of printer drivers (Figure 11-1).

If you have a really old printer, its drivers might not be Vista-compatible. Check the manufacturer's Web site, such as *www.epson.com* or *www.lexmark.com,* or a central driver repository like *www.windrivers.com, to see if there's anything newer.*

Network Printers

If you work in an office where people on the network share a single printer (usually a laser printer), the printer usually isn't connected directly to your computer. Instead, it's elsewhere on the network; your PC's Ethernet cable or wireless antenna connects you to it indirectly.

In general, there's very little involved in ensuring that your PC "sees" this printer. Its icon simply shows up in the Start→Control Panel→Printer folder. (If you don't see it, click "Add a printer" in the toolbar. On the wizard's second screen, you're offered the chance to "Add a network, wireless or Bluetooth printer." That's the one you want.)

— **Note** ———
As you've probably guessed, that's also how you install a wireless or Bluetooth printer.
———

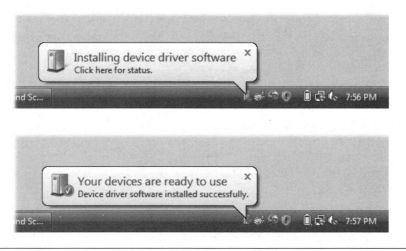

Figure 11-1: You got lucky. Windows dug into its own bag of included drivers and installed the correct one. Let the printing begin.

The Printer Icon

If your driver-installation efforts are ultimately successful, you're rewarded by the appearance of an icon that represents your printer.

Figure 11-2: At first, the toolbar in the Printers window offers few commands. But when you click a particular printer icon, many more useful options appear, as shown here. Many of them duplicate the options that appear when you right-click a printer icon.

This icon appears in the *Printers* window—an important window that you'll be reading about over and over again in this chapter. Exactly how you arrive there depends on how you've set up Vista:

▶ If you've set up your Start menu to display a submenu for the Control Panel (page 152), just choose Start→Control Panel→Printers.

▶ Choose Start→Control Panel, then click Printer (in the Hardware and Sound category).

▶ If you view your Control Panel in *Classic* view (page 152), choose Start→Control Panel, and then open the Printers icon.

▶ You can also make the Printers window show up in your Start menu, which saves you some burrowing if you use this feature a lot. To put it there, right-click the Start button. From the shortcut menu, choose Properties. On the Start Menu tab, click Customize. Scroll down in the list of checkboxes, and finally turn on the Printers checkbox. Click OK twice.

In any case, the Printers window now contains an icon bearing the name you gave your printer during installation (Figure 11-2). This printer icon comes in handy in several different situations, as the rest of this chapter clarifies.

Printing

Fortunately, the setup described so far in this chapter is a one-time-only task. Once it's over, printing is little more than a one-click operation.

Printing from Programs

After you've created a document you want to see on paper, choose File→Print (or press Ctrl+P). The Print dialog box appears, as shown at top in Figure 11-3.

This box, too, changes depending on the program you're using—the Print dialog box in Microsoft Word looks a lot more intimidating than the WordPad version—but here are the basics:

▶ **Name.** If your PC is connected to several printers, or if you've created differently configured icons for the same printer, choose the one you want from this list of printers.

▶ **Page range** controls which pages of the document you want to print. If you want to print only some of the pages, click the Pages option and type in the page numbers you want (with a hyphen, like *3-6* to print pages 3 through 6).

___ Tip _____

> You can also type in individual page numbers with commas, like *2, 4, 9* to print only those three pages—or even add hyphens to the mix, like this: *1-3, 5-6, 13-18*.

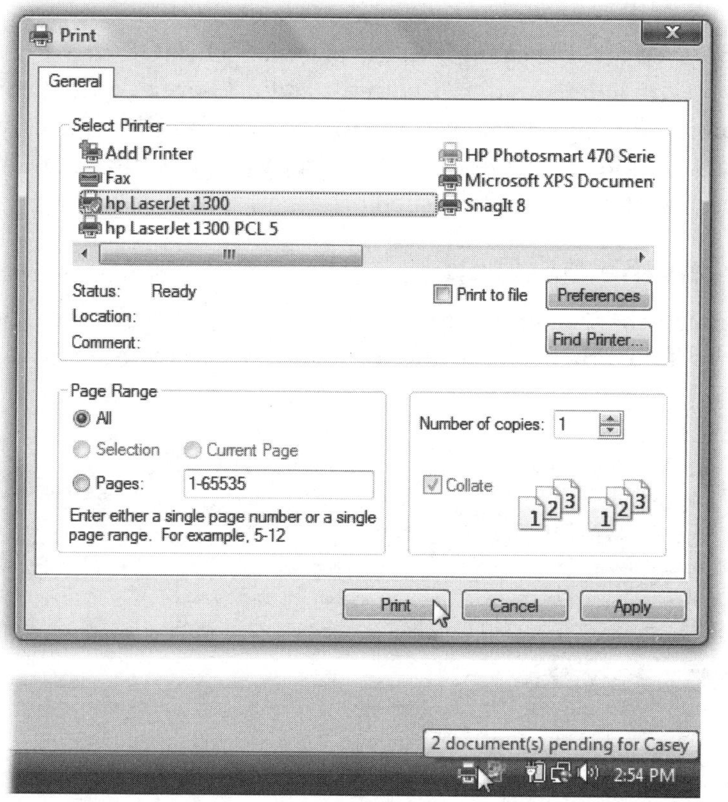

_____

Figure 11-3: Top: The options in the Print dialog box are different for each printer model and each application, so your Print dialog box may look slightly different. For example, here are the Print dialog boxes from Microsoft Word and WordPad. Most of the time, the factory settings shown here are what you want (one copy, print all pages). Just click OK or Print (or press Enter) to close this dialog box and send the document to the printer.

Bottom: During printing, the tiny icon of a printer appears in your notification area. Pointing to it without clicking produces a pop-up tooltip, like this one, that reveals the background printing activity.

Click Current Page to print only the page that contains the blinking insertion point. Click Selection to print only the text you selected (highlighted) before opening the Print dialog box. (If this option button is dimmed, it's because you didn't highlight any text—or because you're using a program that doesn't offer this feature.)

▶ **Number of copies.** To print out several copies of the same thing, use this box to specify the exact amount. You'll get several copies of page 1, then several copies of page 2, and so on—*unless* you also turn on the Collate checkbox, which produces complete sets of pages, in order.

When you've finished making changes to the print job, click OK or Print, or press Enter. Thanks to the miracle of *background printing*, you don't have to wait for the document to emerge from the printer before returning to work on your PC. In fact, you can even exit the application while the printout is still under way, generally speaking. (Just don't put your machine to sleep until it's finished printing.)

Printing from the Desktop

You don't necessarily have to print a document while it's open in front of you. You can, if you wish, print it directly from the desktop or an Explorer window in any of three ways:

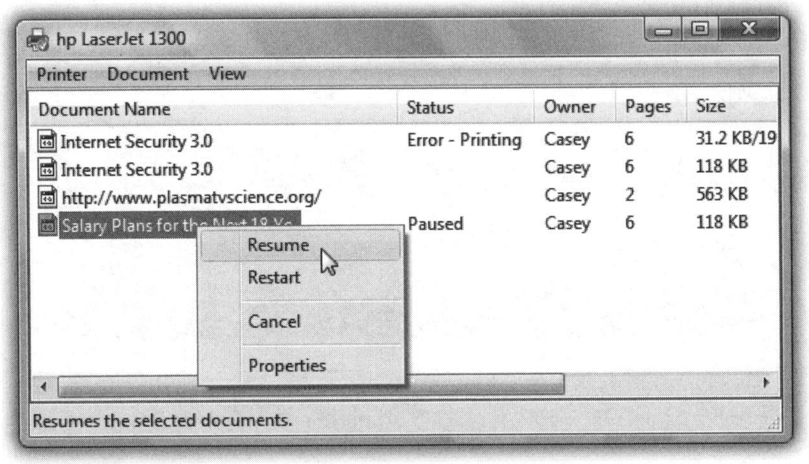

Figure 11-4: The first document, called "Internet Security 3.0," has begun printing; the bottom one, you've put on hold. Several other documents are waiting. By right-clicking documents in this list, you can pause or cancel any document in the queue—or all of them at once.

- Right-click the document icon, and then choose Print from the shortcut menu. Windows launches the program that created it—Word or Excel, for example. The Print dialog box appears, letting you specify how many copies you want and which pages you want printed. When you click Print, your printer springs into action, and then the program quits automatically (if it wasn't open when you started the process).

- If you've opened the Printers window, you can drag a document's icon directly onto a printer icon.

- If you've opened the printer's own print queue window (Figure 11-4) by double-clicking the Printers icon in your Printers window, you can drag any document icon directly into the list of waiting printouts. Its name joins the others on the list.

These last two methods bypass the Print dialog box, and therefore give you no way to specify which pages you want to print, nor how many copies. You just get one copy of the entire document.

Controlling Printouts

Between the moment when you click OK in the Print dialog box and the arrival of the first page in the printer's tray, there's a delay. Usually, it's very brief, but when you're printing a complex document with lots of graphics, the delay can be considerable.

Fortunately, the waiting doesn't necessarily make you less productive, since you can return to work on your PC, or even quit the application and go watch TV. An invisible program called the *print spooler* supervises this background printing process. The spooler collects the document that's being sent to the printer, along with all the codes the printer expects to receive, and then sends this information, little by little, to the printer.

___ Note _____

> The spooler program creates huge temporary printer files, so a hard drive that's nearly full can wreak havoc with background printing.

_____

To see the list of documents waiting to be printed—the ones that have been stored by the spooler—open the Printers window, and then double-click your printer's icon to open its window.

The printer's window lists the documents currently printing and waiting; this list is called the *print queue* (or just the *queue*), as shown in Figure 11-4. (Documents in the list print in top-to-bottom order.)

You can manipulate documents in a print queue in any of the following ways during printing:

▶ **Put one on hold.** To pause a document (put it on hold), right-click its name, and then choose Pause from the shortcut menu. When you're ready to let the paused document continue to print, right-click its listing and choose Resume (Figure 11-4).

▶ **Put them all on hold.** To pause the printer, choose Printer→Pause Printing from the window's menu bar. You might do this when, for example, you need to change the paper in the printer's tray. (Choose Printer→Pause Printing again when you want the printing to pick up from where it left off.)

▶ **Add another one.** As noted earlier, you can drag any document icon directly *from its disk or folder window* into the printer queue. Its name joins the list of printouts-in-waiting.

▶ **Cancel one.** To cancel a printout, click its name and then press the Delete key. If you click Yes in the confirmation box, the document disappears from the queue; it'll never print out.

▶ **Cancel all of them.** To cancel the printing of all the documents in the queue, choose Printer→Cancel All Documents.

Sharing a Printer

If you have more than one PC connected to a network, as described in Chapter 16, they all can use the same printer. In the old days, this convenience was restricted to expensive network printers like laser printers. But in Windows Vista, you can share even the cheapest little inkjet that's connected to the USB port of one computer.

To begin, sit down at the computer to which the printer is attached. Choose Start→Network; in the Network window, click "Network and Sharing Center" on the toolbar. Proceed as described in Figure 11-5.

Once you've *shared* the printer, other people on the network can add it to their own Printers windows. Before you begin, though, be aware that nobody can hook into the

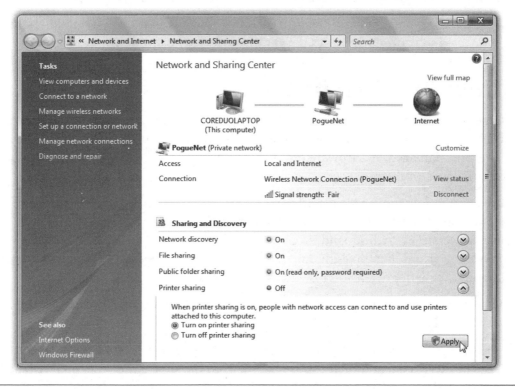

Figure 11-5: How to turn on printer sharing: Expand the V-shaped arrow where it says "Printer sharing," and click "Turn on printer sharing." Click Apply. Authenticate yourself (page 127).

shared-printer PC without an *account* on that PC (Chapter 15)—one with a password. Printer sharing doesn't work with blank-password accounts.

1. **Choose Start→Control Panel. Click "Hardware and Sound," then "Printer," then "Add a printer."**

   The "Choose a local or network printer" window appears.

2. **Click "Add a network, wireless or Bluetooth printer."**

   After a pause while your PC searches, you see a window populated by all the printers that are available to the other PC.

3. **Click the icon of the printer you want to use, and then click Next. On the "which driver" page, click Next again. Finally, type a name for the printer (as you want it to appear on your PC), and then click Next. On the final screen, click Finish.**

   The shared printer appears in *your* Printers window, even though it's not directly connected to your machine. It's now available for any printing you want to do.

Printer Troubleshooting

If you're having a problem printing, the first diagnosis you must make is whether the problem is related to *software* or *hardware*. A software problem means the driver files have become damaged. A hardware problem means there's something wrong with the printer, the port, or the cable.

Test the printer by sending it a generic text file from the command line. To perform such a test, locate a text file or create one in Notepad. Then choose Start→All Programs→Accessories→Command Prompt; send the file to the printer by typing *copy filename.txt prn* and then pressing Enter. (Of course, remember to type the file's actual name and three-letter extension instead of *filename.txt.*)

If the file prints, the printing problem is software-related. If it doesn't work, the problem is hardware-related.

For software problems, reinstall the printer driver. Open the Printers window, right-click the printer's icon, and then choose Delete from the shortcut menu. Then reinstall the printer as described at the beginning of this chapter.

If the problem seems to be hardware-related, try these steps in sequence:

- ▶ Check the lights or the LED panel readout on the printer. If you see anything besides the normal "Ready" indicator, check the printer's manual to diagnose the problem.

- ▶ Turn the printer off and on to clear any memory problems.

- ▶ Check the printer's manual to learn how to print a test page.

- ▶ Check the cable to make sure both ends are firmly and securely plugged into the correct ports.

FREQUENTLY ASKED QUESTION

Microsoft XPS = Adobe PDF

What, exactly, is Microsoft XPS? I see an icon for it in my Print dialog box.

Well, you know how Microsoft always comes up with its own version of anything popular? PalmPilot, iPod, Web browser, whatever?

Its latest target is the PDF document, the brainchild of Adobe.

A PDF document, of course, is a file that opens up on any kind of computer—Mac, Windows, Unix, anything—looking exactly the way it did when it was created, complete with fonts, graphics, and other layout niceties. The recipient can't generally make changes to it, but can search it, copy text from it, print it, and so on. It's made life a lot easier for millions of people because it's easy, free, and automatic.

And now Microsoft wants a piece o' dat. Its new Microsoft XPS document format is pretty much the same idea as PDF, only it's Microsoft's instead of Adobe's.

To turn any Windows document into an XPS document, just choose File→Print. In the Print dialog box, choose Microsoft XPS Document Writer as the "printer," and then click Print. You're asked to name it and save it.

The result, when double-clicked, opens up in Internet Explorer. (Yes, Internet Explorer is the new Acrobat Reader.) You might not even notice the two tiny toolbars that appear above and below the main browser window, but they offer the usual PDF-type options: save a copy, find a phrase, jump to a page, zoom in or out, switch to double-page view, and so on.

Microsoft plans to release XPS readers for other versions of Windows—and, eventually, other kinds of computers. Even so, Microsoft has a long battle ahead if it hopes to make the XPS format as commonplace as Acrobat.

But then again, long battles have never fazed it before.

▶ Test the cable. Use another cable, or take your cable to another computer/printer combination.

Another way to check all of these conditions is to use the built-in Windows *troubleshooter*—a wizard specifically designed to help you solve printing problems. To run, choose Start→Help and Support. Type *printing troubleshooting* into the search box and press Enter. Click "Troubleshoot printer problems" to open that article.

If none of these steps leads to an accurate diagnosis, you may have a problem with the port, which is more complicated. Or even worse, the problem may originate from your PC's motherboard (main circuit board), or the printer's. In that case, your computer (or printer) needs professional attention.

Fonts

Some extremely sophisticated programming has gone into the typefaces that are listed in the Fonts dialog boxes of your word processor and other programs. They use *OpenType* and *TrueType* technology, meaning that no matter what point size you select for these fonts, they look smooth and professional—both on the screen and when you print.

Managing Your Fonts

Windows comes with several dozen great-looking fonts: Arial, Book Antiqua, Times New Roman, and so on. But the world is filled with additional fonts. You may find them on Web sites or in the catalogs of commercial typeface companies. Sometimes you'll find new fonts on your system after installing a new program, courtesy of its installer.

To review the files that represent your typefaces, open the Fonts icon in the Control Panel. As Figure 11-6 illustrates, it's easy and enlightening to explore this folder.

To remove a font from your system, drag its file icon out of this window, right-click it and then choose Delete from the shortcut menu, or highlight it and then choose File→Delete. To install a new font, drag its file icon into this window (or choose File→Install New Font, and then navigate to, and select, the font files you want to install).

Either way, you'll see the changes immediately reflected in your programs' Font dialog boxes.

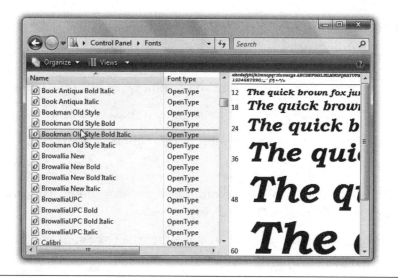

Figure 11-6: All of your fonts sit in the Fonts folder. You'll frequently find an independent font file for each style of a font: bold, italic, bold italic, and so on. Click a font's name to see how it looks at various sizes. Double-click a font's icon to open that preview into a window of its own.

Faxing

One of Vista's most spectacular features is its ability to turn your PC's built-in fax modem into a fax machine. This feature works like a charm, saves all kinds of money on paper and fax cartridges, and may even spare you the expense of buying a physical fax machine.

Faxing in Windows Vista is a much more official feature than it was in Windows XP, where it wasn't even installed automatically. Now there's a new program just dedicated to faxing: Windows Fax and Scan.

Sending a fax is even easier on a PC than on a real fax machine; you just use the regular File→Print command, exactly as though you're making a printout of the onscreen document. When faxes come *in,* you can opt to have them printed automatically, or you can simply read them on the screen.

— Note ——

The Fax and Scan program is available only in the Business, Enterprise, and Ultimate editions of Windows Vista.

Sending a Fax from Any Program

The one big limitation of PC-based faxing is that you can only transmit documents that are, in fact, *on the computer*. That pretty much rules out faxing notes scribbled on a legal pad, clippings from *People* magazine, and so on (unless you scan them first).

If you're still undaunted, the procedure for sending a fax is very easy.

1. **Open up whatever document you want to fax. Choose File→Print.**

   The Print dialog box appears.

2. **Click the Fax icon (or choose Fax from the Name drop-down list, as shown in Figure 11-7), and then click OK or Print.**

   The very first time you try faxing, you encounter the Fax Setup Wizard. It first asks you to type a name for your fax modem.

   Next, it wants you to specify what happens when someone sends a fax to *you* (that is, when the phone line that your PC is connected to "rings"). Click Automatically if you want Windows to answer incoming calls after five rings, assuming that if you haven't picked up by that time, the incoming call is probably a fax.

   If you choose "Notify me," each incoming call triggers an onscreen message, asking you whether you want the PC to answer as a fax machine. And if you choose "I'll choose later," you can postpone the decision and get on with sending your first fax.

Note _____

At this point, the Windows Firewall, rather stupidly, may interrupt to ask if it's OK for Windows Fax and Scan to run. Click Unblock.

   Finally, you arrive in a new Vista program called Windows Fax and Scan. It looks a heck of a lot like an email program, complete with an Inbox, a Sent Items folder, and so on. In fact, a New Fax window (like a New Message window) awaits you (Figure 11-7, middle).

3. **Type the recipient's fax number into the "To:" box.**

   Or click the tiny envelope next to "To:" to open up your Windows Contacts list. Double-click the name of the fax-equipped buddy you want.

4. **If you want a cover page, choose a cover-page design from the Cover Page pop-up menu.**

If you do, then a new text box opens up, where you can type a little note, which also appears on the cover page.

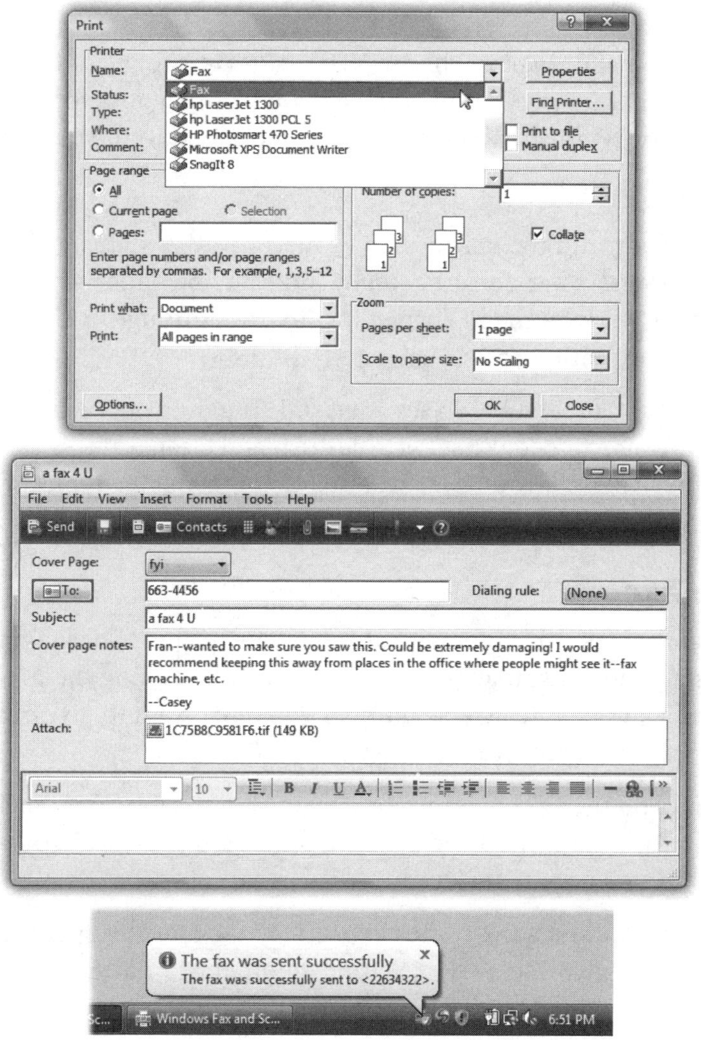

Figure 11-7: Top: To send a fax, pretend that you're printing the document—but choose Fax as the printer. Middle: Address and send the fax. Bottom: Good news! This old-fashioned technology actually worked.

> You can ignore the main message box at the bottom of the window for now. It's intended for creating faxes from thin air, as described below, rather than faxes that began life as documents on your PC.

At this point, you may want to choose View→Preview (or click the tiny Preview icon on the toolbar) to give it a final inspection before it goes forth over the airwaves. When you're finished looking it over, click Send in the toolbar.

5. **Click Send.**

   Your modem dials, and the fax goes on its merry way. A status dialog box appears (although its progress bar doesn't actually indicate how much time remains). You can go do other work on the PC; when the fax goes through, a cheerful message appears in your notification area (Figure 11-7, bottom).

Your recipient is in for a real treat. Faxes you send straight from your PC's brain emerge at the receiving fax machine looking twice as crisp and clean as faxes sent from a standalone fax machine. After all, you never scanned them through a typical fax machine's crude scanner on your end.

Receiving Faxes

There are several reasons why you may *not* want your PC to receive faxes. Maybe you already have a standalone fax machine that you use for receiving them. Maybe your house only has one phone line, whose number you don't want to give out to people who might blast your ear with fax tones.

But receiving faxes on the PC has a number of advantages, too. You don't pay a cent for paper or ink cartridges, and you have a handy, organized software program that helps you track every fax you've ever received.

Exactly what happens when a fax comes in is up to you. Start by opening Windows Fax and Scan; then choose Tools→Fax Settings. Authenticate yourself (page 127), and proceed as shown in Figure 11-8.

You'll see that you have two options for receiving faxes:

▶ **Manual.** This option is an almost-perfect solution if your PC and your telephone share the same phone line—that is, if you use the line mostly for talking, but occasionally receive a fax. From now on, every time the phone rings, a balloon in your notification area announces: "Incoming call from [the phone number]. Click here to answer this call as a fax call." (See Figure 11-8, middle.)

When you do so, your PC answers the phone and begins to receive the fax. To see it, open Fax and Scan.

▶ **Answer automatically.** Use this option if your PC has a phone line all to itself. In this case, incoming faxes produce a telephone-ringing sound, but there's otherwise no activity on your screen until the fax has been safely received. Once again, received faxes secrete themselves away in your Fax Console program.

While you're setting things up in the Fax Settings dialog box, don't miss the "More options" button. It's the gateway to two useful features:

▶ **Print a copy to.** If you like, Windows can print out each incoming fax, using the printer you specify here. Of course, doing so defeats the environmental and cost advantages of viewing your faxes onscreen, but at least you've got something you can hold in your hand.

▶ **Save a copy to.** Ordinarily, incoming faxes are transferred to your Fax and Scan program. If you turn on this option, however, you can direct Windows to place a *duplicate* copy of each one—stored as a graphics file—in a folder of your choice. (Either way, it's handy to know that these are standard TIFF graphics files that you can email to somebody else—or even edit.)

To look at the faxes you've received, open Fax and Scan. Click the Inbox to see a list of faxes that have come in—and then double-click one to open it up (Figure 11-8, bottom).

___ Tip _____

> Another great way to capitalize on the power of your PC for fax purposes is to sign up for J2 or eFax (*www.j2.com* and *www.efax.com*). These services issue you your own personal fax number. And here's the twist—all faxes sent to that number arrive at your PC as email attachments.
>
> The brilliance of the system, of course, is that you don't need another phone line for this, and you can get these faxes anywhere in the world, even on the road. And here's the best part: as of this writing, both of these services are absolutely free. (You might consider reserving a separate email address just for your J2 or eFax account, however, since waves of junk mail are part of the "free" bargain.)

_____

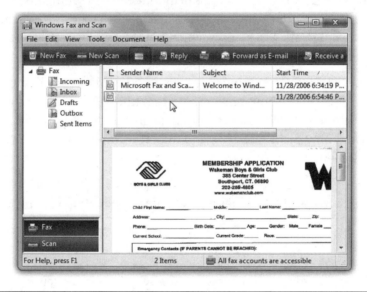

Figure 11-8: Top left: Click the General tab, then turn on "Allow device to receive fax calls." If you choose "Automatically answer," you can also specify how many rings go by before the PC answers; you don't want it answering regular incoming voice calls before you've had a chance to pick up.

Top right: Uh-oh! You're getting a call! Click the balloon itself if you think it's a fax. Windows Fax and Scan takes over and begins to download the fax. This window is cleverly known as the Fax Status Monitor. Bottom: The incoming fax winds up in your Inbox, just as though it's a particularly old-fashioned email message.

EXPANDING YOUR HARDWARE

12

- ▶ External Gadgets
- ▶ Installing Cards in Expansion Slots
- ▶ Troubleshooting Newly Installed Gear
- ▶ Driver Signing
- ▶ The Device Manager

A PC contains several pounds of wires, slots, cards, and chips—enough hardware to open a TrueValue store. Fortunately, you don't have to worry about making all of your PC's preinstalled components work together. In theory, at least, the PC maker did that part for you. (Unless you built the machine yourself, that is. In that case, best of luck.)

But adding *new* gear to your computer is another story. For the power user, hard drives, flash drives, cameras, printers, scanners, network cards, video cards, keyboards, monitors, game controllers, palmtop cradles, and other accessories all make life worth living. When you introduce a new piece of equipment to the PC, you must hook it up and install its *driver*, the software that lets a new gadget talk to the rest of the PC.

The driver issue is a chronic, nagging worry for the average Windows fan, however. Drivers conflict; drivers are missing; drivers go bad; drivers go out of date.

Fortunately, in Vista, Microsoft continues to hammer away at the driver problem. Vista comes with thousands upon thousands of drivers for common products already built in, and Microsoft deposits dozens more on your hard drive, behind the scenes, with every Windows Update (page 334). Chances are good that you'll live a long and happy life with Windows Vista without ever having to lose a Saturday manually configuring new gizmos you buy for it, as your forefathers did.

This chapter guides you through installing accessory gadgets and their drivers—and counsels you on what to do when the built-in, auto-recognizing drivers don't do the trick.

External Gadgets

Over the years, various engineering organizations have devised an almost silly number of different connectors for printers, scanners, and other *peripherals* (Figure 12-1 shows a typical assortment). The back panel—or front, or even side panel—of your PC may include any of these connector varieties.

USB Jacks

Man, you gotta love USB (Universal Serial Bus). The more of these jacks your PC has, the better.

The USB jack itself is a compact, thin, rectangular connector that's easy to plug and unplug. It often provides power to the gadget, saving you one more cord and one more bit of clutter. And it's hot-pluggable, so you don't have to turn off the gadget (or the PC) before connecting or disconnecting it.

___ Tip _____

> Be careful, though, not to yank a USB flash drive or hard drive out of the PC when it might be in the middle of copying files.

USB accommodates a huge variety of gadgets: USB scanners, mice, phones, keyboards, printers, palmtop cradles, digital cameras, camcorders, hard drives, and so on.

Most new PCs come with at least two USB ports, often on the front and back panels.

___ Note _____

> Today's USB gadgets and PCs offer *USB 2* jacks—a faster, enhanced form of USB. You can still plug the older, slower USB 1.1 gadgets into USB 2 jacks, and vice versa—but you'll get the older, slower speed.

Other Jacks

At one time, the backs of PC were pockmarked with all manner of crazy jacks: serial ports, PS/2 ports, SCSI ports, parallel ports, keyboard ports. Today, all of these connec-

---

UP TO SPEED

Of Hubs and Power

If your PC doesn't have enough built-in USB jacks to handle all your USB devices, you can also attach a USB *hub* (with, for example, four or eight additional USB ports), in order to attach multiple USB devices simultaneously.

Whether the jacks are built-in or on a hub, though, you have to be aware of whether or not they're *powered* or *unpowered* jacks.

Unpowered ones just transmit communication signals with the USB gadget. These kinds of USB gadgets work fine with

unpowered jacks: mice, keyboards, flash drives, and anything with its own power cord (like printers).

Powered USB jacks also supply current to whatever's plugged in. You need that for scanners, Webcams, hard drives, and other gadgets that don't have their own power cords but transmit lots of data.

The bottom line? If a gadget isn't working, it may be because it requires a powered jack and you've given it an unpowered one.

---

tors are rapidly disappearing, thanks to the all-powerful superiority of the USB jack.

Here's what else you may find on the modern PC, though:

▶ **FireWire port.** Not all PCs come with this special, rectangle-with-one-V-shaped-end jack, but it's a winner nevertheless. (Various companies may also call it IEEE 1394 or i.Link.) It's a hot-pluggable, extremely high-speed connector that's ideal for digital camcorders (for video editing) and external hard drives.

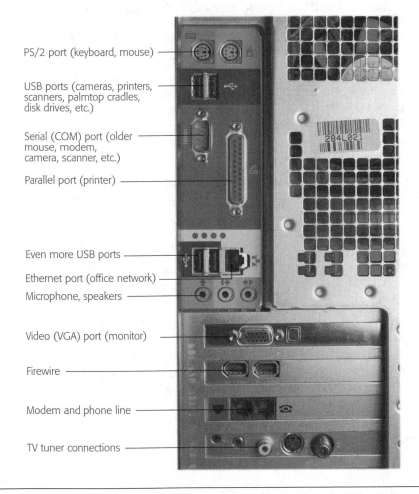

Figure 12-1: The back panel of a typical PC. Not every computer has every kind of jack, and the standard assortment is evolving. But these days, you can generally count on a basic collection like the one shown here.

▶ **Bluetooth adapters.** Bluetooth is a fascinating short-range wireless technology. Don't think of it as a networking scheme—it's intended for the elimination of *cable clutter*. Once you've equipped your printer, PC, and Palm organizer with Bluetooth adapters, your computer can print to the printer, or HotSync with your Palm, from up to 30 feet away.

▶ **PC card or ExpressCard slot.** These slots are found primarily on laptops. They accommodate miniature expansion cards, which look like metal Visa cards. Each card adds a useful feature to your laptop: an Ethernet port, a cellular high-speed modem, a WiFi networking antenna, and so on.

Tip

Hundreds of PC cards are available, for thousands of laptop models. The industry is now pushing a narrower type of card, however, called ExpressCard, which fits into a narrower kind of slot. (Actually, there are *two* ExpressCard types—one narrow, and one *really* narrow.) Just make sure, before you buy any card, that it fits the kind of slot your laptop has.

▶ **Video (VGA) or DVI port.** The VGA connector is a narrow female port with fifteen holes along three rows. Most monitors are designed to plug into either a VGA jack or the more modern DVI (digital visual interface) jack, which has a total of 28 pins and is designed for modern digital LCD screens.

▶ **Game port.** This connector, which is usually part of a sound card, is a wide female port that accepts joysticks and steering wheels.

Connecting New Gadgets

In books, magazines, and online chatter about Windows, you'll frequently hear people talk about *installing* a new component. In many cases, they aren't talking about physically hooking it up to the PC—they're talking about installing its driver software.

The really good news is that Vista comes equipped with thousands of drivers for gadgets, especially USB gadgets. When you plug the thing into the PC for the first time, Vista autodetects its presence, digs into its trunk for the driver, and installs it automatically. Only a flurry of balloons in the notification area lets you know what's going on (Figure 12-2).

If Windows can't find the driver, a dialog box appears, suggesting that you insert whatever software-installation disc came with the gadget.

And now, the fine print:

▶ Usually the process shown in Figure 12-2 is all it takes—that is, you start by plugging the device in. Sometimes, though, you're supposed to install the driver before connecting the gizmo. (Check the manual.)

▶ Usually, the device should be turned on before you plug it in. Again, though, check the manual, because some of them are supposed to be switched on during the installation.

In either case, your gear is now completely installed—both its hardware and its software—and ready to use.

Figure 12-2: Installing a USB gadget is usually no more involved than plugging it into the PC. Vista takes it from there. All you have to do is wait for the "successfully installed message"—and all of this is a one-time ritual for a given device.

Installing Cards in Expansion Slots

Modems and adapter cards for video, TV, sound, network cabling, disk drives, and tape drives generally take the form of circuit boards, or *cards*, that you install inside your PC's case. These slots are connected to your PC's *bus,* an electrical conduit that connects all the components of the machine to the brains of the outfit: the processor and memory.

The two common (and mutually incompatible) kinds of slots are called *ISA* and *PCI*. Knowing the difference isn't especially important. What *is* important is knowing what type of slots your computer has free, so you can purchase the correct type of expansion card.

___ Note: _____
> There's also a third type of slot in many of today's computers, called AGP (Accelerated Graphics Port). This slot is almost always occupied by a graphics card.
_____

Installing a card usually involves removing a narrow plate (the *slot cover*) from the back panel of your PC, which allows the card's connector to peek through to the outside world. After unplugging the PC and touching something metal to discharge static, unwrap the card, and then carefully push it into its slot until it's fully seated.

___ Note _____
> Depending on the type of card, you may have to insert one end first, and then press the other end down with considerable force to get it into the slot. A friendly suggestion, however: don't press so hard that you flex and crack the motherboard.
_____

Troubleshooting Newly Installed Gear

If, when you connect a new component, Windows doesn't display a "successfully installed" message like the one at the bottom of Figure 12-2, it probably can't "see" your new device.

▶ If you've installed an internal card, make sure that it's seated in the slot firmly (after shutting down your computer, of course).

▶ If you attached something external, make sure that it's turned on, has power (if it came with a power cord), and is correctly connected to the PC.

In either case, before panicking, try restarting the PC. If you still have no luck, try the Add New Hardware Wizard described in the box on page 305. (And if even *that* doesn't work, call the manufacturer.)

If your new gadget didn't come with a disk (or maybe just a disk with drivers, but no installer), then hooking it up may produce a "Found New Hardware" balloon in the notification area, but no message about happy success. In that case, click the balloon to make the New Hardware Wizard appear. Proceed as shown in Figure 12-3.

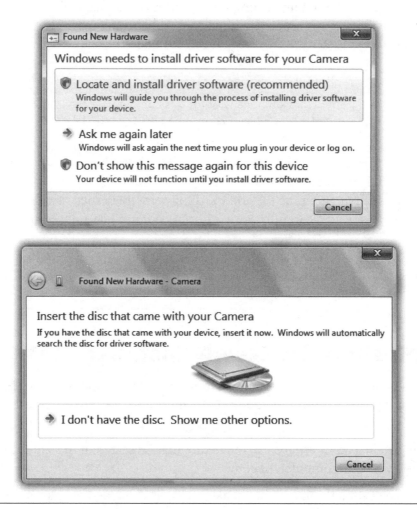

Figure 12-3: Top: If you have the drivers on a CD from the manufacturer, select the first option, "Locate and install driver software."

Bottom: Now Windows asks for the driver CD. Windows either finds the compatible driver and installs it automatically, or offers you a choice of several. If you do not, in fact, have the CD, click "I don't have the disc." You'll be offered two final, fatalistic options: "Check for a solution" (Windows dials the mother ship on the off chance that a driver has miraculously cropped up since its last update), or "Browse my computer," designed for people who have downloaded a driver from the Web on their own.

Driver Signing

Every now and then, when you try to install the software for one new gadget or another, you'll see a warning box that says, "Windows can't verify the publisher of this driver software."

It's not really as scary as it sounds. It's just telling you that Microsoft has not tested this driver for Windows Vista compatibility and programming solidity. (Technically speaking, Microsoft has not put its digital signature on that driver; it's an *unsigned driver.*)

___ Note _____

> In very rare circumstances, you may also see messages that say, "This driver software has been altered" or "Windows cannot install this driver software." In those cases, go directly to the hardware maker's Web site to download the official driver software; Windows is trying to warn you that hackers may have gotten their hands on the driver version you're trying to install.

In theory, you're supposed to drop everything and contact the manufacturer or its Web site to find out if a Vista-certified driver is now available.

In practice, just because a driver isn't signed doesn't mean it's no good; it may be that the manufacturer simply didn't pony up the testing fee required by Microsoft's Windows Hardware Quality Labs. After all, sometimes checking with the manufacturer isn't even possible—for example, it may have gone to that great dot-com in the sky.

FREQUENTLY ASKED QUESTION
Driver vs. Driver

Which is better: the drivers that come with Windows, or the drivers I've downloaded from the manufacturer's Web site?

In many cases, they're the same thing. The drivers included with Windows usually did come from the hardware's manufacturer, which gave them to Microsoft. However, you should still use the drivers that came from your gadget's manufacturer whenever possible, especially if you got them from the manufacturer's Web site. They're likely to be newer versions than the ones that came with Windows.

So most people just plow ahead. If the installation winds up making your system slower or less stable, you can always uninstall it, or rewind your entire operating system to its condition before you installed the questionable driver. (Use System Restore, described on page 328, for that purpose. Windows automatically takes a snapshot of your working system just before you install any unsigned driver.)

___ Tip _____

> If you'd rather not contend with the "unsigned driver" message every time you install something, you can shut it up—but it's a lot of work. The trick is to press F8 each time you turn on the PC. On the black screen shown on page 343, choose Disable Driver Signature Enforcement. (Come to think of it, it's not really worth the effort.)

_____

The Device Manager

The Device Manager is a technical but extremely powerful tool that lets you trouble-shoot and update drivers for gear you've already installed. It's a master list of every component that makes up your PC: floppy drive, CD-ROM drive, keyboard, modem, and so on (Figure 12-4). It's also a status screen that lets you know which drivers are working properly, and which ones need some attention.

You can open the Device Manager in any of three ways:

▶ Right-click Computer (in your Start menu or on the desktop); choose Properties from the shortcut menu. In the Systems Properties dialog box, click the Device Manager link at top left.

▶ Choose Start→Control Panel; in Classic view, double-click Device Manager.

▶ Choose Start→Run. In the Run dialog box, type *devmgmt.msc* and press Enter.

In each of these cases, you're asked to authenticate yourself (page 127). You then arrive at the screen shown in Figure 12-4.

Red Xs and Yellow !s: Resolving Conflicts

A yellow exclamation point next to the name indicates a problem with the device's driver. It could mean that either you or Windows installed the *wrong* driver, or that the device is fighting for resources being used by another component. It could also mean that a driver can't find the equipment it's supposed to control. That's what happens to your Webcam driver, for example, if you've detached the Webcam.

A red X next to a component's name usually indicates either that it just isn't working, or that you've deliberately disabled it, as described below. At other times, the X is the result of a serious incompatibility between the component and your computer, or the component and Windows. In that case, a call to the manufacturer's help line is almost certainly in your future.

— Tip _____

To find out which company actually created a certain driver, double-click the component's name in the Device Manager. In the resulting Properties dialog box, click the Driver tab, where you'll see the name of the company, the date the driver was created, the version of the driver, and so on.

Figure 12-4: The Device Manager lists *types* of equipment; to see the actual model(s) in each category, you must expand each SUBLIST by clicking the + symbol. A device that's having problems is easy to spot, thanks to the red Xs and yellow exclamation points.

Duplicate devices

If the Device Manager displays icons for duplicate devices (for example, two modems), remove *both* of them. (Right-click each, and then choose Uninstall from the shortcut menu.) If you remove only one, Windows will find it again the next time the PC starts up, and you'll have duplicate devices again.

If Windows asks if you want to restart your computer after you remove the first icon, click No, and then delete the second one. Windows won't ask again after you remove the second incarnation; you have to restart your computer manually.

When the PC starts up again, Windows finds the hardware device and installs it (only once this time). Open the Device Manager and make sure that there's only one of everything. If not, contact the manufacturer's help line.

Resolving resource conflicts

If the "red X" problem isn't caused by a duplicate component, double-click the component's name. Here you'll find an explanation of the problem, which is often a conflict in resources (see Figure 12-5).

Turning Components Off

If you click to select the name of a component, the icons at the top of the Device Manager window spring to life. The one on the far right is the Disable button (Figure 12-4), which makes your PC treat the component in question as though it's not even there.

You can use this function to test device conflicts. For example, if a red X indicates that there's a resource conflict, you can disable one of the two gadgets, which may clear up a problem with its competitor.

When you disable a component, a red X appears next to the component's listing in the Device Manager. To undo your action, click the device's name and click the Enable button in the toolbar (formerly the Disable button).

Updating Drivers

If you get your hands on a new, more powerful (or more reliable) driver for a device, you can use the Device Manager to install it.

Newer isn't *always* better, however; in the world of Windows, the rule "If it ain't broke, don't fix it" contains a grain of truth the size of Texas.

WORKAROUND WORKSHOP

The Add Hardware Wizard

Microsoft really, really hopes that you'll never need the Add Hardware Wizard. (But if you do, choose Start→Control Panel; in Classic view, double-click Add Hardware.)

This little program is a holdover from Windows past, designed for very old, pre-Plug-and-Play gadgets that Windows doesn't autorecognize when you plug them in.

Begin by connecting the new gear; turn off the computer first, if necessary. Turn the machine on again, and then open the Add Hardware Wizard program.

The wizard makes another attempt to detect the new equipment and install its driver. If a happy little "Found New Hardware" balloon appears in your notification area, all is well; the wizard's work is done. If not, you're walked through the process of specifying exactly *what* kind of gadget seems to have gone missing, choosing its manufacturer, insert-

ing its driver disc, and so on.

Install the hardware that I manually select from a list. If you choose this option and click Next (or if the previous option fails), the wizard displays a list of device types, as shown here. From that list, find and select the type of hardware you want to install—"Imaging devices" for a digital camera or a scanner, for example, "PCMCIA adapters" for a PC card, and so on. (Click Show All Devices if you can't figure out which category to choose.)

Click Next to forge on through the wizard pages. You may be asked to select a port or configure other settings. When you click the Finish button on the last screen, Windows transfers the drivers to your hard drive. (Along the way, you may be instructed to insert the Windows Vista DVD.) As a final step, you may be asked to restart the PC.

Figure 12-5: The General tab should have all the information you need to resolve a problem. Any resource with a conflict is marked with a red X "not working" icon. If you click "Check for solutions," your PC sends a silent signal back to the mother ship, Microsoft, in hopes of finding that there's a newer driver or a compatibility patch available for downloading.

In the Device Manager, click the component's name, and then click the Update Driver Software button in the toolbar (identified in Figure 12-4). The Update Device Driver Wizard walks you through the process.

Along the way, the wizard offers to search for a better driver, or to display a list of drivers in a certain folder so you can make your own selection. In either case, you may have to restart the PC to put the newly installed driver into service.

Driver Rollback

Suppose that you, the increasingly proficient PC user, have indeed downloaded a new driver for some component—your scanner, say—and successfully installed it using the instructions in the previous paragraphs. Life is sweet—until you discover that your scanner no longer scans in color.

In this situation, you'd probably give quite a bit for the chance to return to the previous driver, which, though older, seemed to work better. That's the beauty of Driver Rollback. To find it, open the Device Manager (page 302), click the component in question, and then click the Properties button. There, you'll find the Roll Back Driver button (shown in Figure 12-6).

Windows Vista, forgiving as always, instantly undoes the installation of the newer driver, and reinstates the previous driver.

Figure 12-6: When you double-click a component listed in your Device Manager and then click the Driver tab, you find four buttons and a lot of information. The Driver Provider information, for example, lets you know who is responsible for your current driver—Microsoft or the maker of the component. Click the Driver Details button to find out where on your hard drive the actual driver file is. Or click Update Driver to install a newer version, the Roll Back Driver button to reinstate the earlier version, or the Uninstall button to remove the driver from your system entirely—a drastic decision.

Incidentally, you can also get to the Roll Back Driver button in the Properties dialog box for a device. To get there, double-click the component's name, and then click the Driver tab shown here.

GETTING HELP

13

- ▶ Navigating the Help System
- ▶ Remote Assistance
- ▶ Getting Help from Microsoft

Windows Vista may be better than any version of Windows before it, but improving something means *changing* it. And in Windows Vista, a *lot* has changed.

Fortunately, help is just around the corner—of the Start menu, that is. Windows now has a completely new electronic Help system; some of its "articles" even offer links that perform certain tasks *for* you. It may take all weekend, but eventually you should find written information about this or that Windows feature or problem.

This chapter covers not only the Help system, but also some of the ways Vista can help prevent you from *needing* help—like backing up your files for safety and keeping your PC's guts running smoothly.

Navigating the Help System

To open the Help system, choose Start→Help and Support, or press F1. The Help and Support window appears, as shown in Figure 13-1. From here, you can home in on the help screen you want using one of two methods: clicking your way from the Help home page, or using the Search command.

Help Home Page

The home page shown in Figure 13-1 contains three basic areas:

▶ At the top: buttons for six broad categories of help, like Windows Basics, Security and Maintenance, What's new?, and Troubleshooting.

▶ In the middle: links to seeking help from other human beings via the Internet.

▶ At the bottom: links to help articles that Microsoft believes answer some of the top questions. At the very bottom of the window are a couple of links to help Web sites.

If one of the broad topics at the top corresponds with your question, click it to see a list of subtopics. The subtopic list leads you to another, more focused list, which in turn leads you to an even narrower list. Eventually you'll arrive at a list that actually produces a help page.

Tip

If you seem to have misplaced your contact lenses, you can adjust the type size used by the Help Center. Click the Options button (top right of the window), and then, from the pop-up menu, choose Text Size. Its submenu offers a choice of five font sizes, from Smallest to Largest.

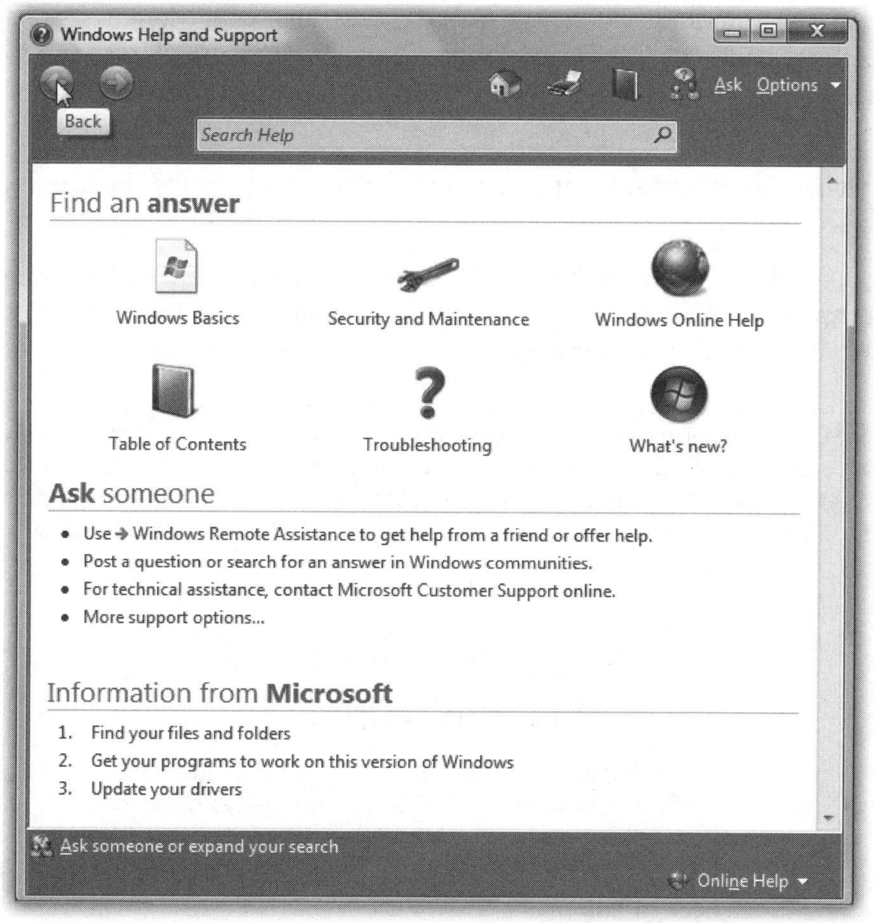

Figure 13-1: The Back, Forward, Home, and Search controls on the Help system's toolbar may look like the corresponding tools in a Web browser, but they refer only to your travels within the Help system. Other buttons at the top let you print a help article or change the type size.

Search the Help Pages

By typing a phrase into the Search Help box at the top of the main page and then pressing Enter (or clicking the tiny magnifying glass button), you instruct Windows to rifle through its 10,000 help pages to search for the phrase you typed.

Here are a few pointers:

- When you enter multiple words, Windows assumes that you're looking for help screens that contain *all* of those words. For example, if you search for *video settings*, help screens that contain both the words "video" and "settings" (although not necessarily next to each other) appear.

- If you would rather search for an exact phrase, put quotes around the search phrase ("video settings").

- Once you've clicked your way to an article that looks promising, you can search within that page, too. Open the Options pop-up menu (upper-right corner of the Help window) and choose "Find (on this page)."

Tip

When you're on a laptop at 39,000 feet, you probably don't have an Internet connection. In that case, you may prefer that Windows not attempt to search Microsoft's help site on the Internet. Open the Options pop-up menu (top right), choose Settings, and turn off "Include Windows Online Help and Support when you search for help." Click OK.

GEM IN THE ROUGH

Links in Help

Along with the nicely rewritten help information, you'll find, here and there in the Help system, a few clickable links.

Sometimes you'll see a phrase that appears in green type; that's your cue that clicking it will produce a pop-up definition.

Sometimes you'll see blue links to other help screens.

And sometimes you'll see a brand new Vista element: help links that *automate* the task you're trying to learn. These good-

ies, denoted by a blue compass icon, offer you two ways of proceeding: either Windows can do the *whole* job for you, or it can show you step by step, using blinking, glowing outlines to show you exactly where to click.

There aren't nearly enough of these automated help topics—but when you stumble onto one, turn down the lights, invite the neighbors, and settle back for an unforgettable five minutes of entertainment.

Drilling Down

If you're not using the same terminology as Microsoft, you won't find your help topic by using the Search box. Sometimes, you may have better luck unearthing a certain help article by drilling down through the Table of Contents.

Start by clicking the little book icon at the top of the window; it's called the Browse button, but it opens a tidy, clickable table of contents. If a topic's icon looks like a little book, that means you'll be treated to even *more* topic listings. If its icon looks like a page with a ? symbol, clicking it opens an actual help article (Figure 13-2).

Figure 13-2: As you arrive on each more finely grained sub-table of sub-contents, you'll see an indented list of topics in the top part of the window. These >> brackets illustrate the levels through which you've descended on your way to this help page; you can backtrack by clicking one of these links.

Remote Assistance

You may think you know what stress is: deadlines, breakups, downsizing. But nothing approaches the frustration of an expert trying to help a PC beginner over the phone—for both parties.

The expert is flying blind, using Windows terminology that the beginner doesn't know. Meanwhile, the beginner doesn't know what to look for and describe on the phone. Every little step takes 20 times longer than it would if the expert were simply seated in front of the machine. Both parties are likely to age ten years in an hour.

Fortunately, that era is at an end. Windows' Remote Assistance feature lets somebody having trouble with the computer extend an invitation to an expert, via the Internet. The expert can actually see the screen of the flaky computer, and even take control of it by remotely operating the mouse and keyboard. The guru can make even the most technical tweaks—running utility software, installing new programs, adjusting hardware drivers, even editing the Registry (Appendix B)—by long-distance remote control. Remote Assistance really *is* the next best thing to being there.

Remote Assistance: Rest Assured

Of course, these days, most people react to the notion of Remote Assistance with stark terror. What's to stop some troubled teenager from tapping into your PC in the middle of the night, rummaging through your files and reading your innermost thoughts?

Plenty. First of all, you, the help-seeker, must begin the process by sending a specific Second, the remote-control person can only *see* what's on your screen. She can't actually manipulate your computer unless you grant another specific permission.

Finally, you must be present *at your machine* to make this work. The instant you see something fishy going on, a quick tap on your Esc key disconnects the interloper.

Remote Assistance, Step by Step

If you're the one who wants help, first make sure that your PC has been set up to allow Remote Assistance (and remote control).

Choose Start→Control Panel. Click Classic View; double-click the System icon. In the links at left, click "Remote settings," and then authenticate yourself (page 127).

Here before you is the master switch for permitting remote connections. If you click Advanced (the button, not the tab), you'll find two other key security options:

▶ **Allow this computer to be controlled remotely.** If this is turned on, your guru will be able to operate your PC, not just see what's onscreen.

▶ **Invitations.** These options let you specify how quickly an invitation to a guru expires. Of course, nobody can get into your PC without a confirmation by you, while you're seated in front of it. Even so, it may give you an extra level of comfort knowing that after, say, three hours of waiting for your guru to come home and get your invitation, the window of opportunity will close.

Click OK twice to close the dialog boxes.

Now you're ready to send the invitation itself:

1. **Choose Start→Help and Support.**

   The Help and Support Center appears, as described earlier in this chapter.

2. **Click "Windows Remote Assistance."**

   You'll see this item under the "Ask someone" heading. After a moment, a window appears. It wants to know if you're the helper or the helpee.

3. **Click "Invite someone you trust to help you."**

   The phrase "you trust"—new in Windows Vista—is Microsoft's little way of reminding you that whoever you invite will be able to see anything you've got open on the screen. (Those who would rather keep that private know who they are.)

   In any case, now the "How do you want to invite someone?" screen appears.

   ___ Tip _____

   If you click "Save this invitation as a file" at this point, Vista invites you to save a *ticket file*—a standalone invitation file—to your hard drive. You'll have to do that if you have a Web-based email account like Google Mail, Hotmail, or Yahoo Mail. (Make up a password first—see step 5, below, for an explanation—and then attach the file you've saved in this step when sending a message to your guru.)

   Saving the file is also handy because you can save some steps by resending it to your guru the next time you're feeling lost.

   _____

4. **Click "Use email to send an invitation."**

Now Vista wants you to make up a password. It's designed to ensure that your guru, and only your guru, can access your machine. (Of course, you need to find some way of *telling* that person what the password is—maybe calling on the phone or sending a separate email.)

5. **Type a password into both boxes and then click Next.**

Figure 13-3: Both parties have to be very, very sure that they want this connection to take place. Top (expert's screen): You must type in the password provided by the struggling novice who asked for help.

Bottom (beginner's screen): You must confirm one last time that you really want a visitation from someone who's technically savvier than you are.

You're going to be sending your invitation via email. If you've never set up email on this PC, Vista automatically opens up Windows Mail and begins the email account-setup wizard. (The window may be *behind* the Remote Assistance window; check your taskbar.)

If you have working email, then your email program now opens, and Windows actually composes an invitation message *for* you. "Hi," it begins. "I need help with my computer. Would you please use Windows Remote Assistance to connect to my computer so you can help me?"

You're welcome to edit this message, of course, perhaps to something that does a little less damage to your ego.

6. **Type your guru's email address into the "To:" box, and then send the message.**

   Windows sends an electronic invitation to your Good Samaritan.

Now there's nothing to do but sit back, quietly freaking out, and wait for your guru to get the message and connect to your PC. (See the next section.)

If your buddy accepts the invitation to help you, then the message shown at top in Figure 13-3 appears, asking if you're absolutely, positively sure you want someone else to see your screen. If you click Yes, the assistance session begins.

If you get a note that your expert friend wants to take control of your PC (Figure 13-3, bottom), and that's cool with you, click OK.

Now watch in amazement and awe as your cursor begins flying around the screen, text types itself, and windows open and close by themselves (Figure 13-4).

As noted earlier, if the expert's explorations of your system begin to unnerve you, feel free to slam the door by clicking the "Stop sharing" button on the screen—or just by pressing the Esc key. Your friend can still see your screen, but can no longer control it. (To close the connection completely, so that your screen isn't even visible anymore, click the Disconnect button.)

Getting Help from Microsoft

If you run into trouble with installation—or with any Windows feature—the world of Microsoft is filled with sources of technical help. For example, you can follow any of

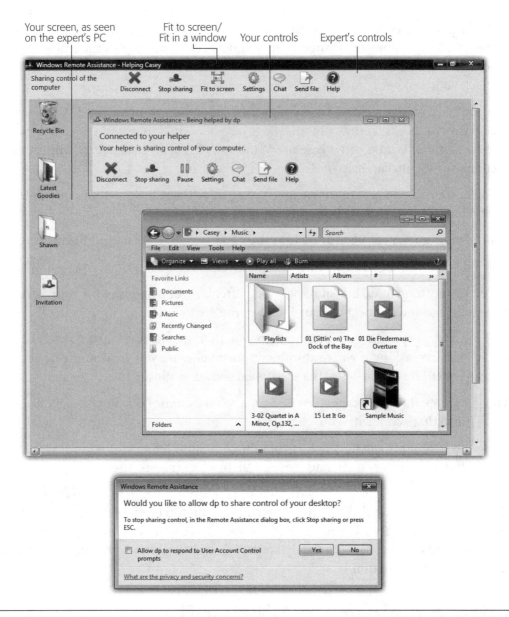

Your screen, as seen on the expert's PC

Fit to screen/ Fit in a window

Your controls

Expert's controls

Figure 13-4: Top: This is what your friendly neighborhood guru sees while watching you, the flailing beginner, from across the Internet. Your guru will soon be ready to tell you what you're doing wrong. Bottom: This is what you see, desperate grasshopper, as your guru wants to do more than see your screen—he wants to control it. If you turn on the "Allow to respond" checkbox, this person will also be able to authenticate certain system changes as he goes (page 127).

these avenues, all of which have direct links from the home page of the Help system (choose Start→Help and Support):

- **Windows communities.** This link takes you to some Internet newsgroups (bulletin boards) pertaining to Windows and Windows issues. You can post questions to the multitudes all over the Internet and return later to read the answers.

- **Microsoft Customer Support pages.** This Web site offers a summary of all the different ways you can get help from Microsoft: phone numbers, pricing plans, links to other help sources, and so on.

  You'll discover there that if you bought Vista separately (that is, it didn't come on your computer), you can call Microsoft for free during business hours. The company is especially interested in helping you get Windows installed. In fact, you can call as often as you like on this subject.

  After that, you can call for everyday Windows questions for free—twice. You'll be asked to provide your 20-digit product ID number, which you can look up by right-clicking Computer in your Start menu and clicking the Properties tab. The not-toll-free number is listed in the packaging of your Vista installation DVD.

  (If Windows came preinstalled on your machine, on the other hand, you're supposed to call the computer company with your Windows questions.)

  Once you've used up your two free calls, you can still call Microsoft—for $35 per incident. (They say "per incident" to make it clear that if it takes several phone calls to solve a particular problem, it's still just one problem.) This service is available 24 hours a day; the U.S. number is (800) 936-5700.

  --- Tip ---
  If you're not in the United States, direct your help calls to the local Microsoft office in your country. You'll find a list of these subsidiaries at *http://support.microsoft.com.*

- **Microsoft website for IT professionals.** This link takes you to a special Web site for network administrators, programmers, and other IT (information technology) pros. At this site you'll find special articles on deployment, corporate security, and so on.

- **Windows Online Help and Support.** This is the mother lode: the master Web site for help and instructions on running Windows Vista. You can search it, use its links to other pages, read articles, study FAQs (frequently asked questions), or burrow into special-topic articles.

Of course, a lot of these online articles are built right into the regular Help system described at the beginning of this chapter. Unless you've turned off "Include Windows Online Help and Support when you search for help," you generally don't have to go online to search a second time.

BACKUPS, MAINTENANCE, AND TROUBLESHOOTING

14

▶ Automatic Backups

▶ System Restore

▶ Windows Update

▶ Four Speed Tricks

▶ Safe Mode and the Startup Menu

▶ Startup Repair

PC troubleshooting is among the most difficult propositions on earth, in part because your machine has so many cooks. Microsoft made the operating system, another company made the computer, and dozens of others contributed the programs you use every day. The number of conflicts that can arise and the number of problems you may encounter is nearly infinite. That's why, if you were lucky, you bought your PC from a company that offers a toll-free, 24-hour help line. You may need it.

In the meantime, Vista is crawling with special diagnostic modes, software tools, and workarounds designed to revive a gasping or dead PC. Some are clearly intended only for licensed geeks. Others, however, are available even to mere mortals armed with no more information than, "It's not working right."

Whether you get it working or not, however, there's one constant that applies to novices and programmers alike—you're always better off if you have a backup copy of your files. This chapter covers the entire cycle of bad things happening to good people: backing up your files and maintaining your equipment to *prevent* trouble, and fixing problems once they arise.

Automatic Backups

Consider that the proximity of your drive's spinning platters to the head that reads them is roughly the same proportion as the wheels of an airliner flying at 500 miles per hour, 12 inches off the ground. It's amazing that hard drives work as well, and as long, as they do.

Still, a hard drive is nothing more than a mass of moving parts in delicate alignment, so it should come as no surprise that every now and then, disaster strikes. That's why backing up your data (making a safety copy) on a regular basis is an essential part of using a PC. There's a lot of valuable stuff on your hard drive: all of your photos, the addresses and phone numbers, a lifetime's worth of email, and so on.

In a corporation, a network administrator generally does the backing up for you and your co-workers. But if you use Windows Vista at home, or in a smaller company that doesn't have network nerds running around to ensure your files' safety, you'll be happy to know about the Backup and Restore feature. It's a brand-new Vista feature that makes it simple to do your own backups.

Backup Hardware

If you have a home or small business network, backing up to a folder on another PC on your network is a wise idea. An inexpensive external hard drive makes a super-convenient backup disk, too.

The advantage of blank CDs and DVDs, though, is that you can store them somewhere else: in a fireproof box, a safe deposit box at the bank, or the trunk of your car. Keep them anywhere except in your office, so your data is safe even in the case of fire or burglary.

___ Tip ___

You can't back up a laptop's files when it's running on battery power. The program won't let you—it's too worried about losing juice in the middle of the operation.

Creating a Backup

Once you've decided to back up your PC and also figured out what you're going to back it up *onto*, proceed like this:

1. **Choose Start→Control Panel. Under the System and Maintenance heading, click "Back up your computer."**

   Now Backup and Restore Center opens (Figure 14-1).

2. **Click "Back up files."**

   "Back up files" is what most people use most of the time. It can back up your photos, music, videos, email, documents, compressed files, and just about anything else *except* for your programs—and Windows itself.

3. **Authenticate yourself (page 127).**

   Now Windows looks through your system, locating hard disks and removable drives. The Back Up Files screen appears, offering you the chance to specify where you want to store the backup copies.

4. **Choose a backup drive.**

   If you're backing up to a hard disk or removable disk, select "On a hard disk, CD, or DVD." From the drop-down list, choose the drive you want to back up to.

USB flash drives and memory cards show up in this list, too. Flash drives make particularly handy backup disks because they're small, inexpensive, and can store several gigabytes
of data.

If you're backing up to a folder that's shared on a networked PC (page 375), select
"On a network," then browse to the folder. You may have to type in a user name and
password to use that folder, depending on how you've set up sharing on the PC.

If you have more than one hard disk on your PC, you're now asked to choose which
ones you want included in the backup. Make your choice.

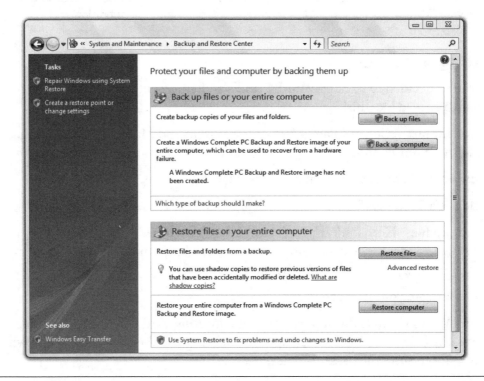

Figure 14-1: The primary purpose of this screen is to back up and restore your PC. But on the left-
hand side, you'll also find links for creating a restore point, and for using System Restore to revert
your PC to a previous time.

5. **Click Next.**

Now you get to choose which *kinds* of files to back up: Pictures, Music, Videos, E-mail, Documents, and several others.

6. **Turn on the checkboxes for the kinds of files you want backed up** (Figure 14-2, top). **Click Next.**

You can now set up a schedule for automatic, unattended backups, which should bring *enormous* peace of mind to anyone who's been, until now, living dangerously (Figure 14-2, bottom).

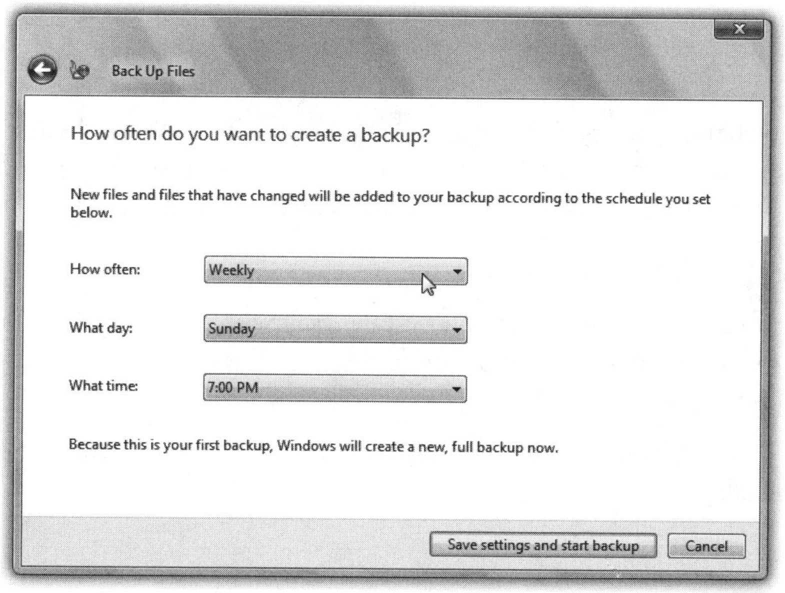

Figure 14-2: Top: As noted earlier in this chapter, Vista intends to back up *all* files of that generic file type—so Documents backs up Word .doc files, Excel .xls files, PowerPoint .ppt files, Adobe .pdf files, and others. You can't specify that you want only *certain* files or folders backed up.

Bottom: Choose a schedule for the automatic backups. For best results, choose times of day when you know that the computer will be turned on.

7. **Click "Save settings and start backup."**

   Backup goes to work, copying your files to their new backup location. The process may take several seconds or several hours, depending on how much you're copying.

   You can continue to work on your PC; copying takes place in the background. You'll be notified once the backup is complete.

From now on, your PC backs itself up, on the schedule you set for it. When Windows Vista creates a new backup, it only backs up new files or files that have changed since the last backup; it doesn't waste its time backing up files that haven't been touched.

Note _____

If you've set your PC to back up to CDs or DVDs, make sure that there's a blank disc available at the appointed time; otherwise, the backup won't happen.

If you want to change your backup settings—back up on a different schedule, say, or add or take away file types—return to the Backup and Restore Center, and click "Change backup settings." From here, you can change anything about your backup.

Restoring Files from a Backup

When your good luck runs out, and you find yourself with a virus/drive crash/meddlesome toddler who threw out an important folder, you'll be glad indeed that you had a backup. This is the payoff.

Fortunately, Vista lets you restore individual files and folders—you don't have to restore all files in one fell swoop.

Tip _____

Perform regular test restores to make sure your data is retrievable from the backup disks. (Consider restoring your files to a test folder—not the folder where the files came from—so you don't wind up with duplicates.) There's no other way to be absolutely sure that your backups are working properly.

Here are the steps. (They assume that, if your whole hard drive did indeed die, you have already replaced it and reinstalled Windows Vista.)

1. **Choose Start→Control Panel. Under the System and Maintenance heading, click "Back up your computer."**

You're back at the Backup and Restore Center.

2. **Click "Restore files."**

   A screen appears, asking whether you want to restore files from your most recent backup, or from a previous backup.

3. **Click "Files from the latest backup" or "Files from an older backup" and click Next.**

   If you choose to restore from a previous backup, you'll be shown a list of backup dates; choose the one you want.

   Now you arrive at the weird little screen shown in Figure 14-3.

4. **Click "Add files" or "Add folders," and specify what files and folders you want brought back to life from your backup copies.**

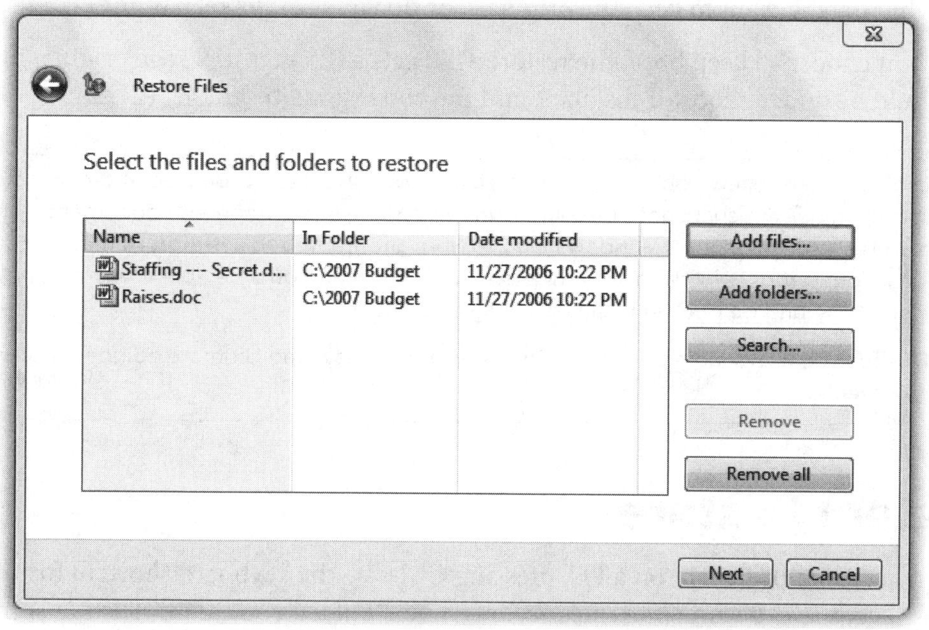

Figure 14-3: When you restore files, you don't have to restore every single file you've backed up. Click Add Files or Add Folders (shown here), and a screen appears where you can select the specific files or folders you want to restore.

Click "Add files" to restore individual files, or "Add folders" to restore individual folders. Note that at this point, although it may look like you're browsing through your hard disk, you're not. You're only browsing the backup that you made.

You can also *search* for files, if you're not sure where a file is that you want to back up. Click Search, type what you're looking for, and then add the file or files.

5. **Click Next. Indicate where you want the restored files put.**

   You can restore files to their original locations, or to a different folder on your PC.

6. **Click "Start restore."**

   Backup now starts copying files and folders *back* from the backup to your hard drive.

   If you've chosen to save files to their original locations, you may be asked what you want to happen if the original files are *still there.* Do you want the backup copies to "win," do you want to keep the originals, or do you want to keep both?

   If you choose to keep both, the restored file gets a (2) after it. So the original file would be budget.doc, for instance, and the copy would be budget (2).doc.

--- **Note** _____

There's another new backup feature in Vista, too: Complete PC Backup. It creates a *disk image*—a perfect snapshot—of your *entire hard* drive at this moment: documents, email, pictures, and so on, *plus* Windows, *and* all your programs and settings. Someone could steal your *entire hard drive,* or your drive could die, and you'd be able to install a new, empty one and be back in business inside of an hour.

This feature is available only in the Business, Enterprise, and Ultimate editions of Vista, however.

_____

System Restore

As you get more proficient on a PC, pressing Ctrl+Z—the keyboard shortcut for Undo—eventually becomes an unconscious reflex. In fact, you can sometimes spot veteran Windows fans twitching their Ctrl+Z fingers even when they're not near the computer—after knocking over a cup of coffee, locking the car with the keys inside, or blurting out something inappropriate in a meeting.

Vista offers one feature in particular that you might think of as the mother of all Undo commands: System Restore. This feature alone can be worth hours of your time and hundreds of dollars in consultant fees.

The pattern of things going wrong in Windows usually works like this: the PC works fine for a while, and then suddenly—maybe for no apparent reason, but most often following an installation or configuration change—it goes on the fritz. At that point, wouldn't it be pleasant to be able to tell the computer: "Go back to the way you were yesterday, please"?

System Restore does exactly that. It "rewinds" your copy of Windows back to the condition it was in before you, or something you tried to install, messed it up.

--- Tip _____

> If your PC manages to catch a virus, System Restore can even rewind it to a time before the infection—*if* the virus hasn't gotten into your documents in such a way that you re-infect yourself after the system restore. An up-to-date antivirus program is a much more effective security blanket.

_____

In fact, if you don't like your PC after restoring it, you can always restore it to the way it was *before* you restored it. Back to the future!

About Restore Points

System Restore works by taking snapshots of your operating system. Your copy of Vista has been creating these memorized snapshots, called *restore points,* ever since you've been running it. When the worst comes to pass, and your PC starts acting up, you can use System Restore to rewind your machine to its configuration the last time you remember it working well.

Windows automatically creates landing points for your little PC time machine at the following times:

▶ After every 24 hours of real-world time (unless your PC is turned off all day; then you get a restore point the next time it's turned on).

▶ Every time you install a new program or install a new device driver for a piece of hardware.

▶ When you install a Windows Update.

▶ When you make a backup using Windows Backup.

▶ Whenever you feel like it—for instance, just before you install some new component.

To create one of these checkpoints *manually*, choose Start→Control Panel. In Classic view, open Backup and Restore Center; in the task pane at left, click "Create a restore point or change settings." Authenticate yourself (page 127).

Now the System Properties dialog box appears, already open to the System Protection tab (Figure 14-4). Click Create, type a name for the restore point, click Create

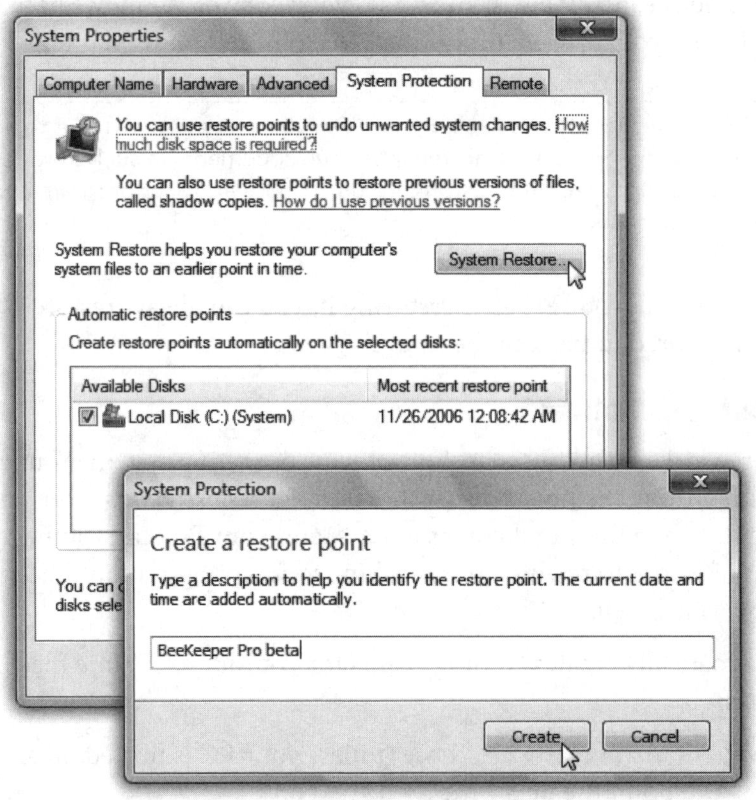

Figure 14-4: Background: The System Protection tab of the System Properties dialog box is where you manage the System Restore feature.

Foreground: Here's you, creating a manual restore point just before installing a program in which you don't have 100 percent confidence.

again, and the restore point is created. Don't include the date and time in the name of the restore point; you'll see that when you get around to doing an actual restoration.

As you can well imagine, storing all these copies of your Windows configuration consumes quite a bit of disk space. Out of the box, System Restore can use up to 15 percent of every hard drive—that adds up quickly!

That's why Windows Vista automatically begins *deleting* restore points when it's running out of disk space. That's also why the System Restore feature stops working if your hard drive is very full.

And that's *also* why you should run the System Restore feature promptly when your PC acts strangely.

Performing a System Restore

If something goes wrong with your PC, here's how to roll it back to the happy, bygone days of late last week—or this morning, for that matter:

1. **Choose Start→Control Panel. In Classic view, open Backup and Restore Center. In the task pane at left, click "Repair Windows using System Restore." Authenticate yourself (page 127).**

   The "Restore system files and settings" screen appears (Figure 14-5).

2. **If you want to use the recommended restore point, click Next. Otherwise, skip to step 5.**

   Windows recommends that you use the most *recent* restore point. When you click Next, it asks you to confirm your decision.

3. **Close all open files and programs. Click Finish.**

   You have one more chance to back out: Windows asks if you *really* want to continue.

4. **Click Yes.**

   Windows goes to town, reinstating your operating system to reflect its condition on the date you specified. Leave your PC alone while this occurs.

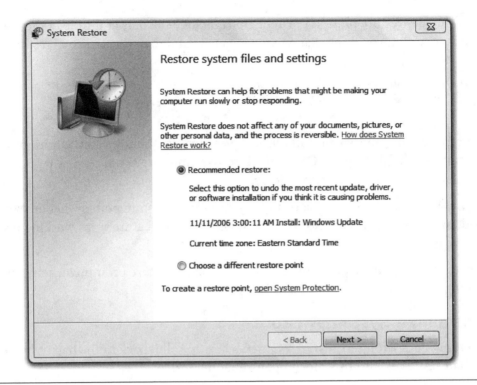

Figure 14-5: When you use System Restore, you'll be shown the date and time of your most recent restore point, as well as why the restore point was created—for example, because you installed a new piece of software, or because you applied a Windows Update. That's a clue as to which restore point you should use.

When the process is complete, the computer restarts automatically. When you log back in, a message shown appears, welcoming you back to the past.

5. **If you want a different restore point, select "Choose a different restore point," and then click Next.**

    Now you see a list of all restore points (which Windows also calls checkpoints) that have been created in the last five days (Figure 14-6). For each checkpoint, you'll see the time, date, and a description. If you want to see checkpoints from before five days ago, turn on the "Show restore points older than 5 days" checkbox.

6. **Click the checkpoint you want, and then click Next.**

    You'll be asked to confirm that you want to use that checkpoint.

7. Close all files and programs. Click Finish.

Windows restores your PC to the past, as outlined in step 2.

Tip

If rewinding your system to the golden days actually makes matters worse, you can always reverse the entire Restore process. To do so, choose Start→Control Panel. In Classic view, open Backup and Restore Center. In the task pane at left, click "Repair Windows using System Restore." From the System Restore screen that appears, click Undo System Restore. Click Next, click Finish, click Yes, and wait for the process to reverse itself.

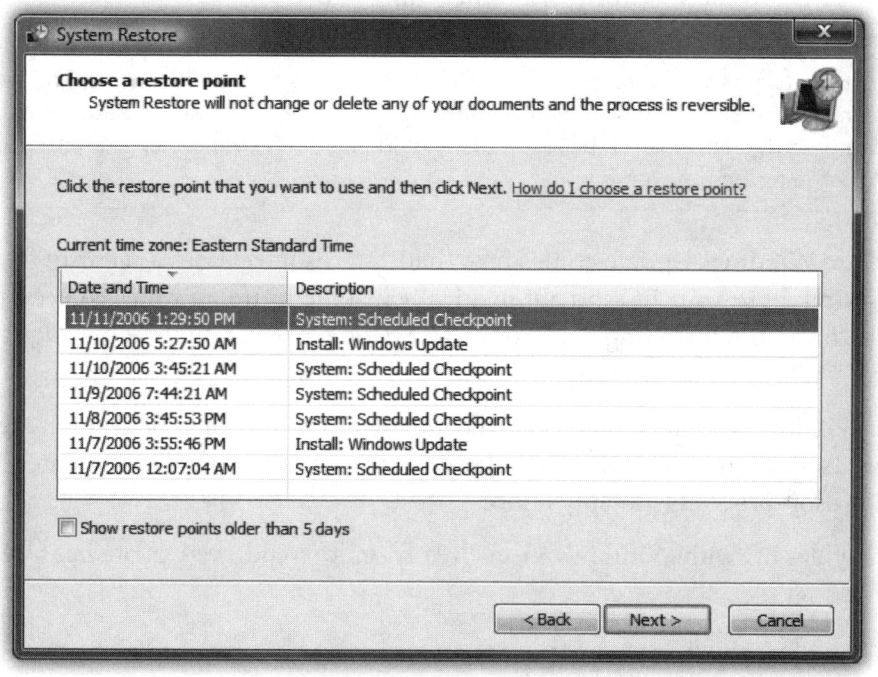

Figure 14-6: The Description column for checkpoints shows you why the restore points were created—for example, because a Windows Update was installed. You can provide your own names for restore points only when you create them manually. (You'll see their names here.)

Windows Update

Windows Vista is far more secure than previous versions of Windows, but Microsoft isn't running around saying, "You don't need an antivirus program anymore." The hackers will have a *much* harder time of it, but with 50 million lines of code to explore, they're sure to break in somehow.

Microsoft and other security researchers constantly find new security holes—and as soon as they're found, Microsoft rushes a patch out the door to fix it. But creating a patch is one thing; actually getting that patch installed on multiple millions of copies of Windows Vista around the world is another thing entirely.

> **Note**
>
> In fact, it's Microsoft's *patches* that usually alert hackers to the presence of the security hole in the first place! They exploit the fact that not everyone has the patch in place instantly. (Which brings up the question: should Microsoft even be creating the patches? But that's another conversation.)

That's where Windows Update comes in. When Microsoft releases a security fix, it gets delivered straight to your PC and automatically installed. (If you want, you can first review the fix before installing it, although few people have enough knowledge to judge its value.)

In Vista, Windows Update's job has been expanded. It doesn't just deliver patches to Windows itself; it can also send you better drivers for your hardware and patches to other Microsoft products, notably Office.

If you bought a PC with Windows Vista already on it, Windows Update has already been turned on.

Fiddling with Windows Update

To adjust Windows Update, choose Start→Control Panel. Click System and Maintenance→Windows Update. If there are any available updates that you haven't yet installed, you'll see them here (Figure 14-7).

If you click Change settings, the screen pictured in Figure 14-8 appears. The four options here correspond to four levels of trust people have in Microsoft, the mother ship:

The best option for most people is the one called "Install updates automatically (recommended)." Translation: "Download and install all patches automatically. We trust in thee, Microsoft, that thou knowest what thou do-est." (All of this will take place in the middle of the night—or according to whatever schedule you set on this screen—so as not to inconvenience you.)

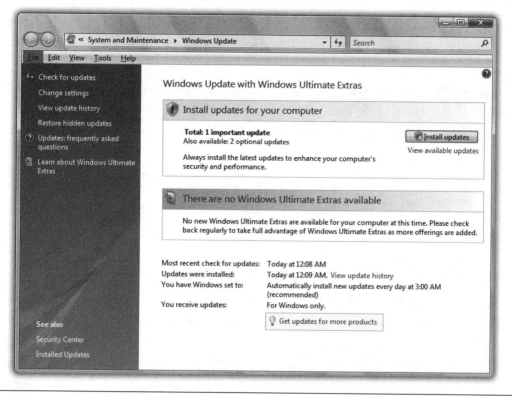

Figure 14-7: If there are any available updates that you haven't yet installed, you can install them by clicking "Install updates." To get details about an update, click "View available updates."

Removing Updates

If an update winds up making life with your PC worse instead of better, you can remove it. Head to Control Panel→Programs→View Installed Updates, right-click an update, and then select Remove.

___ **Note** _____

You can't remove all updates, however. Security-related updates are usually nonremovable.

_____

There's one problem with this action. The next time Windows Updates does it job, it will *re*install the update you just removed.

The workaround is to *hide* the update so that it doesn't get downloaded and installed again. Open Windows Update, and then click "Check for updates."

After Windows finds updates, click "View available updates." Right-click the update you don't want; select "Hide update." From now on, Windows Update ignores the update.

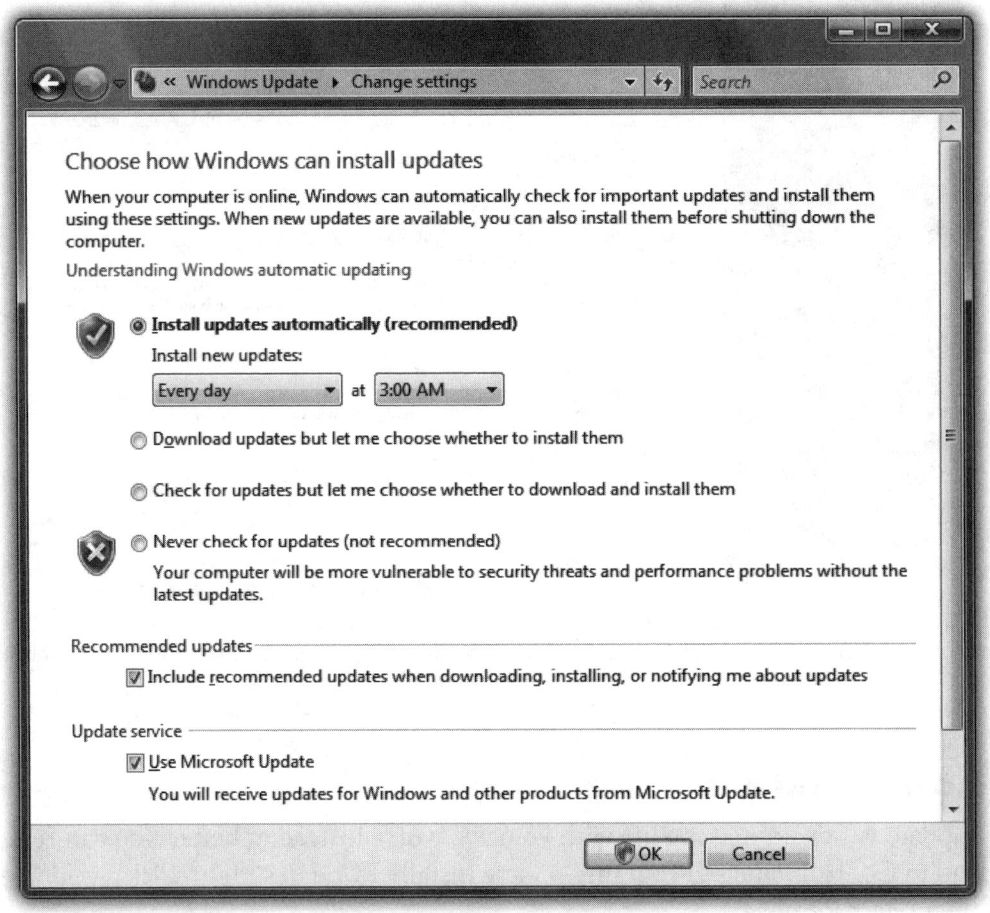

Figure 14-8: Windows Vista's auto-update feature can ask that you be notified either before the software patch is downloaded (third choice) or after it's been downloaded and is ready to install (second choice). You can also permit the updates to be updated and then installed automatically, on a schedule that you specify (top choice).

If, later, you change your mind, click "Restore hidden updates," select the update you want installed, and then click Restore.

Four Speed Tricks

It's a fact of computing. Every PC seems to get slower the longer you own it.

There are plenty of reasons, mostly having to do with the fact that a computer is fastest when it's new and empty:

- ▶ The hard drive has loads of free space.
- ▶ The boot process hasn't yet been cluttered up by startup code deposited by your programs.
- ▶ Few background programs are constantly running, eating up your memory.
- ▶ You haven't yet drained away horsepower with antivirus and automatic backup programs.
- ▶ Every year, the programs you buy or download are more demanding than the previous year's software.

Some of the usual advice about speeding up your PC applies here, of course: install more memory or a faster hard drive.

But in Windows Vista, here and there, nestled among the 50 million lines of Vista code, you'll find some *free* tricks and tips for giving your PC a speed boost. For example:

SuperFetch

Your PC can grab data from RAM (memory) hundreds of times faster than from the hard drive. That's why it uses a *cache,* a portion of memory that holds bits of software code that you've used recently. After all, if you've used some feature or command once, you may want to use it again soon—and this way, Windows is ready for you. It can deliver that bit of code nearly instantaneously the next time.

When you leave your PC for a while, however, background programs (virus checkers, backup programs, disk utilities) take advantage of the idle time. They run themselves when you're not around—and push out whatever was in the cache.

That's why, when you come back from lunch (or sit down first thing in the morning), your PC is especially sluggish. All the good stuff—*your* stuff—has been flushed from the cache and returned to the much slower hard drive, to make room for those background utilities.

SuperFetch attempts to reverse that cycle. It attempts to keep your most frequently used programs in the cache all the time. In fact, it actually *tracks you* and your cycle of work. If you generally fire up the computer at 9 a.m., for example, or return to it at 1:30 p.m., SuperFetch will anticipate you by restoring frequently used programs and documents to the cache.

There's no on/off switch for SuperFetch, and nothing for you to configure. It's on all the time, automatic, and very sweet.

ReadyBoost

Your PC can get to data in RAM (memory) hundreds of times faster than it can fetch something from the hard drive. That's why it uses a *cache,* a portion of memory that holds bits of software code that you've used recently.

The more memory your machine has, the more that's available for the cache, and the faster things should feel to you. Truth is, though, you may have a bunch of memory sitting around your desk at this moment that's *completely wasted*—namely, USB flash drives. That's perfectly good RAM that your PC can't even touch if it's sitting in a drawer.

That's the whole point of ReadyBoost: to use a flash drive as described above as additional cache storage. You can achieve the same effect by installing more RAM, of course, but that job can be technical (especially on laptops), forbidden (by your corporate masters), or impossible (because you've used up all your PC's RAM slots already).

To take advantage of this speed-boosting feature, just plug a USB flash drive into your computer's USB jack.

___ Note _____

Both the flash drive *and* your PC must have USB 2.0 or later. USB 1.1 is too slow for this trick to work.

_____

In any case, the AutoPlay dialog box now opens, as shown in Figure 14-9 (top). Click "Speed up my system"; in the flash device's Properties dialog box (which opens automatically), turn on "Use this device." That box is shown in Figure 14-9, bottom.

That's all there is to it. Your PC will now use the flash drive as an annex to its own built-in RAM, and you will, in theory, enjoy a tiny speed lift as a result.

And now, the fine print:

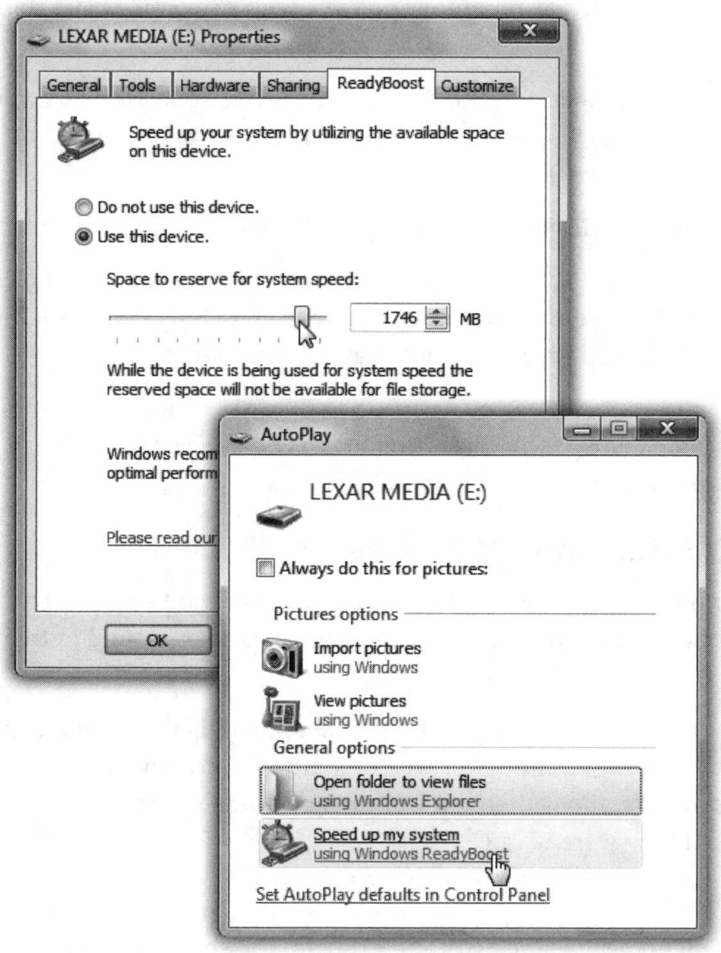

Figure 14-9: Lower right: The AutoPlay dialog box opens when you insert a flash drive. "Speed up my system" is the English version of the term *ReadyBoost*.

Top left: You can decide for yourself how much of the flash drive's storage is used for ReadyBoost purposes, although you won't notice any speed difference unless the real-to-flash memory ratio is 2.5 to 1 or lower.

▶ Not all flash drives are equally fast, and therefore not all work with ReadyBoost. Look closely at the drive's packaging to see if there's a Vista ReadyBoost logo. (Technically speaking—very technically—its throughput must be capable of 2.5 MB per second for 4 K random reads, and 1.75 MB per second for 512 K random writes.)

▶ ReadyBoost works only with memory gadgets with capacities from 256 megabytes to 4 gigabytes.

▶ Once you've set aside space on the flash drive for ReadyBoost, you can't use it for storing everyday files. (Unless, of course, you change the settings in its Properties dialog box or reformat it.)

▶ You can use one flash drive per PC, and one PC per flash drive.

▶ The biggest speed gains appear when you have a 1-to-1 ratio between real PC memory and your flash drive. For example, if your PC has 1 gigabyte of RAM, adding a 1-gig flash drive should give you a noticeable speed boost.

The speed gains evaporate as you approach a 2.5-to-1 ratio. For example, suppose your PC has 1 gigabyte of RAM and you add a 256-megabyte flash drive. That's an 8-to-1 ratio, and you won't feel any acceleration at all.

Shutting Off Bells and Whistles

Vista, as you know, is all dressed up for "Where do you want to go today?" It's loaded with glitz, glamour, special effects, and animations. And every one of them saps away a little bit of speed.

With any luck, your PC is a mighty fortress of seething gigahertz that brushes off that kind of resource-sapping as though it were a mere cloud of gnats. But when things start to bog down, remember that you can turn off some of the bells and whistles—and recover the speed they were using.

Here's how.

Open the Start menu. Right-click Computer; from the shortcut menu, choose Properties. In the System control panel that appears, click "Advanced system settings" at left. Authenticate yourself (page 127).

Now, on the Advanced tab (Figure 14-10, top), click the uppermost Settings button. You've just found, in the belly of the beast, the complete list of the little animations that make up Vista's Windows dressing (Figure 14-10, bottom). For example, "Animate windows when minimizing and maximizing" makes Windows present a half-second animation showing your window actually shrinking down onto the taskbar when you minimize it. "Show shadows under mouse pointer" produces a tiny shadow beneath

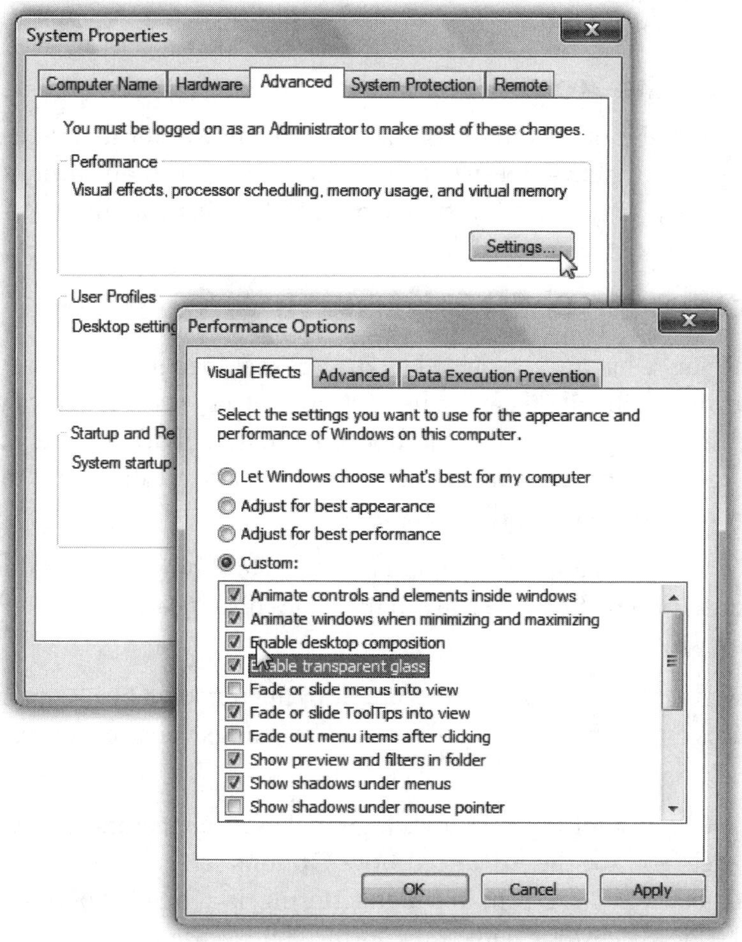

Figure 14-10: Top left: The Advanced tab of the System Properties dialog box offers three Settings buttons. The one you want is at the top.

Bottom right: Depending on the speed and age of your machine, you may find that turning off all of these checkboxes produces a snappier, more responsive PC—if a bit less Macintosh-esque. (Leave "Use visual styles on windows and buttons" turned on, however, if you like the new, glossy look of Windows Vista.)

your cursor, as though it were floating a quarter-inch above the surface of your screen.

With one click—on "Adjust for best performance"—you can turn off all of these effects. Or, if there are some you can't live without—and let's face it, tooltips just aren't the same if they don't *fade* into view—click Custom, and then turn off the individual checkboxes for the features you don't need.

Toning Down the Aero

Aero is the new visual look of Windows Vista, but the power for its visual effects—drop shadows, transparency, glitz—doesn't grow on trees. If you can do without some of it, you gain another itty-bitty speed boost. See page 104 for instructions.

Safe Mode and the Startup Menu

If the problems you're having are caused by drivers that load just as the computer is starting up, turning them all off can be helpful. At the very least, it allows you to get into your machine to begin your troubleshooting pursuit. That's precisely the purpose of the Startup menu—a menu most people never even know exists until they're initiated into its secret world by a technically savvy guru.

Making the Startup menu appear is a matter of delicate timing. First, **restart the computer. Immediately after the** BIOS startup messages disappear, **press the F8 key (on the top row of most keyboards).**

The BIOS startup messages—the usual crude-looking text on a black screen, filled with copyright notices and technical specs—are the first things you see after turning on the computer.

If you press the F8 key after the Windows logo makes its appearance, you're too late. But if all goes well, you see the Advanced Boot Options screen (Figure 14-11). Displayed against a black DOS screen, in rough lettering, is a long list of options that includes Safe Mode, Safe Mode with Networking, Safe Mode with Command Prompt, Enable Boot Logging, and so on. Use the arrow keys to "walk through" them.

Here's are the most important Startup menu commands:

▶ **Safe Mode.** Safe Mode starts up Windows in a special, stripped-down, generic, somewhat frightening-looking startup mode—with the software for dozens of hardware and software features *turned off*. Only the very basic components work: your mouse, keyboard, screen, and disk drives. Everything else is shut down and cut off.

In short, Safe Mode is the tactic to take if your PC *won't* start up normally, thanks to some recalcitrant driver.

Once you select the Safe Mode option on the Startup menu, you see a list, filling your screen, of every driver that Windows is loading. Eventually, you're asked to log in.

Your screen now looks like it was designed by drunken cavemen, with jagged, awful graphics and text. That's because in Safe Mode, Windows doesn't load the driver for your video card. (It avoids that driver, on the assumption that it may be causing the very problem you're trying to troubleshoot.) Instead, Windows loads a crude, generic driver that works with *any* video card.

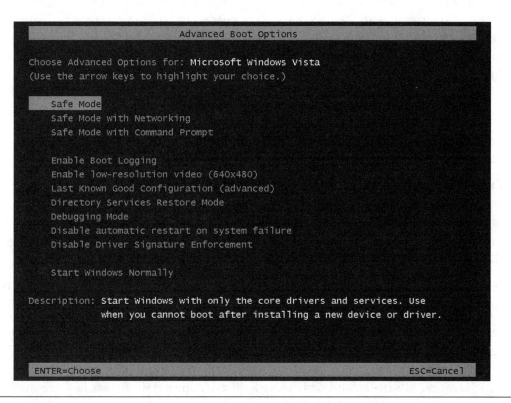

```
                      Advanced Boot Options

Choose Advanced Options for: Microsoft Windows Vista
(Use the arrow keys to highlight your choice.)

    Safe Mode
    Safe Mode with Networking
    Safe Mode with Command Prompt

    Enable Boot Logging
    Enable low-resolution video (640x480)
    Last Known Good Configuration (advanced)
    Directory Services Restore Mode
    Debugging Mode
    Disable automatic restart on system failure
    Disable Driver Signature Enforcement

    Start Windows Normally

Description: Start Windows with only the core drivers and services. Use
             when you cannot boot after installing a new device or driver.


ENTER=Choose                                            ESC=Cancel
```

Figure 14-11: Let's hope you never need to see this screen. It's the Advanced Boot Options screen—a graphically uninteresting, but troubleshootingly critical starting point. To make a selection, press the up or down arrow keys to walk through the list. Press Enter when you've highlighted the option you want.

The purpose of Safe Mode is to help you troubleshoot. If you discover that the problem you've been having is now gone, you've at least established that the culprit is one of the drivers that Windows has now turned off. Safe Mode also gives you full access to the technical tools of Windows Vista, including System Restore (page 328), the Device Manager (page 302), the Backup and Restore Center, and Help. You might use the Device Manager, for example, to roll back a driver that you just updated (page 306), or System Restore to undo some other installation that seems to have thrown your PC into chaos.

If this procedure doesn't solve the problem, contact a support technician.

▶ **Safe Mode with Networking.** This option is exactly the same as Safe Mode, except that it also lets you load the driver software needed to tap into a network, if you're on one, or onto the Internet—an arrangement that offers a few additional troubleshooting possibilities, like being able to access files and drivers on another PC or from the Internet. (If you have a laptop that uses a PC Card networking card, however, this option still may not help you, since the PC Card driver itself is still turned off.)

▶ **Safe Mode with Command Prompt.** Here's another variation of Safe Mode, this one intended for ultra–power users who are more comfortable typing out geeky text commands than using icons, menus, and the mouse.

▶ **Enable VGA Mode.** In this mode, your PC uses a standard VGA video driver that works with all graphics cards, instead of the hideously ugly generic one usually seen in Safe Mode. Use this option when you're troubleshooting video-display problems— problems that you're confident have less to do with drivers than with your settings in the Display control panel (which you're now ready to fiddle with).

(Of course, VGA means 640 x 480 pixels, which looks huge and crude on today's big monitors. Do not adjust your set.)

▶ **Last Known Good Configuration.** Here's yet another method of resetting the clock to a time when your PC was working correctly, in effect undoing whatever configuration change you made that triggered your PC's current problems. It reinstates whichever set of drivers, and whichever Registry configuration, was in force the last time the PC was working right. (This option, however, isn't as effective as the System Restore option, which also restores operating-system files in the process.)

▶ **Start Windows Normally.** This option starts the operating system in its usual fashion, exactly as though you never summoned the Startup menu to begin with. The Normal option lets you tell the PC, "Sorry to have interrupted you...go ahead."

Startup Repair

You might play by all the rules. You might make regular backups, keep your antivirus software up to date, and floss twice a day. And then one day, you get your reward: the PC won't even start up. You can't use any of Vista's software troubleshooting tools, because you can't even get to Windows.

In those most dire situations, Microsoft is pleased to introduce Startup Repair, known to techies as WinRE (Windows Recovery Environment). As shown in Figure 14-12, it's a special recovery mode that runs from the *Windows DVD* so that it can fix whatever's damaged or missing on the hard drive's copy of Windows.

___ **Note** _____

> Depending on who sold you your PC, you might not have a traditional Windows DVD. Your PC company might even have replaced Startup Repair with a similar tool; check its Web site or manual.

_____

To open Startup Repair, follow these steps:

1. **Start up from your Vista installation DVD.**

   Insert the DVD. Then restart the PC—but as it's coming to life, press the F8 key. Your PC says something like, "Press a key to boot from CD or DVD." So do it—press a key.

   After a moment, the Vista installation screen appears (Figure 14-12, top). But you're not going to install Windows—not yet.

2. **Click "Repair your computer."**

   It's a link at the lower-left corner. Now you're asked which copy of Windows you want to repair. Chances are you've got only one.

3. **Click your copy of Windows.**

   Now the Recovery Environment appears (Figure 14-12, bottom).

At this point, you have some powerful tools available to help you out of your PC's mess.

Figure 14-12: If your hard drive won't even let you in, insert your original Vista installation DVD. Top: At the main installation screen, click "Repair your computer." Specify which copy of Windows you want to repair (not shown). Bottom: The new Startup Repair suite, at your disposal.

Because you're running off the DVD, you can perform surgeries on the hard drive that you wouldn't be able to if the hard drive itself were in control. That'd be like trying to paint the floor under your own feet.

Your options are:

▶ **Startup Repair.** If there is indeed a missing or damaged file in your copy of Windows, click this link to trigger an automatic repair job. You're running off the original installation DVD, for heaven's sake, so it's extremely easy for Startup Repair to reach into its bag of spare parts if necessary.

▶ **System Restore.** Remember System Restore, described earlier in this chapter? When better to rewind your Windows installation to a healthier, happier time than right now? Click this link to choose a restore point. With any luck, the rewinding job will include restoring the undamaged startup files that your PC needs right about now.

▶ **Windows Complete PC Restore.** If you, the proud owner of the Business, Enterprise, or Ultimate edition of Vista, have taken advantage of the Complete PC backup feature (which makes a snapshot of the entire hard drive, programs and all), then you're in luck. You have at your disposal a complete disk image of your hard drive, presumably made when the disk was working fine. It's like super System Restore. Click this link to copy the whole schmear back onto your hard drive. (Of course, you'll lose any documents or settings you've changed since the backup was made.)

▶ **Windows Memory Diagnostic Tool.** Click this link if you suspect that it's your RAM (memory), not the hard drive, that's causing your problems. The software does a quick check to make sure your memory hardware is actually working right.

▶ **Command Prompt.** If you're lucky enough to know what you're doing at the command prompt (a black window where you type out text commands), you're in luck. You can use it to issue commands and perform repair surgery.

Thanks to these powerful tools, there's less reason than ever to pay $35 for the privilege of talking to some technician named "Mike" who's actually in India, following a tech-support script that instructs you to first erase your hard drive and reinstall Windows from scratch.

PART FIVE:
THE VISTA NETWORK

ACCOUNTS
(AND LOGGING ON)

15

▶ Introducing User Accounts

▶ Accounts

▶ Fast User Switching

▶ Logging On

For years, teachers, parents, tech directors, and computer lab instructors struggled to answer two difficult questions. How do you rig one PC so that several different people can use it throughout the day, without interfering with each other's files and settings? And how do you protect a PC from getting fouled up by mischievous (or bumbling) students and employees?

Introducing User Accounts

Windows Vista was designed from the ground up to be a multiple-user operating system. Anyone who uses the computer must *log on*—click (or type) your name and type in a password—when the computer turns on. Upon doing so, you discover the Windows universe just as you left it, including these elements:

▶ **Desktop.** Each person sees his own shortcut icons, folder icons, and other stuff left out on the desktop.

▶ **Start menu.** If you reorganize the Start menu, as described in Chapter 5, you won't confuse anybody else who uses the machine. No one else can even *see* the changes you make.

▶ **Documents folder.** Each person sees only her own stuff in the Documents folder.

▶ **Email.** Windows maintains a separate stash of email messages for each account holder—along with separate Web bookmarks, a Windows Messenger contact list, and other online details.

▶ **Favorites folder.** Any Web sites, folders, or other icons you've designated as Favorites appear in *your* Favorites menu, and nobody else's.

▶ **History and cookies.** Windows maintains a list of recently visited Web sites independently for each person; likewise, it stores a personal collection of *cookies* (Web site preference files).

▶ **Control Panel settings.** Windows memorizes the preferences each person establishes using the Control Panel (page 152), including keyboard, sound, screen saver, and mouse settings.

▶ **Privileges.** Your user account also determines what you're allowed to do on the network and even on your own computer: which settings you can change in the Control Panel, and even which files and folders you can open.

Behind the scenes, Windows stores *all* these files and settings in a single folder—your Personal folder, the one that bears your name. You can open it easily enough; it's at the top right of the Start menu.

This feature makes sharing the PC much more convenient, because you don't have to look at everybody else's files (and endure their desktop design schemes). It also adds a layer of security, making it less likely for a marauding 6-year-old to throw away your files.

__ Tip __

Even if you don't share your PC with anyone and don't create any other accounts, you might still appreciate this feature because it effectively password-protects the entire computer. Your PC is protected from unauthorized fiddling when you're away from your desk (or if your laptop is stolen).

If you create an account for a second person, when she turns on the computer and signs in, she'll find the desktop exactly the way it was as factory-installed by Microsoft: basic Start menu, nature-photo desktop picture, default Web browser home page, and so on. She can make the same kinds of changes to the PC that you've made, but nothing she does will affect your environment the next time *you* log on. You'll still find the desktop the way you left it: *your* desktop picture fills the screen, the Web browser lists *your* bookmarks, and so on.

In other words, the multiple-accounts feature has two components: first, a convenience element that hides everyone else's junk; and second, a security element that protects both the PC's system software and other people's work.

If you're content simply to *use* Windows, that's really all you need to know about accounts. If, on the other hand, you have shouldered some of the responsibility for *administering* Windows machines—if it's your job to add and remove accounts, for example—read on.

__ Note __

The following discussion is intended for ordinary people whose computers are connected to a small home or office network, or no network at all. If you work in a mega-corporation (one with a so-called domain network that's run by a highly paid network geek), things are a little different. Among other things, you aren't responsible for creating and managing accounts.

Accounts

To see what accounts are already on your PC, choose Start→Control Panel, and then, under User Accounts and Family Safety, click "Add or remove user accounts."

You're asked to authenticate yourself (page 127), and then you see a list of existing accounts (Figure 15-1).

If you see more than one account here—not just yours—then one of these situations probably applies:

▶ You created them when you installed Windows Vista.

Figure 15-1: This screen lists everyone for whom you've created an account. From here, you can create new accounts or change people's passwords. (Hint: To change account settings, just click the person's name on the bottom half of the screen. Clicking the "Change an account" link at the top requires an extra click.)

- You bought a new computer with Vista preinstalled, and created several accounts when asked to do so the first time you turned on the machine.

- You upgraded the machine from an earlier version of Windows. Vista gracefully imports all of your existing accounts.

If you're new at this, on the other hand, there's probably just one account listed here: yours. This is the account that Windows created when you first installed it.

Administrator vs. Standard Accounts

It's important to understand the phrase that appears just under each person's name. On your own personal PC, the word Administrator probably appears underneath yours.

Because you're the person who installed Vista, the PC assumes that you're one of its *administrators*—the technical wizards who will be in charge of it. You're the teacher, the parent, the resident guru. You're the one who will maintain this PC and who will be permitted to make system-wide changes to it.

You'll find settings all over Windows that *only* people with Administrator accounts can change. For example, only an administrator is allowed to create or delete accounts and passwords on the PC; install new programs (and certain hardware components); make changes to certain Control Panel programs that are off limits to non-administrators; and see and manipulate *any* file on the machine.

There's another kind of account, too, for people who *don't* have to make those kinds of changes: the Standard account.

Now, until Vista came along, people doled out Administrator accounts pretty freely. You know: the parents got Administrator accounts, the kids got Standard ones.

The trouble is, an Administrator account *itself* is a kind of security hole. Any time you're logged in with this kind of account, any nasty software you may have caught from the Internet is *also,* in effect, logged in—and can make changes to important underlying settings on your PC, just the way a human administrator can.

Put another way: If a Standard account holder manages to download a computer virus, its infection will be confined to his account. If an *administrator* catches a virus, on the other hand, every file on the machine is at risk.

In Vista, therefore, Microsoft recommends that *everyone* use Standard accounts—even you, the wise master and owner of the computer!

So how are you supposed to make important Control Panel changes, install new programs, and so on?

That's a lot easier in Vista. Using a Standard account no longer means that you can't make important changes. In fact, you can do just about everything that an Administrator account can—*if* you know the *name and password* of a true Administrator account.

—— **Note** ——

Every Vista PC can (and must) keep at least one Administrator account on hand, even if you rarely log in with that account.

Whenever you try to make a big change, you're asked to authenticate yourself. As described on page 127, that means supplying an Administrator account's name and password, even though you, the currently logged-in person, are a lowly Standard account holder (Figure 15-2).

The idea is that if you really *are* a Standard account holder, you can call over an Administrator to approve the change you're making. And if you really are the PC's owner, you know the Administrator account's password anyway, so it's no big deal.

Now, making broad changes to a PC when you're an Administrator *still* presents you with those "prove yourself worthy" authentication dialog boxes. The only difference is that you, the Administrator, can click Continue to bypass them, rather than having to type in a name and password.

You'll have to weigh this security/convenience tradeoff. But you've been warned: the least vulnerable PC is one where everyone uses Standard accounts.

Adding an Account

Once you've opened the Manage Accounts window in the Control Panel, it's easy to create a new account: click the "Create a new account" link shown in Figure 15-1. (You see this link only if you are, in fact, an administrator.)

The next screen asks you to name the account and choose an account type: Administrator or Standard.

When you're finished with the settings, click Create Account (or press Enter). After a moment, you return to the User Accounts screen (Figure 15-1), where the new person's name joins whatever names were already there. You can continue adding new accounts forever or until your hard drive is full, whichever comes first.

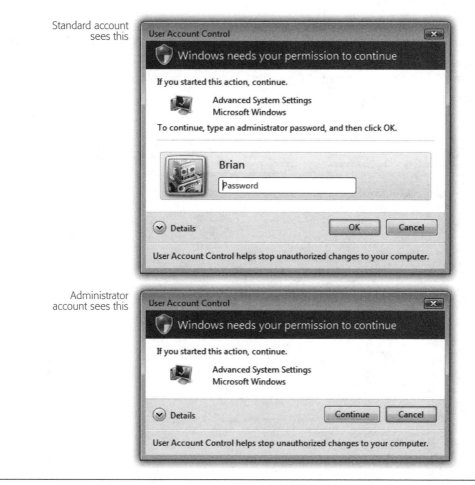

Standard account sees this

Administrator account sees this

Figure 15-2: Top: If you're a Standard account holder, installing a program or making PC-wide changes in the Control Panel requires your filling in this dialog box with an Administrator's name and password.

Bottom: If you're logged in as an Administrator, you can just click Continue to get past the box. You've already supplied your name and password (when you logged in!).

Editing an Account

Although the process of creating a new account is swift and simple, it doesn't offer you much in the way of flexibility. You don't even have a chance to specify the new person's password, let alone the tiny picture that appears next to the person's name and at the top of the Start menu (rubber ducky, flower, or whatever).

That's why the next step in creating an account is usually *editing* the one you just set up. To do so, once you've returned to the main User Accounts screen (Figure 15-1), click the name or icon of the freshly created account. You arrive at the screen shown at the top in Figure 15-3, where—if you are an administrator—you can choose from any of these options:

Figure 15-3: Top: Here's the master menu of account-changing options that you can see.

Bottom: You're supposed to type your password twice, to make sure you didn't introduce a typo the first time. (The PC shows only dots as you type, to guard against the possibility that some villain is snooping over your shoulder.)

- **Change the name.** Click "Change the account name." You'll be offered the opportunity to type in a new name for this person and then click the Change Name button—just the ticket when one of your co-workers gets married or joins the Witness Protection Program.

- **Create a password.** Click this link if you'd like to require a password for access to this person's account (Figure 15-3, bottom). Capitalization counts.

  The usual computer book takes this opportunity to stress the importance of having a long, complex password, such as a phrase that isn't in the dictionary, something made up of mixed letters and numbers, and *not, by the way,* the word "password." This is excellent advice if you create sensitive documents and work in a corporation.

  But if you share the PC only with a spouse or a few trusted colleagues in a small office, you may have nothing to hide. You may see the multiple-users feature more as a convenience (for keeping your settings and files separate) than a way of protecting secrecy and security.

  In these situations, there's no particular need to dream up a convoluted password. In fact, you may want to consider setting up *no* password—leaving both password blanks empty. Later, whenever you're asked for your password, just leave the Password box blank. You'll be able to log on and authenticate yourself that much faster each day.

  If you do decide to provide a password, you can also provide a *hint* (for yourself or whichever co-worker's account you're operating on). This is a hint that anybody can see (including bad guys trying to log on as you), so choose something meaningful only to you. If your password is the first person who ever kissed you plus your junior-year phone number, for example, your hint might be "first person who ever kissed me plus my junior-year phone number."

  Later, when you log in and can't remember your password, leave the Password box empty and hit Enter. You'll wind up back at the login screen to try again—but this time, your hint will appear just below the Password box to jog your memory.

- **Remove the password.** By removing the password, you open up the opportunity for this person to replace it with something better.

  By the way, be careful when you remove someone else's password after they've been using the computer for a while. If you do, you'll wipe out various internal security features of their accounts, including encrypted files, access to their stored Web site passwords, and stored passwords for shared folders and disks on the network (Chapter 16). See the box below for details.

▶ **Change the picture.** The usual sign-in screen (Figure 15-1) displays each account holder's name, accompanied by a little picture. When you first create the account, however, it assigns a picture to you at random—and not all of the pictures are necessarily appropriate for your personality.

Passwords Within Passwords

The primary password that you or your administrator sets up in the User Accounts program has two functions. You already know that it lets you log on each day, so you can enter your Windows world of desktop clutter, Start menu tailoring, Web bookmarks, and so on.

But what you may not realize is that it's also the master key that unlocks all the *other* passwords associated with your account: the passwords that Internet Explorer memorizes for certain Web sites, the passwords that get you into shared disks and folders on the network, the password that protects your encrypted files, the password that protects your .NET Passport (and its Wallet for electronic payments, if you set one up), and so on. The simple act of logging onto your account also unlocks all of these other secure areas of your PC life.

But remember that anyone with an Administrator account can *change* your password at any time. Does that mean that whoever has an Administrator account—

your teacher, boss, or teenager, for example—has full access to your private stuff? After you leave the household, company, or school, what's to stop an administrator from changing your password, thereby gaining access to your electronic-brokerage account (courtesy of its memorized Internet Explorer password), buying stuff with your Passport Wallet, and so on?

Fortunately, Microsoft is way ahead of you on this one. The instant an administrator changes somebody else's password, Windows *wipes out* all secondary passwords associated with the account. That administrator can log onto your account and see your everyday files, but not Web sites with memorized passwords, and so on.

Note that if you change your *own* password—or if you use a Password Reset Disk, described in these pages—none of this applies. Your secondary passwords survive intact. It's only when *somebody else* changes your password that this little-known Windows security feature kicks in, sanitizing the account for your protection.

If you like one of the selections that Microsoft has provided, just click it to select it as the replacement graphic. If you'd rather use some other graphics file on the hard drive instead—a digital photo of your own face, for example—you can click the "Browse for more pictures" link. You'll be shown a list of the graphics files on your hard drive so you can choose one, which Windows then automatically scales down to postage-stamp size.

▶ **Set up Parental Controls.** Whenever you edit a Standard account, this link is available, on the premise that this person is either a child or someone who acts like one. See page 219 for the Parental Controls details.

▶ **Change the account type.** Click this link to change a Standard account into an Administrator account, or vice versa.

▶ **Delete the account.** See page 362.

You're free to make any of these changes to any account at any time; you don't have to do it immediately after creating the account.

Tip

The Start menu offers a big, fat shortcut to the Edit Account dialog box shown in Figure 15-3: just click your picture at the top of the open Start menu.

The Forgotten Password Disk

As described above, Windows contains a handy hint mechanism for helping you recall your password if you've forgotten it.

But what if, having walked into a low-hanging branch, you've completely forgotten both your password *and* the correct interpretation of your hint? In that disastrous situation, your entire world of work and email would be locked inside the computer forever. (Yes, an administrator could issue you a new password—but as noted in the box on the facing page, you'd lose all your secondary passwords in the process.)

Fortunately, Windows offers a clever solution-in-advance: the Password Reset Disk. It's a CD or USB flash drive (not a floppy, as in Windows XP) that you can use like a physical key to unlock your account, in the event of a forgotten password. The catch is, you have to make this disk *now,* while you still remember your password.

To create this disk, insert a blank CD or a USB flash drive. Open/ the Start menu and click your picture (top right). The "Make changes to your account" window opens (Figure 15-3).

The first link in the task pane says, "Create a password reset disk." Click that to open the Forgotten Password Wizard. Click through it, supplying your current password when you're asked for it. When you click Finish, remove the CD or flash drive. Label it, and don't lose it!

___ Tip _____

Behind the scenes, Vista saves a file onto the CD or flash drive called *userkey.psw*. You can guess what that is.

_____

When the day comes that you can't remember your password, leave the Password box empty and hit Enter. You'll wind up back at the login screen; this time, in addition to your password hint, you'll see a link called "Reset password." Insert your Password Reset CD or flash drive and then click that link.

A Password Reset Wizard now helps you create a new password (and a new hint to remind you of it). You're in.

Even though you now have a new password, your existing Password Reset Disk is still good. Keep it in a drawer somewhere, for use the next time you experience a temporarily blank brain.

Deleting Accounts

It happens—somebody graduates, somebody gets fired, somebody dumps you. Sooner or later, you may need to delete an account from your PC.

To delete a user account, open the User Accounts program, click the appropriate account name, and then click "Delete the account."

Windows now asks you if you want to preserve the contents of this person's Documents folder. If you click the Keep Files button, you'll find a new folder, named for the dearly departed, on your desktop. (As noted in the dialog box, only the documents, the contents of the desktop, and the Documents folder are preserved—but *not* programs, email, or even Web favorites.) If that person ever returns to your life, you can create a new account for him and copy these files into the appropriate folder locations.

If you click the Delete Files button, on the other hand, the documents are gone forever.

Fast User Switching

Suppose you're signed in, and you've got things just the way you like them. You have eleven programs open in carefully arranged windows, your Web browser is downloading some gigantic file, and you're composing an important speech in Microsoft Word. Now Chris, a co-worker/family member/fellow student, wants to duck in to do a quick email check.

In the old days, you might have rewarded Chris with eye-rolling and heavy sighs, or worse. If you chose to accommodate the request, you would have had to shut down your whole ecosystem—interrupting the download, closing your windows, saving your work, and exiting your programs. You would have had to log off completely.

Thanks to Fast User Switching, however, none of that is necessary. All you have to do is press the magic keystroke, ⊞+L. (Or, if you've misplaced your keyboard, you can choose Start→Switch User.)

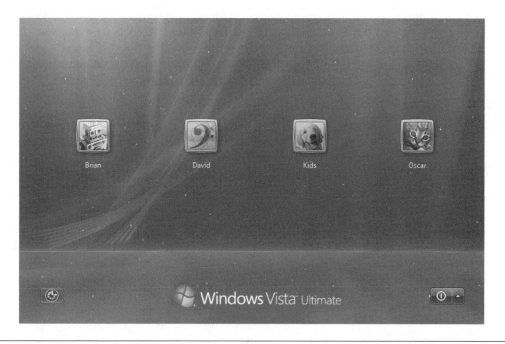

Figure 15-4: At this moment, you have several alternatives. If you click the ⏻ button (lower-right corner of the screen), you can make the computer turn off, restart, sleep, and so on—maybe because you're in a sudden panic over the amount of work you have to do. Or you can just log in.

Now the Welcome screen (Figure 15-4) appears, ready for the next person to sign in. Looking at the screen now, you may *think* you've just logged off in the usual way.

But look at it closely: the word *Locked* indicates that you haven't actually logged off at all. Instead, Windows has *memorized* the state of affairs in your account—complete with all open windows, documents, and programs—and shoved it into the background.

By clicking Switch User, Chris (or whoever) can now sign in normally, do a little work, or look something up. When Chris logs out, the Welcome screen comes back once again, at which point *you* can log on again. Without having to wait more than a couple of seconds, you find yourself exactly where you began, with all programs and documents still open and running.

The Double-Thick Security Trick

If you first turn on the machine. You don't proceed to the Classic logon box (Figure 15-5) until you first press Ctrl+Alt+Delete.

This somewhat inconvenient setup is intended as a security feature. By forcing you to press Ctrl+Alt+Delete to bypass the initial Welcome box, Windows rules out the possibility that some sneaky program (such as a Trojan-horse program), designed to *look* like the Classic logon box, is posing *as* the Classic logon box—in order to "capture" the name and password you type there.

This two-layer logon system is what you get when you add your PC to a network

Press CTRL + ALT + DELETE to log on

domain during the Windows Vista installation. If you want to use it on a workgroup machine, you can, but you have to do a little digging to find it. Press ⊞+R to open the Run dialog box; type *control Userpasswords2,* and then press Enter. Authenticate yourself (page 127). You see a strange-looking program—the old-style User Accounts box. Click the Advanced tab.

At the bottom of the Advanced tab, turn on "Require users to press Ctrl+Alt+Delete," and then click OK. From now on, turning on the PC greets you not with a logon screen, but with the unfakeable Welcome box shown here.

Logging On

When it comes to the screens you encounter when you log onto a Windows Vista computer, your mileage may vary. What you see depends on how your PC has been set up. For example:

You Get the Windows Welcome Screen

This is what people on standalone or workgroup computers see most of the time (Figure 15-4).

To sign in, click your account name in the list. If no password is required for your account, you proceed to your Windows desktop with no further interruption.

If there *is* a password associated with your account, you'll see a place for it (Figure 15-5). Type your password and then press Enter (or click the blue arrow button).

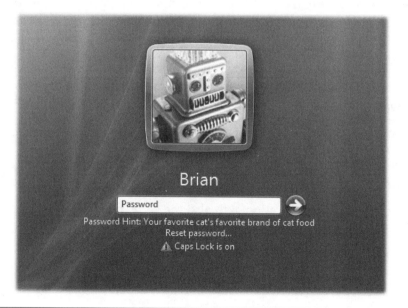

Figure 15-5: Here's what you see after at least one unsuccessful attempt to plug in your password. If you've created a password reset disk (page 361), you'll see a note here suggesting that you go grab it.

There's no limit to the number of times you can try to type in a password. With each incorrect guess, you're told, "The user name or password is incorrect," and an OK button appears to let you try again. The second time you try, your *password hint* appears, too (page 359), as shown in Figure 15-5.

> **Tip**
>
> If your Caps Lock key is pressed, another balloon lets you know. Otherwise, because you can't see anything on the screen as you type except dots, you might be trying to type a lowercase password with all capital letters.

You Zoom Straight to the Desktop

If you are the sole account holder, and you've set up no password at all for yourself, you can cruise all the way to the desktop without any stops.

This password-free scenario, of course, is not very secure; any evildoer who walks by your machine when you're in the bathroom has complete access to all of your files (and all of your password-protected Web sites). But if you work in a home office, for example, where the threat of privacy invasion isn't very great, it's by far the most convenient arrangement.

Setting it up requires a few extra-techy steps. They're described in a free bonus document that await on this book's "Missing CD" at *www.missingmanuals.com.*

You Get the "Press Ctrl+Alt+Delete to Begin" Dialog Box

If you work in a big corporation, you may encounter a message, when you turn on the PC, instructing you to press Ctrl+Alt+Delete (the "three-fingered salute") to begin.

This is the most secure configuration, and also the least convenient, as described in the box on page 364.

SETTING UP A NETWORK AND SHARING FILES

16

▶ Kinds of Networks

▶ Sharing an Internet Connection

▶ The Network and Sharing Center

▶ Sharing Files

▶ Accessing Shared Files

It's a rare Windows Vista machine indeed that isn't connected, sooner or later, to some kind of office network (sometimes known as a *local area network,* or *LAN*). And no wonder: the payoff is considerable. Once you've created a network, you can copy files from one machine to another just as you'd drag files between folders on your own PC. Everyone on the network can consult the same database, phone book, or calendar. When the workday's done, you can play games over the network. You can even store your MP3 music files on one computer and listen to them on any other. Most importantly, you can share a single printer, cable modem or DSL Internet connection, fax modem, or phone line among all the PCs in the house.

If you work at a biggish company, you probably work on a *domain network,* which is quite a big, hairy, technical deal. You, lucky thing, won't have to fool around with building or designing a network, because your job, and your PC, presumably came with a fully functioning network (and a fully functioning geek responsible for running it).

If you work at home, or if you're responsible for setting up a network in a smaller office, this chapter is for you. It guides you through the construction of a less formal *workgroup network,* which ordinary mortals can put together.

You'll soon discover that, when it comes to simplicity, setting up a network has a long way to go before it approaches, say, setting up a desk lamp. It involves buying equipment, hooking up (or even installing) network adapter cards, and configuring software. Fortunately, Vista's Network and Sharing Center makes the software part as painless as possible.

Kinds of Networks

You can connect your PCs using any of several different kinds of gear. Many of the world's offices are wired with *Ethernet cable,* but wireless networks (also called WiFi) are very popular for small offices and homes. Here and there, a few renegades are even installing networking systems that rely on the phone or power lines already in the walls.

This isn't a book about network design, let alone the art of snaking wires through plaster walls. The rest of this chapter assumes that you've performed some kind of wired or wireless network installation already.

Sharing an Internet Connection

If you have broadband (high-speed) Internet service, like a cable modem or DSL service, you're a very lucky individual. Not only do you get spectacular speed when surfing the Web or doing email, but you also have a full-time connection. You never have to wait for a modem to dial (screeching all the way), and wait again for it to disconnect.

If your broadband company didn't supply a piece of equipment (like a wireless or Ethernet router) for sharing that connection with more than one computer, shame on them!

Fortunately, setting up such a system is fairly easy, and practically a requirement if your home or office has more than one PC. There are two ways to go about it.

Get a Broadband Router

A router (a *gateway* in Microsoft lingo) is a little box, about $60, that connects directly to the cable modem or DSL box. It provides multiple Ethernet jacks—which look like slightly fattened telephone jacks—to accommodate your wired PCs. The Internet signal is automatically shared among all the PCs connected to the router.

Use Internet Connection Sharing

Internet Connection Sharing (ICS) is a built-in Vista feature that *simulates* a router. Like a hardware router, ICS distributes a single Internet connection to every computer on the network—but unlike a router, it's free. You just fire it up on the *one* PC that's connected directly to your cable modem or DSL box—or, as networking geeks would say, the *gateway* or *host* PC.

But there's a downside: if the gateway PC is turned off or goes into Sleep mode, nobody else in the house can go online.

Also, the gateway PC requires *two* network connections: one that goes to the cable modem or DSL box, and another that connects it your network.

It might be two Ethernet cards, two WiFi cards, or—most commonly of all, especially for laptops—one Ethernet and one WiFi card. One connects to the Internet (for example, via a cable modem, DSL box, or WiFi), and the other goes to the hub or the router to distribute the signal to the other computers.

If you decide to use Internet Connection Sharing, make sure the gateway PC can already get onto the Internet, on its own, before you attempt to enable ICS.

Choose Start→Control Panel. Open Network. At the top, click "Network and Sharing Center." At left, click "Manage network connections."

Right-click the icon of the network connection you want to share. From the shortcut menu, choose Properties. Authenticate yourself (page 127), and then click the Sharing tab. Finally, turn on "Allow other network users to connect through this computer's Internet connection," shown in Figure 16-1, and click OK.

Thereafter, other computers on the network can share the gateway PC's Internet connection, even if they're running earlier versions of Windows, or even Mac OS X and Linux. In fact, they don't need to be computers at all: you can use ICS to share your Internet connection with a video game console or palmtop!

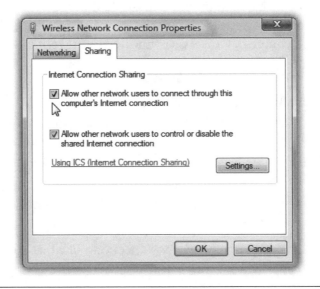

Figure 16-1: Internet Connection Sharing lets you broadcast your cable modem/DSL's signal to all of the grateful, connectionless computers in the house. Your savings: the price of a hardware router.

And now the fine print:

▶ Internet Connection Sharing doesn't work with domain networks, DNS servers, gateways, or DHCP servers (you know who you are, network geeks).

▶ The "receiving" PCs (the ones that will share the connection) can't have static (fixed) IP addresses. To check, sit down at each one. Choose Start→Control Panel. In Classic view, open Network Connections.

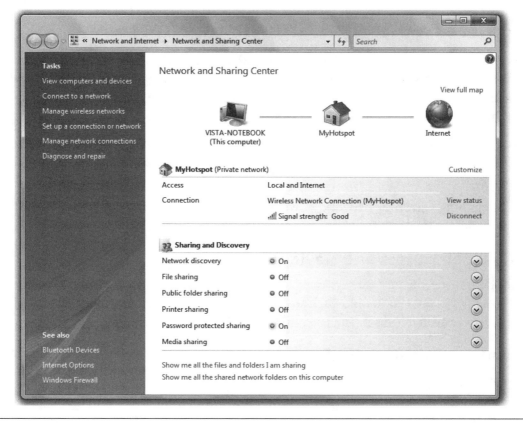

Figure 16-2: The Network and Sharing Center is where you specify how Vista talks to the network. The network map at the top gives you, at a glance, reassurance that you're connected both to your network and to the Internet.

Right-click the icon of the network connection; from the shortcut menu, choose Properties. Authenticate yourself (page 127). Double-click "Internet Protocol Version 4 (TCP/IPv4); turn on "Obtain an IP address automatically."

▶ The gateway machine is now the only thing protecting you from all the worms, Trojans, and bad guys on the Internet. If, on the advice of some cable modem technician during a spasm of troubleshooting, you momentarily plug one of the "downstream" PCs directly into the cable modem, you might forget that it has no protection at all.

The Network and Sharing Center

Once you've set up the networking equipment, Vista does a remarkable job of determining how to configure everything. To see how well it's doing, visit the Network and Sharing Center. This, by the way, is where you set up the sharing of files, folders, printers, and multimedia files over the network.

To open the Center, choose Start→Control Panel. In Classic view, open the Network and Sharing Center (Figure 16-2). It gives you an excellent central status screen for your network.

To *do* anything with your network, however, you generally refer to the options listed in the task pane at the left side. Here's a summary.

"View computers and devices"

Click here to view icons that represent all the computers in your network, as shown in Figure 16-3. You can double-click any of the icons in this view to see which shared resources are available on it (such as music, files, folders, and printers).

"Connect to a network"

This option brings up a list of available networks, including wireless networks and dial-up connections. Select a network and click Connect to establish a connection to it. You can disconnect from your current network by selecting it and clicking Disconnect.

In Figure 16-4, for example, the dialog box shows The Dude Behind You (a computer-to-computer network, probably set up by another user in the same Internet café); Cox25, which seems to be a neighbor's wireless network (and is password-protected); and linksys, which is a wide-open network.

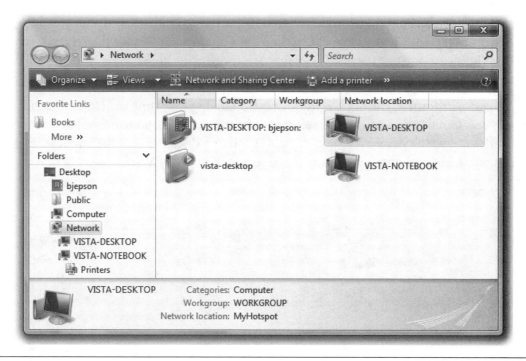

Figure 16-3: This view shows all the computers and other networked gadgets in your vicinity. You can see that VISTA-DESKTOP has two entries for shared music and photos: the bottom-left icon lets you browse to see which users are sharing media, and the top-left icon takes you directly to bjepson's shared music library.

"Manage wireless networks"

This option lets you control how Vista connects to wireless networks. You can drag and drop them to choose the priority of each network. That is, if Vista detects *two* wireless networks where you are, it will connect to the one closer to the top of the list.

If you're on a home or office network, clicking "View full map" makes Vista query the computers and devices on your network and draw a map of the results.

"Customize"

The first time you connect to a network, you're asked to specify whether it's a public or private network. This choice determines how friendly your computer will be with other devices on the network.

On a public network, like a wireless hot spot, Vista tries to be as stealthy as possible in an effort to keep your laptop invisible to bad guys attempting to sniff the airways. On a private (home or office) network, Vista is much more open about what it's sharing with other computers and people.

If you click Customize, the Set Network Location dialog box appears. Here, you can switch between public and private, select which icon you want to use to represent the network, or give the network a new name. (This name doesn't affect the wireless ID of the network, but it changes the name that appears in many of Vista's network dialog boxes.)

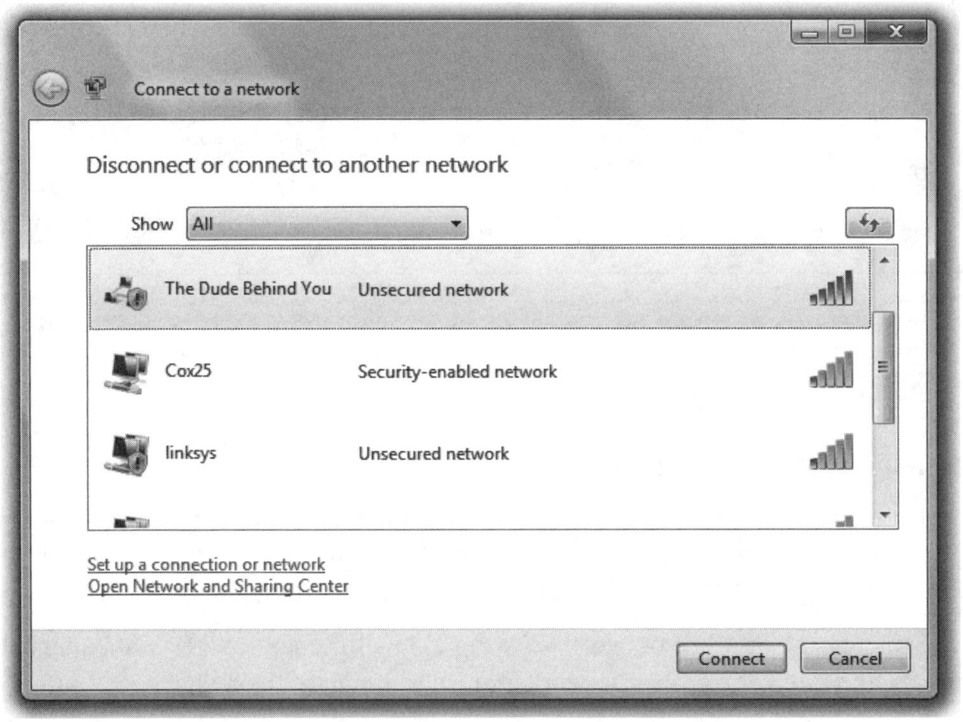

Figure 16-4: This view of all available networks is especially useful if you're a laptopper. How do you know what WiFi networks are available in the spot where you're standing? Here, in this master list. (Hit F5 to refresh the list—for example, if a new network has just come online.)

You can also click "Merge or delete network locations" to combine two or more locations into one, or delete a location that's no longer needed.

Testing the Network

After all of this setup, here's how you can find out whether or not the gods are smiling on your new network. Start by choosing Start→Network.

The network window opens, revealing the folders and disks that your machine can "see" on other computers in the network. You should see the names and icons of the other computers you've set up, as shown in Figure 16-9. In the following pages, you can find out how to burrow into these icons, using the files and folders of other networked PCs exactly as though they were on your own computer.

Tip

All recent generations of Windows can "see" each other and work joyously side-by-side on the same network. On older machines, you would open the equivalent window by double-clicking the My Network Places or Network Neighborhood icon on the desktop instead of using the Start menu.

If you don't see the icons for your other computers, something has gone wrong. Check to see that:

▶ Your cables are properly seated in the network adapter card and hub jacks.

▶ Your router, Ethernet hub, or wireless access point is plugged into a working power outlet.

▶ Your networking card is working. To check, open the System program in Control Panel→System and Maintenance. Click Device Manager. Look for an error icon next to your networking card's name. See Chapter 12 for more on the Device Manager.

If you don't find a problem, visit the Network and Sharing Center and click Diagnose and Repair. If it has no suggestions that solve the problem, you'll have to call Microsoft or your PC company for help.

Sharing Files

Whether you built the network yourself or work in an office where somebody has done that work for you, all kinds of fun can come from having a network. You're now ready to share the following components among the various PCs on the network:

- ▶ **Printers.** You don't need a printer for every PC; all of the PCs can share a much smaller number of printers. If several printers are on your network—say, a high-speed laser printer for one computer and a color printer on another—everyone on the network can use whichever printer is appropriate to a particular document.

- ▶ **Your Internet connection.** Having a network means that all the PCs in your home or office can share a single connection (page 369).

- ▶ **Files, folders, and disks.** No matter what PC you're using on the network, you can open the files and folders on any *other* networked PC, as long as the other PCs' owners have made these files available for public inspection. That's where *file sharing* comes in, and that's what this section is all about.

The uses for file sharing are almost endless. At its simplest, you can use file sharing to finish writing a letter in the bedroom that you started downstairs at the kitchen table—without having to carry a flash drive around. But you can also store your library of MP3 music files on one computer and play them from any other computer on the network.

Note _____

Your network might include a Vista PC, a couple of Windows XP machines, Windows 95, 98, or Me machines, and even Macs. That's perfectly OK; all of these computers can participate as equals in this party. This chapter points out whatever differences you may find in the procedures.

Getting a slick file-sharing system going involves two steps:

- ▶ Sharing the files on one computer on the network; and

- ▶ Knowing how to reach them from the other computers.

That's the structure of this section.

Sharing Files: Two Methods

It's not easy being Microsoft. You have to write *one* operating system that's supposed to please *everyone,* from the self-employed first-time PC owner to the network administrator for General Motors. Clearly, the two might have slightly different attitudes toward the need for security and flexibility.

That's why Windows Vista offers two ways to share files:

▶ **The Public folder.** It's a folder on every Vista PC that's free for anyone on the network to access, like a grocery store bulletin board. Super-convenient, super-easy.

There are only two downsides, and you may not care about them. First, you have to move or copy files *into* the Public folder before anyone else can see them. Depending on how many files you wish to share, this can get tedious.

Second, this method isn't especially secure. If you worry about people rummaging through the files and deleting or vandalizing them, or if bad things could happen if the wrong person in your building gets a look at them, well, then, don't use this method. But if it's just you and your spouse—and you trust your spouse—the Public-folder method makes a lot of sense. (Besides, you can still give the Public folder a password.)

▶ **Any folder.** You can also make any ordinary folder available for inspection by other people on the network. This method means that you don't have to move files into the Public folder, for starters. It also gives you elaborate control over who is allowed to do what to your files. You might want to permit your company's executives to see and edit your documents, but allow the peons in accounting only to see them. And Andy, that unreliable goofball in sales? You don't want him even seeing what's in your shared folder.

The Public Folder Method

Behind the scenes, the Public folder (there's one per PC) sits in the Local Disk (C:)→Users folder.

To find it faster, open any Explorer window, and then click Public in the Navigation pane (Figure 16-5).

Within the Public folder, Microsoft has thoughtfully suggested an internal folder structure: Public Documents, Public Music, Public Pictures, and so on. (They start out empty, except for some sample files in the music, pictures, and videos folders.) You can use these folders, if you like, or replace them with whatever folders you prefer.

Job One is to drag into them any files and folders you want to share with all comers on the network.

Before you go live with your Public folder, though, you have a few more administrative details to take care of, all of which are designed to let you fiddle with the convenience/security balance:

▶ **Set up accounts.** Ordinarily, each person who wants to get into your PC from the network requires an account (Chapter 15). They already have accounts on their own machines, of course, but you need to create corresponding ones on your machine.

— Tip —

If the names and passwords you create for them on your machine are *exactly* the same as the accounts on their own machines, you'll make life simpler for them. They won't see the "Connect to" login box shown in Figure 16-9 every time they connect—they'll go straight to your stuff.

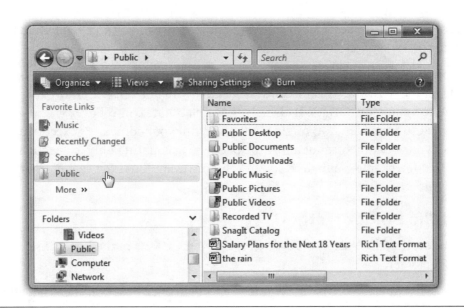

Figure 16-5: The Public folder is a central public square, a shared meeting point for all PCs on the network. Anything in one of these folders is available to anyone on the network—free and clear. You can find the Public folder listed either among the links (top left) or in the Folder list (bottom left).

▶ **Turn off the password requirement (optional).** Anyone who doesn't have an account can see what's in the Public folder, open it, and make their own copies of it—but can't make changes to it. Such people can't add files, delete anything, or edit anything. (Technically, they'll be using the Guest account feature of every Windows PC.)

To set up password-free access, choose Start→Control Panel. Under the Network and Sharing heading, click "Set up file sharing." You arrive at the Network and Sharing Center.

As shown in Figure 16-6, "Public folder sharing" comes turned on. Out of the box, it requires your guests to type their names and passwords when connecting (page 384). But if you expand the "Password protected sharing" panel as shown in Figure 16-6, you'll see that you can turn *off* the requirement for a password. Now anyone will be able to see what's in your Public folder, even without an account on your machine.

To make your changes stick click Apply, and then authenticate yourself (page 127).

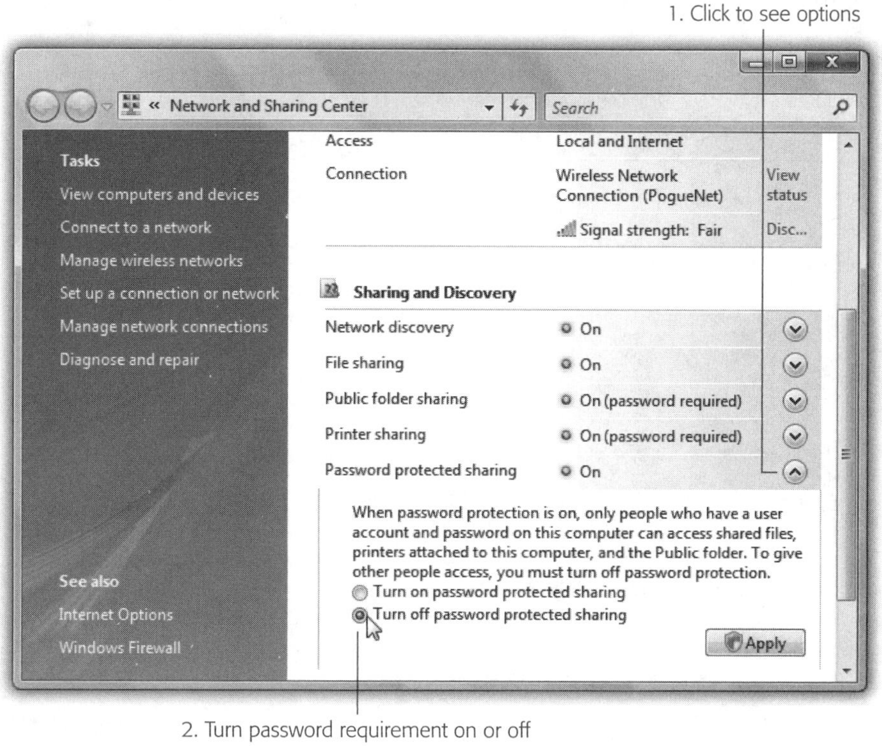

Figure 16-6: Here's how to turn off the requirement for an account password. Note, however, that you're also turning off the ability for your network guests to make changes to what's in the Public folder. To do that, they need an actual account.

So now that you've set up Public folder sharing, how are other people supposed to access your Public folder? See page 382.

The "Share Any Folder" Method

If the Public folder method seems too simple, restrictive, and insecure to you, then you can graduate to what Microsoft cleverly calls the "share any folder" method. In this scheme, you can make *any* folder available to other people on the network.

This time, you don't have to move your files anywhere; they sit right where you have them. Better yet, files you share this way are available *both* to other people on the network *and* other account holders on the same computer.

Here's how to share a file or folder disk on your PC:

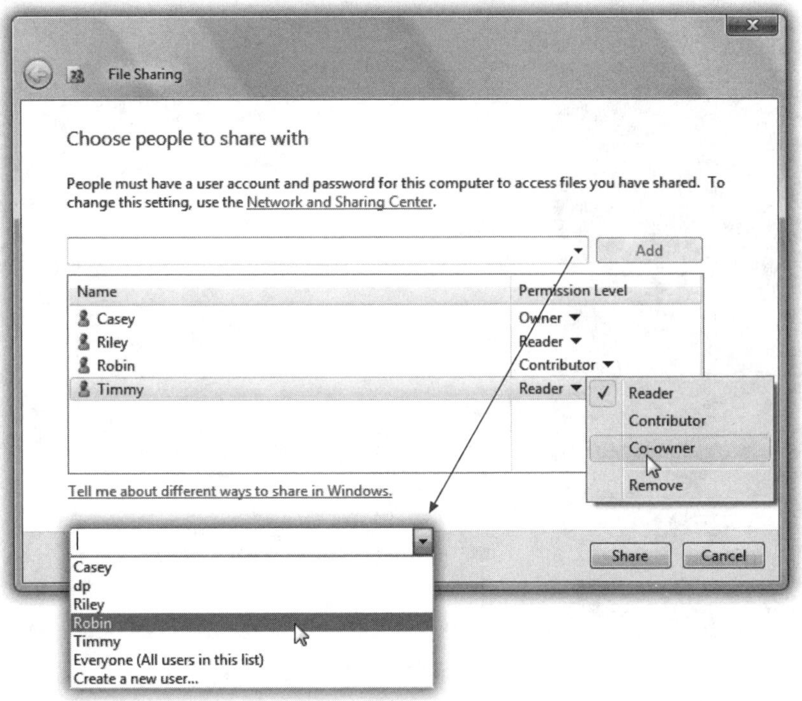

Figure 16-7: The top pop-up menu lists everyone with an account on your PC. One by one, you can add them to the list of lucky sharers of your file or folder (inset)—and then change the degree of access they have to the stuff you're sharing.

1. **In an Explorer window, highlight the file or folder you want to share. On the toolbar, click Share.**

   The "Choose people to share with" dialog box appears (Figure 16-7). You wanted individual control over each account holder's access? You got it.

2. **Choose a person's name from the upper pop-up menu** (Figure 16-7), **and then click Add.**

   This is the list of account holders (Chapter 15).

   If the person who'll be connecting across the network doesn't yet have an account on your machine, choose "Create a new user" from this pop-up menu. (This wording does not imply some kind of sci-fi breakthrough. You are not, in fact, going to create a human being—only an account for an *existing* person.)

   The name appears in the list.

   Now your job is to work through this list of people, specify *how much* control each person has over the file or folder you're sharing.

3. **Click a name in the list. Click the ▾ in the Permission Level column and choose Reader, Contributor, or Co-owner.**

   A *Reader* is someone who gets "look, but don't touch" access. This person can see what's in the folder (or file) and can copy it, but can't delete or change the original.

   Contributors (available for folders only—not files) have much broader access. These people can add, change, or delete files in the shared folder—but only files *that they put there*. Stuff placed there by other people (Owners or Co-owners) appears as "look, but don't touch" to a Contributor.

   A *Co-owner* has the most access of all. This person, like you, can add, change, or delete any file in the shared folder.

   This stuff may sound technical and confusing, but you have no idea how much simpler it is than it was before Vista came along.

4. **Click Share.**

   The "Your folder is shared" dialog box appears. This is more than a simple message, however; it contains the *network address* of the files or folders you shared. Without this address, your colleagues won't know that you've shared stuff, and will have a tough time finding it.

5. **Click e-mail or copy** (Figure 16-8).

The e-mail link opens a new, outgoing message in Windows Mail, letting the gang know that you've shared something and offering them a link to it. The copy link copies the address to the Clipboard, so you can paste it into another program—which is your best bet if Mail isn't your email program of choice.

___ **Note:** _____

Sharing a folder also shares all of the folders inside it, including new ones you create later.
_____

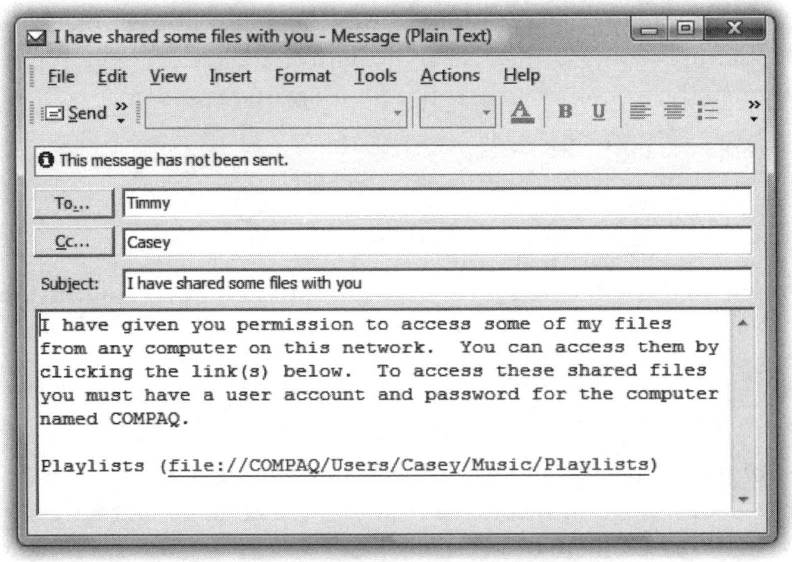

Figure 16-8: This is the message that your colleagues get, letting them know that you've made files and folders available.

Accessing Shared Files

Now suppose you're not you. You're your co-worker, spouse, or employee. You're using your laptop downstairs, and you want access to the stuff that's in a shared folder on the Beefy Main Dell computer upstairs. Here's what to do; the steps are the same whether the Public folder or *any* folder was shared.

1. **Choose Start→Network.**

   The Network window appears, showing icons for all the computers on the network.

   _____ Tip _____

   Alternatively, you can click the Network icon in the Folders list at the left side of every Explorer window. The same Navigation pane is available in the Save and Open dialog boxes of your programs, too, making the entire network available to you for opening and saving files.
   _____

   If you *don't* see a certain computer's icon here, it might be turned off, or off the network. It also might have *network discovery* turned off; that's the feature that lets a PC announce its presence to the network. (Its on/off switch is one of the buttons shown in Figure 16-6.)

   And if you don't see any computers at *all* in the Network window, then network discovery might be turned off on *your* computer.

2. **Double-click the computer whose files you want to open.**

   The Connect To box may now appear (Figure 16-9, top).

3. **Fill in your name and password.**

   This, of course, is a real drag, especially if you access other people's files frequently. Fortunately, you have three time-saving tricks available to you here.

   First, if your name and password are the same on both machines, you get to skip the "Connect to" dialog box.

   Second, if you turn on "Remember my password," then you'll never see this box again. The next time you want to visit the other PC, you'll be able to double-click its icon for instant access.

   Finally, if you're trying to get to someone's Public folder, and you don't need to modify the files, just read or copy them, you don't need a password, ever. Just type *guest* into the "User name" box and click OK. You'll have full read-only access (page 381). And here again, next time, you won't be bothered for a name or password.

__ Tip __

In the unlikely event that you want Vista to *stop* memorizing your password, choose
Start→Control Panel. Click User Accounts and Family Safety, then "Change your account,"
and finally "Manage your network passwords." You'll find a list of every password Vista
has memorized for you; use the Add, Remove, Edit, or "Back up" buttons as suits your
fancy.

4. **Click OK.**

Figure 16-9: Top: Supply your account name and password as it exists on the distant PC, the one
you're trying to access.

If all went well, the other computer's window opens, presenting you with the icons of its shared folders and disks.

Once you've brought a networked folder onto your screen, you can double-click icons to open them, drag them to the Recycle Bin, make copies of them, and otherwise manipulate them exactly as though they were icons on your own hard drive. (Of course, if you weren't given permission to change the contents of the shared folder, you have less freedom.)

Windows Vista for Starters: The Missing Manual

PART SIX: APPENDIX

Appendix The Master Keyboard Shortcut List

APPENDIX

▶ Explorer windows

▶ Instant Search box
(top of each Explorer window)

▶ Working with icons

▶ Navigation pane

▶ Windows-key shortcuts

▶ Login screen

▶ Security screen

▶ Miscellaneous/Editing

Here it is, by popular, frustrated demand: The master list of every secret (or not-so-secret) keystroke in Windows Vista. Clip and post to your monitor (unless, of course, you got this book from the library).

Explorer windows

Highlight the Address bar	Alt+D
Open Previous Locations list (Address bar)	F4
Refresh the window	F5
Open this folder's parent window	Alt+Up arrow
Back (previous window)	Alt+Left arrow or Backspace
Forward	Alt+Right arrow
Cancel the current task or search	Esc
Make menu bar visible	F10 or Alt
Close window	Alt+F4 or Ctrl+W
Open Search window	F3, Ctrl+F, or ⊞+F
Open another window for this folder	Ctrl+N
Full Screen Mode on/off	F11
Open this window's Control menu	Alt+Space
Cycle through open windows	Alt+Tab
Cycle through open windows without closing the menu	Ctrl+Alt+Tab
Open Start menu	⊞ or Ctrl+Esc
Open Task Manager	Ctrl+Shift+Esc
Resize columns to fit their contents	Ctrl+Plus sign (+) on numeric keypad

Instant Search box (top of each Explorer window)

Select the Instant Search box (next to Address bar)	Ctrl+E
Search and open Search Pane	Alt+Enter
Search in Internet Explorer	Shift+Enter
Open a selected program elevated (Start Menu searches)	Ctrl+Shift+Enter

Working with icons

Select all icons in a document or window	Ctrl+A
Select last icon in the window	End
Select first item in the window	Home
Move to last item in the window without selecting it	Ctrl+End
Move to first item in the window without selecting it	Ctrl+Home

Select non-adjacent icons	Ctrl+Arrow keys to move, Space bar to select
Select adjacent icons	Shift+arrow keys Shift with any arrow key
Open a selected icon's shortcut menu	Shift+F10
Rename the selected icon	F2
Open Properties dialog box for the selected icon	Alt+Enter
Move selected icon to the Recycle Bin	Delete or Ctrl+D
Delete selected icon without moving it to the Recycle Bin first	Shift+Delete

Navigation pane

Open all subfolders of selected folder	Num Lock+Asterisk (*) on numeric keypad
Display contents of the selected folder	Num Lock+Plus sign (+) on numeric keypad
Collapse the selected folder	Num Lock+Minus sign (-) on numeric keypad
Collapse folder (if expanded), or select parent folder (if not)	Left arrow
Display folder's contents (if collapsed), or select first subfolder (if not)	Right arrow
View previous folder	Alt+Left arrow
View next folder	Alt+Right arrow

Windows-key shortcuts

Open or close the Start menu	⊞
Open icon in Quick Launch toolbar	⊞+1 (first item), ⊞ +2 (second item), etc.
Open System Properties dialog box	⊞+Break key
Display the desktop, hide all windows	⊞+D
Minimize all Explorer windows	⊞+M
Restore minimized windows to the desktop	⊞+Shift+M
Open Computer window	⊞+E
Search for a file or folder	⊞+F

Search for computers (on a network domain)	Ctrl+⊞+F
Lock your computer or switch users	⊞+L
Run dialog box	⊞+R
Cycle through programs on the taskbar	⊞+T
Open Windows Flip 3-D	⊞+Tab
Bring Windows Sidebar to the front	⊞+Space
Cycle through Sidebar gadgets	⊞+G
Open Ease of Access Center	⊞+U
Open Windows Mobility Center	⊞+X

Login screen

Open Restart/Sleep/Hibernate/Shut Down menu	Alt+S
Highlight other account-holder tiles	Arrow keys

Security screen

Change password	Alt+C
Lock machine	Alt+K
Log off	Alt+L
Open Task Manager	Alt+T
Switch user	Alt+W

Miscellaneous/Editing

Copy	Ctrl+C
Cut	Ctrl+X or Shift+Delete
Paste	Ctrl+V
Undo	Ctrl+Z
Redo	Ctrl+Y
Help	F1
Cycle through parts of a window or dialog box	F6
Create shortcut	Ctrl+Shift-drag an icon
Highlight a block of text	Ctrl+Shift with arrow keys
Move insertion point to next word	Ctrl+Right arrow
Move insertion point beginning of previous word	Ctrl+Left arrow

INDEX

Symbols

→ **symbol,** 4
⊞ **key,** 27
   shortcuts, 159

A

access points *see* **wireless networks**
accounts, 352-364
   administrator vs. standard, 355-356
   changing type, 361
   creating, 356
   defined, 352-353
   deleting, 362
   editing, 357-361
   Fast User Switching, 363-364
   logging in, 365-366
   parental controls, 219-223
   passwords, 359
   pictures, 360-361
   renaming, 359
   Users folder, 85
Add/Remove Programs, 163
Address bar, 44-48
   Back button, 46
   contents list, 46
   Forward button, 46
   Internet Explorer, 228-229
   recent folder list, 46
   recent pages list, 46
   Refresh button, 47
   Search box, 47
   triangles in, 44
administrator accounts, 147, 355-356
Aero (advanced visual design), 24-25
   defined, 24-25
   thumbnail taskbar buttons, 70
   turning off, 104-107, 342
   Windows Flip 3D, 67-68
All Programs menu, 27-28, 124
alphabetizing icons, 58-59
Alt+Tab, 65-67
Alt-clicking, 11
animations, 25
   turning off, 340-342
antivirus, 216-217
Any Folder sharing, 380-382
appearance, 104-120
archived Web pages, 244
arrow notation, 4
arrow pointer *see* **cursor; mouse**
attaching files, 263
authentication, 127
AutoComplete/AutoFill
   in Address bar, 48
   Internet Explorer, 228, 238
   erasing, 229, 238
AutoPlay dialog box, 170

COLOPHON

Due to an annoying and permanent wrist ailment, the author wrote this book by voice, using Dragon Naturally Speaking on an assortment of old and new PCs. The book was created in Microsoft Word XP, whose revision-tracking feature made life far easier as drafts were circulated from author to technical and copy editors. SnagIt (*www.tech-smith.com)* was used to capture illustrations; Adobe Photoshop CS2 and Macromedia Freehand MX were called in as required for touching them up.

The book was designed and laid out in Adobe InDesign CS2 on a PowerBook G4, and Power Mac G5. The fonts used include Formata (as the sans-serif family) and Minion (as the serif body face). To provide the ⊞ and ⏻ symbols, custom fonts were created using Macromedia Fontographer.

The book was generated as an Adobe Acrobat PDF file for proofreading and indexing, and final transmission to the printing plant.

Better than e-books

Buy *Windows Vista for Starters: The Missing Manual* and access the digital edition FREE on Safari for 45 days.

Go to www.oreilly.com/go/safarienabled
and type in coupon code YEDHJGA

Search
thousands of
top tech books

Download
whole chapters

Cut and Paste
code examples

Find
answers fast

Search Safari! The premier electronic reference
library for programmers and IT professionals.